50 Hikes

In the North Georgia Mountains

Walks, Hikes & Backpacking Trips from
Lookout Mountain to the Blue Ridge to the Chattooga River

JOHNNY MOLLOY

First Edition

The Countryman Press
Woodstock, Vermont

DEDICATION

This book is for a great American, James E. Leary.

AN INVITATION TO THE READER

Over time trails can be rerouted and signs and landmarks altered. If you find that changes have occurred on the routes described in this book, please let us know so that corrections may be made in future editions. The author and publisher also welcome other comments and suggestions. Address all correspondence to:

Editor, Fifty Hikes™ Series
The Countryman Press
P.O. Box 748
Woodstock, VT 05091

LIBRARY OF CONGRESS CATALOGING-IN-PUBLICATION DATA

Data has been applied for.

ISBN-13: 978-0-88150-648-8
ISBN-10: 0-88150-648-6

Maps by Mapping Specialists Ltd., Madison, WI
© The Countryman Press
Book design by Glenn Suokko
Text composition by Doug Porter; Desktop Services & Publishing; San Antonio, TX
Cover photograph of Keown Falls and all interior photographs © Johnny Molloy

Copyright © 2006 by Johnny Molloy

First Edition

Published by The Countryman Press
P.O. Box 748
Woodstock, VT 05091

Distributed by W. W. Norton & Company, Inc.
500 Fifth Avenue
New York, NY 10110

Printed in the United States of America

10 9 8 7 6 5 4 3 2 1

OTHER BOOKS BY JOHNNY MOLLOY

A Canoeing & Kayaking Guide to the Streams of Florida

A Canoeing & Kayaking Guide to the Streams of Kentucky (with Bob Sehlinger)

A Paddler's Guide to Everglades National Park

Beach & Coastal Camping in Florida

Beach & Coastal Camping in the Southeast

The Best in Tent Camping: The Carolinas

The Best in Tent Camping: Colorado

The Best in Tent Camping: Florida

The Best in Tent Camping: Georgia

The Best in Tent Camping: Kentucky

The Best in Tent Camping: Southern Appalachian & Smoky Mountains

The Best in Tent Camping: Tennessee

The Best in Tent Camping: West Virginia

The Best in Tent Camping: Wisconsin

Day & Overnight Hikes in Shenandoah National Park

Day & Overnight Hikes in the Great Smoky Mountains National Park

Day & Overnight Hikes in West Virginia's Monongahela National Forest

Day & Overnight Hikes: Kentucky's Sheltowee Trace

Exploring Mammoth Cave National Park

From the Swamp to the Keys: A Paddle through Florida History (with Sandra Friend)

The Hiking Trails of Florida's National Forests, Parks, and Preserves

Land Between the Lakes Outdoor Recreation Handbook

Long Trails of the Southeast

Mount Rogers Outdoor Recreation Handbook

60 Hikes within 60 Miles: San Antonio & Austin (with Tom Taylor)

60 Hikes within 60 Miles: Nashville

Trial by Trail: Backpacking in the Smoky Mountains

Visit the author's web site: www.johnnymolloy.com.

50 Hikes in the North Georgia Mountains at a Glance

HIKE	CITY
1. West Rim Loop Trail at Cloudland Canyon	Trenton
2. East Chickamauga Creek Loop	LaFayette
3. Keown Falls/Johns Mountain Double Loop	Dalton
4. Georgia Pinhoti Trail Primer at Horn Mountain	Dalton
5. Fort Mountain	Chatsworth
6. Gahuti Loop at Fort Mountain State Park	Chatsworth
7. Grassy Mountain Tower via Songbird Trail	Chatsworth
8. Wild Rivers Route	Chatsworth
9. Tearbritches Wilderness Loop	Chatsworth
10. Jacks River Falls via Rice Camp Trail	Chatsworth
11. Emery Creek Falls and Overlook	Chatsworth
12. Panther Creek Falls and Overlook	Chatsworth
13. Cascades of Crenshaw	Chatsworth
14. Penitentiary Loop	Blue Ridge
15. Gennett Poplar on Bear Creek	Ellijay
16. Benton MacKaye Trail near Aska	Ellijay
17. Flat Creek Loop	Ellijay
18. Amicalola Falls Loop	Dawsonville
19. AT Benton MacKaye Legacy Loop	Ellijay
20. Long Creek Falls	Dahlonega
21. Cooper Creek Scenic Area Loop	Dahlonega
22. Preaching Rock via Dockery Lake	Dahlonega
23. Bear Hair Gap Loop	Blairsville
24. Sosebee Cove Nature Trail	Blairsville
25. Coosa Backcountry Loop	Blairsville

DISTANCE (miles)	VIEWS	WATERFALL	CAMPGROUND	TRAILSIDE CAMPING	KID FRIENDLY	COMMENTS
4.9	★	★	★			Some of the best vistas in the state
6.3			★			Remote loop, solitude
4.8	★	★	★		★	Two vistas, great in spring
5.4	★		★		★	One of Georgia's newer trails
2.0	★		★		★	Mysterious rock wall, great for kids
8.2	★	★	★	★		This loop has a little of everything.
4.6	★		★		★	Extensive views and wildlife opportunities
21.9			★	★		55 fords, tough hike, backpacking opportunity
10.1			★			Wilderness hike, many fords
11.2		★	★			Back way to popular falls
7.4	★	★	★			Isolated top-down approach to falls
8.2	★	★	★			Best view in the Cohutta Wilderness
7.2		★	★			Multiple falls on remote trail
13.1			★			Explore high and low, 18 fords
2.9		★			★	See huge tree on loop hike.
6.6		★	★			Fall Branch Falls, solitude beyond the falls
5.7			★			Classic day hike, good winter destination
2.2	★	★	★		★	Highest falls in the East at good state park
4.5	★			★	★	Southern terminus of AT and Benton MacKaye Trail
2.4	★			★	★	Easy hike to falls in rich, deep forest
4.8		★			★	Setting is 1,240-acre Cooper Creek Scenic Area
10.2	★		★	★		Wilderness hike to wide-open vista
4.3	★	★	★		★	Good day hike for all at state park
.5					★	Big trees in botanical area
12.7	★		★	★		Good backpacking loop

50 Hikes in the North Georgia Mountains at a Glance

HIKE	CITY
26. Jarrard Gap AT Loop	Blairsville
27. Blood Mountain Loop	Cleveland
28. DeSoto Falls Double-Decker Hike	Cleveland
29. Cowrock Mountain from Hog Pen Gap	Cleveland
30. Martin's Mine Meander at Smithgall Woods	Cleveland
31. Locust Log Ridge Lookout	Hiawassee
32. Wagon Train Vista/Brasstown Bald	Hiawassee
33. Raven Cliff Falls	Cleveland
34. Chattahoochee Headwaters Hike	Helen
35. Bottoms Loop of Unicoi State Park	Helen
36. Rocky Mountain Loop	Helen
37. High Shoals Waterfall Walk	Helen
38. Tray Mountain	Helen
39. Wolfstake Knob from Dicks Creek Gap	Hiawassee
40. Hemlock Falls	Clayton
41. Southern Nantahala Wilderness Walk	Hiawassee
42. Three Falls of the Tallulah River Valley	Clarkesville
43. James Edmonds Backcountry Loop	Clayton
44. Tennessee Rock Loop	Clayton
45. Panther Creek Falls of Habersham County	Clarkesville
46. Tallulah Gorge Loop	Clarkesville
47. Becky Branch Falls and Martin Creek Falls	Clayton
48. Rabun Bald	Clayton
49. Rabun Bald and Flat Top Mountain via Bartram Trail	Clayton
50. Chattooga Wild and Scenic River Ramble	Clayton

DISTANCE (miles)	VIEWS	WATERFALL	CAMPGROUND	TRAILSIDE CAMPING	KID FRIENDLY	COMMENTS
5.9			★	★	★	Great Georgia mountain primer
5.8	★			★		Extensive views from special peak
2.0	★	★	★		★	Fine recreation destination
3.6	★			★	★	Wide rock face atop mountain
6.5					★	Explore Georgia's gold rush history.
7.4	★					Arkaquah Trail is very beautiful.
3.6	★				★	Georgia's highest peak, plus nearby view
4.9	★	★		★	★	Popular hike to unusual falls
9.4				★		Ridge walk to significant spring
2.2	★		★		★	Family day hike, wildlife interpretation
5.4	★		★	★		Earn your views on this trek.
2.4		★		★	★	Easy hike to two impressive falls
2.4	★			★	★	Multiple vistas from wilderness peak
5.4	★			★		Forgotten and often bypassed vista
1.8		★	★	★	★	Easy hike through scenic gorge to powerful falls
6.2	★			★		Take AT to North Carolina state line and view.
2.4		★	★		★	Two short hikes to three waterfalls, good for kids
7.0	★	★	★	★		Hike at Georgia's highest state park.
2.2	★		★		★	Interpretive trail with view
6.8		★		★	★	Impressive gorge with more impressive waterfall
1.9	★	★	★		★	More scenery per step than any other hike
4.0		★		★	★	Two falls on Bartram Trail
5.8	★			★		Steep hike to Georgia's second-highest peak
9.0	★			★		Solitude aplenty with two vistas on Bartram Trail
19.2		★		★		Backpack along gorgeous river corridor.

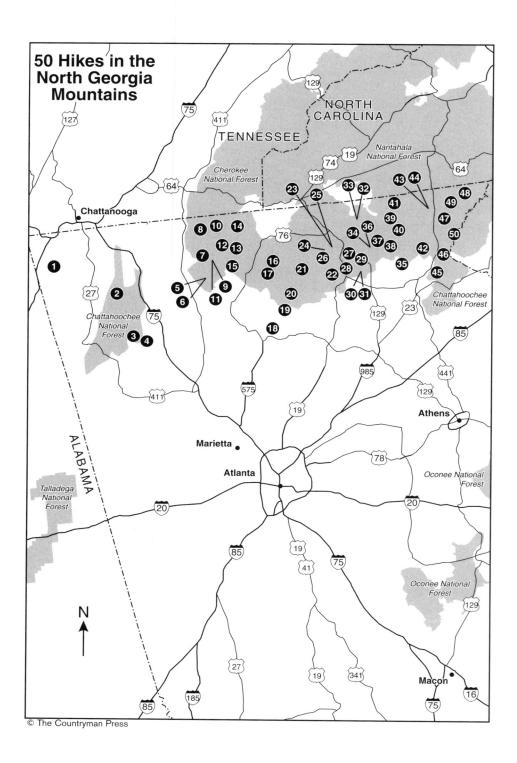

50 Hikes in the North Georgia Mountains

Contents

NORTHEAST GEORGIA MOUNTAINS

Acknowledgments

I would like to thank all the people who went hiking with me in Georgia through the years. Thanks to Ken Ashley, who was the first Georgia hiker I knew. Also, thanks to Francisco Meyer for hiking down Mountaintown Creek, and to John Cox for hiking both the Bartram and Benton MacKaye Trails with me in their entirety, and for the fishing trips in the Cohutta. Thanks to Hunt Cochrane for coming up from Alabama, and to Karen Stokes, Levi Novey, and Wendy Watts for their help. And thanks to Larry Madden of the Georgia Pinhoti Trail Association. Thanks to Tina Dean for meeting me at Tallulah River Gorge. Thanks to Hans "Double H" Hollmann for his input, and to Mike Vess for a shuttle on the Chattooga. A special thanks to all the personnel of the Chattahoochee National Forest and the rangers at all the state parks of North Georgia, and also to all the wonderful hikers I met out on the trail. Y'all reinforced my enthusiasm for hiking in the North Georgia Mountains. And thanks to the rest of my friends and family for backing me up and helping along the way.

Preface

Heading to the North Georgia Mountains was a natural extension of my camping, hiking, and paddling obsession that began in the Smoky Mountains of Tennessee in the early 1980s. My first trip in Georgia was to Cloudland Canyon, led by Calvin Milam. We camped, explored the trails, and enjoyed vistas that opened my eyes to the many outdoor possibilities in the Peach State. More trips covered the Cohutta Mountains and the ridges where the Appalachian Trail (AT) headed from Springer Mountain toward its destination in Maine. Oh, to relive those days of seeing new sights for the first time!

Later, I moved to Atlanta, and adventuring in Georgia became much easier. I explored the mountains from top to bottom, hiking many of the trails included in this guidebook. Time passed, and I was writing outdoor guidebooks, "hiking for keeps" if you will. I eventually pitched the idea for this guidebook, then began systematically exploring the North Georgia Mountains for the best hikes.

It was a real pleasure (most of the time) to travel the trails of North Georgia, from quiet and forgotten Chickamauga Creek to busy Blood Mountain, where the Appalachian Trail reaches its highest point in Georgia. Along the way, I found some unexpected hikes like the Martin Mine Meander at Smithgall Woods that pleasantly surprised this grizzled veteran. And with the joy of completing a book and the sadness of an adventure ended, I finished my research. But I will continue putting my lessons to work, enjoying more of Georgia in future outdoor adventures.

Introduction

This book details 50 excellent hikes in the North Georgia Mountains, from Cloudland Canyon near the Alabama state line to the Chattooga River on the South Carolina border and throughout the mountains in between. Specific emphasis has been placed on the scenic destinations and unique places that make the North Georgia Mountains so special; places like Springer Mountain, the southern terminus of the master path of the East, the Appalachian Trail.

Many of the hikes discussed here take place on the AT. Others travel through the 10 federally designated wilderness areas in the mountains, including the famed Cohutta Wilderness and the less visited Southern Nantahala Wilderness. Hikes of various length and difficulty add diversity to the experiences because sometimes we feel like going on a rugged hike, while other times an easy stroll will do. Time constraints, companions, and season are some of the many considerations in choosing a specific hike. Grandma is not going to feel like fording remote rivers; however, a weekend backpack with your old Scout buddy will likely involve more challenging terrain.

These hikes primarily take place in the Chattahoochee National Forest, which covers 750,000 acres across the North Georgia Mountains. The Chattahoochee not only has hiking trails, but also campgrounds, waterways to float and fish, special scenic areas, botanical areas, hunting, and more. These public lands become more valuable as surrounding areas become more populated with vacation homes and more folks enjoy the superlative scenery the region offers. Georgia state parks are also destinations for those who want to explore the area. Fort Mountain State Park protects a rock wall of unknown origin. And Unicoi State Park makes the most of its setting and offers recreation of all stripes, including, of course, hiking. These are but two examples from the fine state park system of which Georgians should be proud.

No matter what entity manages the land, there is plenty to see in these mountains, from old gold mines to dramatic falls where whitewater is framed in rich forests, to high peaks that offer panoramic views, to a backcountry where bears furtively roam the hollows and trout ply the tumbling streams. You must reach these places by foot. The rewards increase with every footfall beneath the stately oaks of the ridgetops or into deep gorges where waterfalls roar among old-growth trees spared the logger's ax. A respite into the mountains revitalizes both mind and spirit. Smelling the autumn leaves on a crisp afternoon, climbing to a lookout, or contemplating pioneer lives at an old homesite puts our lives into perspective.

That is where this book comes into play. It will help you make every step count, whether you are leading the family on a brief day hike or undertaking a challenging backpack into the back of beyond. Herein you will find many classic North Georgia treks, such as Blood Mountain and Amicalola Falls. However, many hikes are off the beaten path, offering more solitude on the way to lesser known, yet equally scenic, sights such as

There is plenty of interesting wildlife in the North Georgia Mountains.

Martin Branch Falls and Wolfstake Knob. This affords you plenty of opportunities to get back to nature on your own terms.

Two types of day hikes are offered: there-and-back and loop hikes. The former lead to a particular rewarding destination and return via the same trail. The return trip allows you to see everything from the opposite vantage point. You may notice more minute trailside features the second go-round, and returning at a different time of day may give the same trail a surprisingly different character. But to some, returning on the same trail isn't as enjoyable. These hikers just can't stand the thought of covering the same ground twice when there are miles of North Georgia Mountain trails awaiting them. The loop hikes avoid this. Most of these hikes offer solitude that maximizes your experience, though by necessity portions of some hikes traverse potentially busier areas.

Another possibility is an end-to-end hike, which requires a vehicle shuttle between the starting and ending points. There-and-back and loop hikes start and end at the same trailhead.

Day-hiking is the most popular way to explore the North Georgia Mountains, but this book also offers some of the best camping spots for those who want to see the sun rise and set in the mountains. The

lengths of these hikes were chosen primarily for the weekend backpacker. Backpackers should follow all applicable regulations and practice "Leave No Trace" wilderness-use etiquette.

The wilderness experience can unleash your mind and body, allowing you to relax and find peace and quiet. It also enables you to grasp beauty and splendor: a wide rock slab with a window to the wooded valley below, a bobcat disappearing into a laurel thicket, or a snow-covered clearing marking an old homestead. In these lands you can let your mind roam free, to go where it pleases. So get out and enjoy the treasures of the North Georgia Mountains.

HOW TO USE THIS GUIDEBOOK

The 50 hikes are divided into three regions, with individual hikes running in order from west to east within each area. Each hike includes an information box with quick facts about the trek: total distance, hiking time, vertical rise, difficulty, and useful maps.

Here is an example:

Emery Creek Falls and Overlook

Total distance: 7.4 miles there and back

Hiking time: 4¾ hours

Vertical rise: 2,200 feet

Rating: Difficult

Maps: USGS 7.5' Crandall, Dyer Gap, Chattahoochee National Forest

To determine distance I walked (and, in many cases, rewalked) every hike in this guidebook using a Global Positioning System (GPS). You may notice discrepancies between the distances given here and those marked on trailhead signs, in other

Lake Trahlyta from Vogel Overlook

books, or in trail literature distributed by the agencies that administer the trails. Sometimes trail distance is passed down from one government body to the next without anyone knowing where it originated. I have full confidence in the mileages provided here, since I obtained them myself with GPS in hand. Distances are from the trailhead to the destination, not from the parking area.

The hiking time in the above example is 4¾ hours. This is roughly the time an average hiker would spend on the trail, plus a little extra for stops. It's intended to be a baseline from which you can plan your hike. Hiking times will be different for each hiker and hiking group, and adventurers need to consider the physical fitness of the group, rest times desired, eating and drinking breaks, as well as breaks for relaxing and contemplating nature when projecting their own hiking times.

The vertical rise in the above example is 2,200 feet. In this case, the elevation gain is on the return trip from Emery Creek Falls; it's uphill the whole way back. Vertical rise is calculated as the largest uphill change during the hike. This may occur anywhere along the hike, not necessarily on the first climb from the trailhead. And it is not the sum of all climbs during the hike. I obtained the vertical rise from elevation profiles derived from plotting the GPS tracks I created onto a mapping program.

This hike is rated difficult due to the elevation change and the fact that it is a lightly used, remote trail that may be difficult to follow at times. Other hikes range from easy to moderate to difficult. The difficulty rating is largely based on the following factors: trail length, overall trail condition (including trail maintenance), trail "followability," and elevation changes. Longer, rougher hikes with large elevation changes, such as this, are rated difficult. In contrast, a short, level, and well-marked nature trail like the Sosebee Cove Nature Trail is rated easy.

The maps section informs you of maps that could be useful for the hike, in addition to the one provided in the book. The first map, or maps, mentioned are the United States Geographical Survey (USGS) 7.5' quadrangle maps. These "quad maps," as they are known, cover every parcel of land in this country. They are divided into very detailed rectangular maps. Each quad has a name, usually based on a physical feature located within the quad. The Emery Creek Falls hike traverses two quad maps, Crandall and Dyer Gap. Quad maps can be obtained online at www.usgs.gov. The Chattahoochee National Forest map also will be helpful for this hike.

Other maps may offer detailed views of wilderness areas or state park hiking trails. These maps supplement the map included with each hike, although the book maps should be sufficient.

Following the information box is an overview of the hike. This will give you a feel for what to expect, what you might see, trail conditions, and/or important information you might need to consider before undertaking the hike, such as necessary permits, river fords, or challenging driving conditions. Next is a "How to Get There" section, which includes detailed directions from a known and identifiable starting point to the trailhead. Finally, you come to "The Hike," the meat and bones of the trek. Here you will find detailed descriptions of the trails used in the hike, including trail junctions, stream crossings, and interesting human or natural history along the way.

All of this information is designed to help you enjoy an informed, better-executed hike, making the most of your precious time.

The author at Preaching Rock in the Blood Mountain Wilderness

WHAT IT'S LIKE–HIKING THE NORTH GEORGIA MOUNTAINS

It's walking Bear Hair Gap Loop in a thunderstorm;
It's gaining views of green forest lands from Grassy Mountain Tower;
It's fording Conasauga River and noticing the crystalline clarity of the water;
It's smelling the damp rich soil of the hemlock woods of Long Creek Valley;
It's listening to Raven Cliff Falls echo off stone walls;
It's pounding your feet on the rocky AT near Spaniards Knob;
It's seeing abandoned gold mines in Dukes Creek Valley;
It's being eaten up by no-see-ums on Tray Mountain;
It's being awed by the rapids at Dicks Creek Ledge;
It's traveling the maze of trails atop Fort Mountain;
It's being very sore from hiking while camped near Jacks River;
It's absorbing the raw power of the Panther Creek Falls;
It's trying to identify the oaks along the Benton MacKaye Trail;
It's watching snow fall from Woods Hole Trail Shelter;
It's seeing a black bear on the Tearbritches Trail;
It's looking out on barren trees from Preaching Rock;
It's walking amid cathedralesque white pines along Martin Creek;
It's watching the fall colors reflect off Dockery Lake on a calm evening;
It's eating lunch on the rock flats of Cowrock Mountain;
It's reading the interpretive information on the Tennessee Rock Loop;
It's identifying delicate spring wildflowers on Flat Creek;

Introduction 19

It's being disheartened at trash left by thoughtless hikers;
It's watching the water emerge from Chattahoochee Spring;
It's passing an old hardscrabble homestead and wondering what life was like then;
It's missing the Chattooga River Trail as it turns off an old roadbed;
It's the constant birdsong in the Smith Creek watershed;
It's the quiet of the Southern Nantahala Wilderness broken by a white-tailed deer;
It's seeing the ruggedness of the Tallulah River Gorge;
It's falling asleep to a mountain stream while snug in your sleeping bag;
It's seeing tree after tree after tree and appreciating them all;
It's being amazed by the rock walls of Cloudland Canyon;
It's the sheer number of hikers at Springer Mountain;
It's Chickamauga Creek reflecting the green density of the forest;
It's watching turkeys scatter on a wooded hill;
It's just being in the North Georgia Mountains.

CONTACT INFORMATION

Chattahoochee National Forest
1755 Cleveland Highway
Gainesville, GA 30501
770-297-3000
www.fs.fed.us/conf

Georgia State Parks
Department of Natural Resources
205 Butler Street
Atlanta, GA 30334
1-800-864-7275
www.gastateparks.org

1

West Rim Loop Trail at Cloudland Canyon

Total distance: 4.9 miles

Hiking time: 3 hours

Vertical rise: 250 feet

Rating: Moderate

Maps: USGS 7.5' Durham, Cloudland Canyon State Park

Cloudland Canyon, located in the northwest corner of Georgia, is one of the most scenic parks in the state. Here, Daniel Creek cuts its way down Lookout Mountain and forms Sitton Gulch, a rock-rimmed gorge with sheer walls, cliff lines, waterfalls, and vistas that will leave every hiker satisfied that the scenery was worth the effort. Cloudland Canyon has overnight accommodations ranging from cabins to walk-in tent sites, so consider staying the night when you hike this trail. Or at least bring a lunch, as the path starts at an attractive picnic area.

For all its rewards, the trail isn't too hard. First, it offers vistas from near the parking area before leading you on a side trip into the canyon of Sitton Gulch, where there are two waterfalls. It then crosses Daniels Creek and climbs large rock slabs onto the west rim of the gulch, where more views await. Finally, the trail begins its loop on a gentle ascent, then curves back along the rim of Sitton Gulch, where you'll find developed overlooks.

HOW TO GET THERE

From Exit 11 on I-59, take GA 136 east for 8 miles to the state park. Follow the main road to its end, near the scenic overlooks. Alternate directions from Exit 320 on I-75 are as follows: Take GA 136 west through LaFayette for a total of 35 miles to the state park, on your right. The West Rim Loop Trail leaves near Picnic Shelter No. 2.

THE HIKE

Walk toward the edge of the canyon and begin to follow the paved trail to the left,

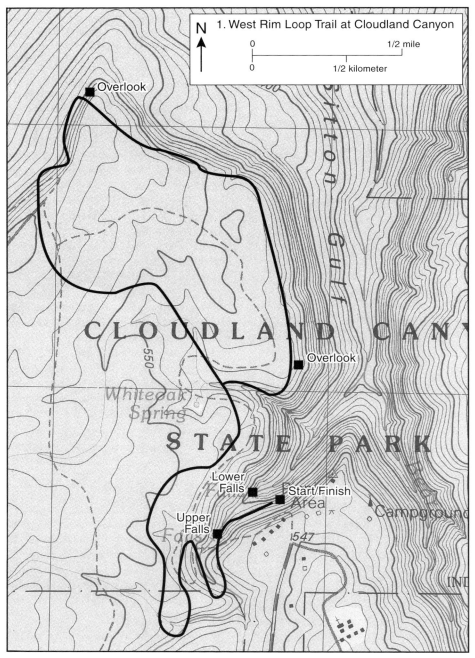

away from the opening of the canyon. You immediately gain grand views into the canyon, beyond the safety rails. The pavement soon gives way to dirt and gravel, as the trail passes behind some of the park cabins. When the water is up you can easily hear the waterfalls crashing in the depths below.

The path is wide, rocky, and rooty. Descend toward Daniels Creek, passing a couple of spur trails leading to overlooks. Pines, oaks, mountain laurel, and rhododendron border the trail. At 0.3 mile, reach the spur trail to the waterfalls. This path descends along a sheer bluff, then divides. The upper falls are closer, but hikers have to negotiate many steps. It has a large plunge pool at its base. The lower falls are reached by an engineering marvel of a path, involving untold steps along unstable terrain, which leads to this drop into a pool bordered by rock walls.

The West Rim Loop Trail leaves the junction with the spur trail to the waterfalls and continues descending toward Daniels Creek. Enter a tangle of mountain laurel and rhododendron, which bloom in May and June. The stream gurgles to your right. Reach and cross Daniels Creek by footbridge. An attractive pool lies just below the bridge. The path ascends away from Daniels Creek in a series of switchbacks. Unfortunately, some hikers have chosen to shortcut these switchbacks, creating a maze of trails. Stay with the painted blazes on the trees and you will be okay. Also, know that no park-created paths go directly up and down the hillside. The user-created trails not only add confusion, but also lead to erosion and siltation of Daniels Creek. Stay on the trail.

Watch for a little cave beside the trail as you climb. Regain the edge of the canyon rim in a dry forest. Reach a trail junction at 1.3 miles. A spur trail leads left to the West Rim

Campground. Keep moving forward with the painted blazes. You are soon walking on wide rock slabs. Reach a particularly wide rock slab that extends to the edge of the rim and offers vistas into the upper canyon. Note how the rock slab open to the sun is bleached white, while other parts are darker. Be careful, as deep crevasses divide some of the biggest slabs. The path runs along the edge of the rim in brushy vegetation. Wooden safety rails are in place in the most precarious locations. Partial views continue to your right.

The West Rim Loop Trail leaves the edge of Sitton Gulch and turns into a side creek, which has created its own mini-canyon. Dip down and come alongside the unnamed branch and reach the loop portion of the hike. To your right, across a small wooden bridge, is your return route. Stay left and continue up the creek, which is flowing quietly, as the water has a negligible descent, a hanging canyon if you will. Continue a moderate climb up the creek in an upland hardwood forest dotted with white pines. Pass the spur trail to the walk-in tent camping area, then step over what remains of the unnamed branch of the creek.

The woods become more piney as the trail makes a gentle upturn, passing an area of exposed rock slabs well away from the canyon rim. Reach and cross a park road. Just ahead is a partial overlook to the west. The town of Trenton and the Lookout Creek valley are below. The trail turns right and levels off, meandering among a thicket of Table Mountain pines broken by big boulders. Blackberry bushes, with their thorny vines, crowd the trail in summer where tree cover is sparse.

The trail dips to its most northerly point, then reaches a spur trail to a fantastic overlook at 2.6 miles. Walk the short piece

Cloudland Canyon

down to a jutting rock and behold Lookout Valley and views beyond to the Tennessee River and the state of Tennessee to the north. The west brow of Lookout Mountain stretches off to the northeast, while the far rim of Sitton Gulch stands to the east.

The main path turns back to the south beyond this overlook and cruises along the west rim of Sitton Gulch. Look for blueberry bushes here. Ahead, spur trails lead right from the main path to more park cottages. Stay with the painted blazes. Other spur trails lead left to small outcrops with views of varied openness. Since you are now heading into Sitton Gulch, the canyon is narrowing. The sheer rock walls of the far rim are closer and their detail more impressive.

A second developed overlook is reached by another left-leading spur trail. You can see a branch cutting its own gorge to meet Daniels Creek to form Sitton Gulch Creek. The third developed overlook, at 3.4 miles, offers a view across the canyon at the picnic area where this hike began. Look for the grassy area and wooden safety rails. At this overlook the waterfalls are clearly audible below. From here, the path turns away from the main gorge and travels the bluff line of a mini-canyon. Reach the stream forming the small canyon at a wooden bridge at 3.6 miles. You have been here before, and the loop portion of the hike is complete. Backtrack to Daniels Creek and its bridge, then ascend to the picnic area at 4.9 miles.

2

East Chickamauga Creek Loop

Total distance: 6.3 miles

Hiking time: 3½ hours

Vertical rise: 550 feet

Rating: Moderate

Maps: USGS 7.5' Catlett, Chattahoochee National Forest

Located in a less visited parcel of the Chattahoochee National Forest near LaFayette, this hike makes a circuit through the ridge and valley country of northwest Georgia. A trip here rewards the hiker with solitude amid rich bottomland forests and craggy ridgetop woodlands. Actually, there is more ridgeline walking than creek walking, despite the official national forest name of "Chickamauga Creek Trail." And there is more than one creek. The loop starts on Ponder Creek, a small clear stream, then meanders north and climbs a rocky crease. The path runs quite a distance, zigzagging from old roadbeds to singletrack paths and traveling spur ridges before descending to East Chickamauga Creek. This stream offers a quiet, subtle beauty and a remote feel as the trail heads up the intimate valley, shaded by stately beech trees. A final climb jumps back into the Ponder Creek watershed, where many crossings take you back to your point of origin.

This relatively low elevation hike is best suited for spring, fall, and winter. Summer can be excessively hot. Be aware that this trail isn't as well marked as state park or national park trails, and the trailbed is not as easy to follow as more heavily used national forest trails. That being said, all but complete neophyte hikers should have no trouble following the route. This loop is also a good overnight backpack, with a stop in the flats along Chickamauga Creek.

HOW TO GET THERE

From Exit 320 on I-75, take GA 136 west for 18 miles to Ponder Creek Road. Turn right

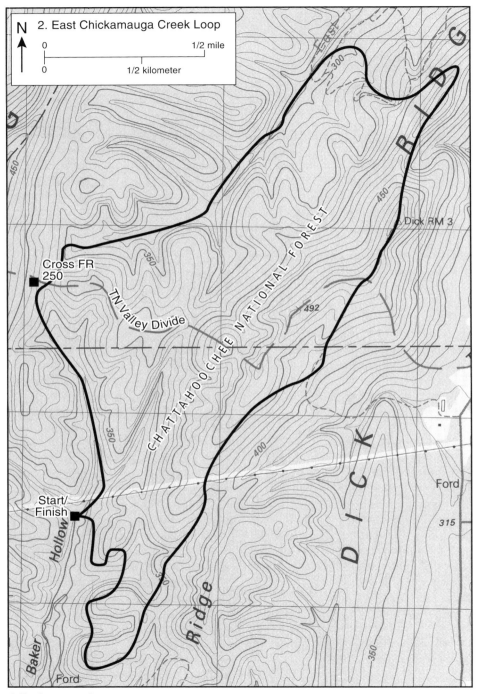

N

2. East Chickamauga Creek Loop

0   1/2 mile

0   1/2 kilometer

300

East   R I D G

450

450

Dick RM 3

Cross FR
250

TN Valley Divide

350

492

C H A T T A H O O C H E E   N A T I O N A L   F O R E S T

350

400

Ford

Start/
Finish

Hollow

315

D I C K

Baker

Ridge

350

Ford

© The Countryman Press

and go 0.6 mile to Forest Road 219. Veer right onto FR 219 for 1.7 miles to dead-end at the trailhead parking area.

THE HIKE

The trail is not immediately evident from the parking lot. Look for it on the right side of the lowermost metal gate. Pick up the Chickamauga Creek Trail and immediately cross Ponder Creek on a wooden footbridge. Turn upstream and briefly trace Ponder Creek before reaching the loop portion of the trail. Turn right here, away from the power-line clearing, and begin working along the side of the steep ridge above.

The narrow path has been leveled, and it winds in and out of dry stream drainages. Look for evidence of a fire from years past—blackened bases of tree trunks and even aged brush on the forest floor. Parts of this loop weave in and out of old burns. Fire is important for the long-term health of pine-oak-hickory forests, which thrive on the ridgelines of northwest Georgia. Periodic fires keep these woodlands open, enrich the soils for the surviving trees, and prevent alteration of the ecosystem by introduction of less fire-tolerant species. See if you can spot the former burn areas.

The hillside above the trail is quite rocky. Climb to reach a gap at 1.4 miles. The path then begins to switchback up the ridgeline. Oaks are the predominant species. Rise to meet an old fire road at 1.8 miles. The road goes up to your right, but keep downhill to your left, dipping briefly and then climbing to reach the power-line clearing at 1.9 miles. Blackberry bushes will be full of ripe fruit in midsummer along the clearing. Cross the power-line clearing and reenter woodland, angling right, still on a narrow footpath. The Chickamauga Creek Trail continues in a northeasterly direction.

Views are available to the east, weather and foliage depending. Make a steady ascent, only to turn back right, still climbing. The path undulates over earthen berms designed to minimize erosion while channeling water off the trail. At 2.7 miles there is a split in the old roadbed. Stay right. The entire trail is marked with white blazes and also has brown plastic posts at confusing places. The walking becomes an easy woods stroll atop the crest of the ridge. But just as you are getting comfortable, the Chickamauga Creek Trail unexpectedly splits left off the ridge at 2.9 miles. Watch closely for this turn, as a game trail continues forward.

The trail once again becomes a footpath and descends in loping switchbacks, then levels off amid an extremely rocky area. Look for the unusual "preachin' rock" here. This rock rises up with a diving board–like extension on top, a perfect pulpit for a circuit-riding minister from days gone by. Move left off the ridge not far past the unusual rock and join another old roadbed that continues downward.

The naked trunks of some pine trees reveal the presence of the southern pine beetle, a native insect that bores into pines and consumes the inner bark. The relationship between the beetle and the pines is natural and cyclical. A cold winter will end the beetle's surge. After the trees fall, the forest floor will open to the sun, increasing the number of summer wildflowers and eventually harboring pines a generation from now. Watch ahead, as the track splits. Stay downhill and to the right, winding toward Chickamauga Creek, which you reach at 4.2 miles. It is off to your right, and you will hear it when flows are high.

This branch of Chickamauga Creek is actually East Chickamauga Creek. It flows

"The Pulpit"

north to meet West Chickamauga Creek and leads to the famed Civil War battlefield of the same name, just south of Chattanooga. (Chickamauga National Battlefield is well worth a visit.) The path now levels off and heads upstream. Soon you step over a couple of feeder branches of Chickamauga Creek, then cross the creek itself at 4.5 miles. This small, shallow crystalline stream gurgles gently over rocks, allowing a dry crossing in times of normal flow.

Continue up the slender valley bordered by steep hillsides broken only by feeder branches that form their own tight hollows. Birdsong echoes in this intimate valley that exudes a wild aura. By now you may have noticed the preponderance of beech trees in the creekside flats along Chickamauga Creek. These moisture-loving giants with smooth gray bark show off leaves of gold in the fall. Their large crowns also discourage ground cover below, offering open areas that beckon you to stop. The forest floor is covered with dwarf crested iris, a delicate purple and white wildflower that brightens moist woods in spring.

Cross Chickamauga Creek three more times. By this point, Chickamauga Creek is barely flowing and all feeder branches are intermittent. After the last crossing the path rises steeply to a gap and Forest Road 250 at 5.4 miles.

The ridge dividing Ponder Creek from Chickamauga Creek forms part of what is known as the Tennessee Valley Divide. This divide separates waters of the Tennessee River, which flow into the Ohio and then the Mississippi and on to the Gulf in Louisiana, from waters flowing directly south into the Gulf. Ponder Creek, south of the Tennessee Divide, flows into Armuchee Creek, then into the Oostanula River and the Coosa River, and then the Alabama River, which flows into the Gulf at Mobile Bay.

The Tennessee Valley Divide extends in an easterly line across North Georgia, and much of the Appalachian Trail traverses it here.

The Chickamauga Creek Trail crosses Forest Road 250 at an angle and reenters the woods about 150 feet beyond where it emerged. It is all downhill from here. A rich forest thrives in this valley, though the hillsides are more open from past fires. You step over Ponder Creek six times before crossing over a feeder branch and completing the loop portion of the hike. It is but a short walk back to the trailhead.

3

Keown Falls/Johns Mountain Double Loop

Total distance: 4.8 miles

Hiking time: 3¼ hours

Vertical rise: 850 feet

Rating: Moderate

Maps: USGS 7.5' Sugar Valley, Chattahoochee National Forest

This hike not only features two loops in one hike, but at least two features on two trails. It is like two hikes in one, without the bother of driving to two different trailheads. Start out at a pretty picnic area, which only enhances this adventure, and head up to Keown Falls (pronounced *cow-an*), a low flow, but high drama cascade that tumbles over an under-cut cliff line. From here, climb a little more to an observation deck where you can look out on the ridge and valley country of northwest Georgia. Then join the Johns Mountain Trail and climb onto a ridgeline with another vista from yet another deck. Cruise along the crest of Johns Mountain on a level track before descending back to the Keown Falls Valley, where you begin your second loop by walking under Keown Falls to a second waterfall beyond, more two-for-one pleasure. A steady descent takes you back to the lowlands and the end of your double loop.

HOW TO GET THERE

Take GA 136 west from Exit 320 on I-75 for 14 miles to The Pocket Road. Turn left and go 4.8 miles to Forest Road 702. Turn right and continue 0.6 mile to dead-end at Keown Falls Recreation Area (a parking-fee area). Short gravel paths lead to secluded picnic areas set in a pretty hardwood forest. A pump well and rest rooms complete the package.

THE HIKE

Leave the parking area on the Keown Falls Trail, passing under an A-frame shelter. The gravel trail is lined with mossy rocks, and the creek of Keown Falls runs to your right.

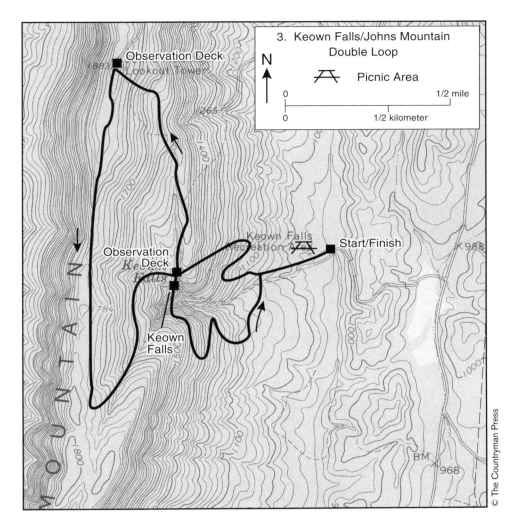

Be aware that this creek can be bone-dry in late summer, early fall, and periods of drought. Early spring is a good time to make this hike, as the temperature will be cooler in this relatively low terrain and the creeks will likely be running. If you must hike this in summer, make it early in the morning.

An open hardwood forest greets hikers on the gentle ascent. Shagbark hickory is a tree of particular interest. It is easily identifiable by its long vertical strips of what appears to be peeling bark. North Georgia is near the edge of this tree's southeastern range. It grows in moist soils of valleys like this one and also on drier upland slopes. Pioneers used the inner bark for making yellow dye.

Soon you pass the first split in the trail. Stay right toward the falls and with the Pinhoti Trail. Step over the stream of Keown Falls at 0.4 mile. The hollow you are ascending narrows and the trail switchbacks up the mountainside, then turns away from the hollow. Pine and mountain laurel thrive on the south-facing slopes. The sparse vegetation makes opens vistas to the south. Keep climbing as more views open. The trail plies a rocky ridgeline and becomes hemmed in by a sheer stone bluff. Stone steps ease the climb.

The path splits. To your left are the lower loop and the base of Keown Falls. Take a short walk over to appreciate this narrow, 40-foot, bridal-veil falls. The cliff line is undercut here and supports a surprising array of viny vegetation.

Backtrack from the falls and continue climbing stone steps along the bluff to soon reach a large wooden observation deck where you can look down on Keown Falls and off in the distance to Horn Mountain and Mill Mountain. This double view should inspire you to continue on to reach the Johns Mountain Trail just a few feet ahead, at 0.7 mile. This is the beginning of your second loop. Turn right here and begin a steady ascent on an old woods road. The rim of the mountain is off to your right and the uppermost portion of the Keown Falls drainage is to your left. Classic pine-oak-hickory woods provide cover over the trail. Blueberries are abundant in the understory.

The trail turns westerly, away from the edge of the mountain, before making a final jump to reach a parking area and an alternate access to the Johns Mountain Trail. You are now at 1,835 feet, having climbed 850 feet. A grassy glade stands to your left and another observation deck overlooks the landscape to the west. You can see Armuchee Valley at your feet, backed by Taylor Ridge. Lookout Mountain forms the long rampart in the rear, beyond Taylor Ridge. For auto drivers who want to look from the observation deck, Forest Road 208 climbs Johns Mountain the easy way.

Here, the Johns Mountain Trail heads south, crosses the grassy glade, and reenters lush woods, soon passing a concrete-block structure that was an ancillary building to a transmitter tower. The path narrows beyond the building. The woods are thick here, despite the presence of many boulders running along the top of the mountain. They are covered with an endless array of lichens and mosses growing in innumerable patterns. They make good relaxation and contemplation spots. The trail is nearly level atop Johns Mountain, and the southbound walking is easy and the views glorious. Look around and off the mountain through the trees, as the hillsides drop off sharply and steeply. Virginia spiderwort and fire pink wildflowers thrive in this environment.

This part of the hike passes too quickly. Almost before you know it, the trail is turning east and the path cruises along the upper edge of a bluff. Partial views open to the east and south. Curve back into the Keown Falls Creek valley to cross a small creek. Ahead, a spur trail to the right leads to the upper edge of an unnamed falls formed by the creek you just crossed—a different falls than Keown. You will shortly see it from below.

Soon you come to another spur trail leading to an outcrop that looks over Keown Falls. Just ahead is a wooden bridge over the stream of Keown Falls. A few more steps take you to the end of the Johns Mountain Trail and the completion of your first loop at 3.8 miles. You have been here before. Backtrack past the wooden observation deck and descend the stone stairs, returning to the base of Keown Falls. Enjoy your second helping of Keown Falls, this time continuing on the trail—the completion of your second loop—under the falls.

This section is the icing on the cake. The path makes its way along the base of a dripping cliff line, where ferns and other vegetation cling to crevices. Ahead is the second

Keown Falls

unnamed falls that you saw from above. This one is about 30 feet high and a bit wider than Keown Falls, although it has less flow.

Descend switchbacks away from the second falls, enjoying more beautiful bluffs that give way to sloping rocky woods. The slope of the hillside moderates as you descend to another junction. You have now completed your double loop. A short walk leads back to the picnic area.

4

Georgia Pinhoti Trail Primer at Horn Mountain

Total distance: 5.4 miles there and back

Hiking time: 3 hours

Vertical rise: 475 feet

Rating: Moderate

Maps: USGS 7.5' Villanow, Chattahoochee National Forest

This there-and-back hike follows a portion of the Pinhoti Trail (PT), which is an evolving long trail in the tradition of the granddaddy of all long trails, the Appalachian Trail. Originally built in Alabama's Talladega National Forest, the Pinhoti Trail has been extended beyond Alabama into Georgia, primarily in the Chattahoochee National Forest.

This section of the Pinhoti on Horn Mountain travels off and on old logging grades before reaching the crest of the mountain after a 400-plus-foot climb. Here it heads south along a rocky ridgeline that well represents the ridge portion of this part of northwest Georgia, known as ridge and valley country, where long parallel mountains are divided by narrow watersheds. This lesser traveled path is a great spring, fall, and winter destination and offers plentiful solitude. Scattered ridgetop views reveal Chestnut Mountain to the east and Johns Mountain to the west. Perhaps walking the Pinhoti atop Horn Mountain will spark your curiosity about other sections of the PT.

HOW TO GET THERE

From Exit 320 on I-75 south of Dalton, take GA 136 west for 10.6 miles to Snake Creek Gap and a parking area on your right. (You'll reach GA 136 Connector after 6.5 miles, but stay right on GA 136 west.)

THE HIKE

The hike starts on the west side of GA 136. After crossing the road from the parking area, leave Snake Creek Gap and join the

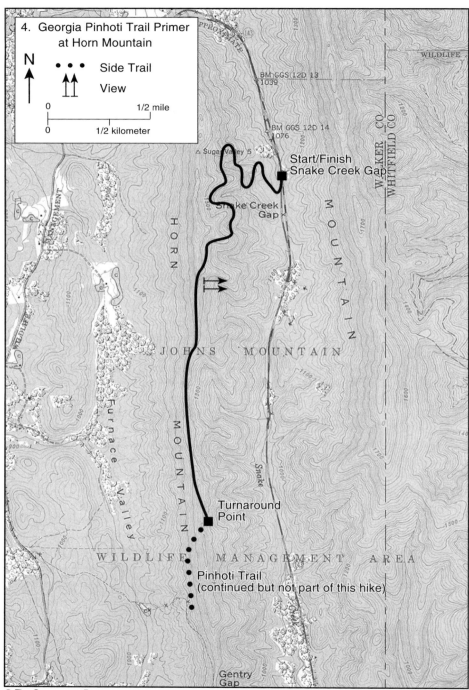

4. Georgia Pinhoti Trail Primer
at Horn Mountain

N

••• Side Trail

↑↑ View

0 ——————— 1/2 mile

0 ——————— 1/2 kilometer

WILDLIFE

BM GGS 12D 13
1039

BM GGS 12D 14
1076

△ Sugar Valley 5

Start/Finish
Snake Creek Gap

Snake Creek
Gap

W KER CO
WHITFIELD CO

HORN

M
O
U
N
T
A
I
N

JOHNS MOUNTAIN

M
O
U
N
T
A
I
N

F
u
r
n
a
c
e

V
a
l
l
e
y

WILDLIFE

Snake

Turnaround
Point

WILDLIFE MANAGEMENT AREA

Pinhoti Trail
(continued but not part of this hike)

Gentry
Gap

© The Countryman Press

The turkey track marks the Pinhoti Trail.

Pinhoti as it traces an old roadbed flanked by a young, spindly forest of pine, sweetgum, and tulip trees. This forest is obviously regenerating after past timbering. The PT makes a switchback to the right. Ferns, blueberry bushes, and gray rocks are scattered on the forest floor. Ahead, the path leaves the old logging grade and becomes a rougher footpath. Overhead the forest is bigger and older. Chestnut oaks are the dominant tree species on this dry mountainside. Pines and hickories are common as well.

Dry, rocky hollows cut into steep hillside, and you see actual flowing water only during storms. The trail joins and leaves old logging grades, which are the only level ground on Horn Mountain and so make logical trailbeds. More switchbacks lead gently but steadily uphill, and the trail nearly doubles back on itself. Pass through areas of nearly pure pine, which generally face south and dominate in dry situations. Mountain laurel also thrives on these slopes. This evergreen

shrub brightens the forest with its white and pink blooms during the month of May. Bush-like sassafras trees also are prevalent. Notice the irregular-shaped leaves that range from the classic "glove" to other forms.

Pass a pipe spring on the uphill side of the trail. This is your only chance for water on Horn Mountain, and even this spring may peter out in late summer and early fall. Leave the last of the former roadbeds a few hundred yards beyond the spring, after crossing a final dry wash. The ascent continues on a rocky singletrack trail. Crest out atop Horn Mountain at 1.7 miles, where the rocky spine of the ridgeline is revealed. You can see Johns Mountain to the west through the trees, especially during winter. The ridgetop of Horn Mountain runs around 1,500 feet high, making it a bit warm in summer. But the steeply sloped mountainsides offer great winter vistas.

The Pinhoti Trail turns south along Horn Mountain. Breaks in the trees up here allow summer and fall wildflowers such as asters to thrive. Another flower, spiderwort, literally lines the trail in places. Its purple flowers with yellow pistils color the woods in late spring. Gnarly Table Mountain pines grow amid the lichen-covered rocks. In other places, thin soils support gently swaying grasses. A vista of Chestnut Mountain opens to the east. A series of fallen trees cleared this view, and new growth will again obscure the view one day. But just as surely, another group of trees will topple in shallow soils atop Horn Mountain, creating another view.

At times, the excessively rocky crest of Horn Mountain forces the PT to slip over to the east side of the mountaintop. However, these rocks, where level, make for good picnicking or resting areas. This entire Horn Mountain part of the PT was "built from scratch" as the Pinhoti Trail. Other sections of the Georgia Pinhoti Trail overlay previously existing national forest trails, with just the addition of the distinctive Pinhoti Trail turkey-track blaze. Where no public lands are available the PT currently traces public roads.

At 2.7 miles, the PT regains the crest of Horn Mountain. Relax here on an old fallen pine trunk, and then backtrack down the way you came to Snake Creek Gap. This area was the site of Civil War action. In late 1864, as Sherman was on his "March to the Sea," Confederate and Union soldiers fought to control Snake Creek Gap, which helped protect the railroad that ran from Chattanooga to Atlanta. The Battle of Resaca was less than a week later. Union soldiers commandeered a train in an attempt to destroy the tracks.

Beyond Snake Creek Gap, the Pinhoti heads over Mill Creek Mountain and beyond to the Cohutta Mountains. The Pinhoti's northern terminus is in Georgia, where it meets another long trail, the Benton MacKaye. There are currently over 151 miles of the Pinhoti Trail in the state. Georgia could be called the state of long trails, as the Appalachian Trail starts here at Springer Mountain on its journey to Maine up the spine of the Appalachians.

In addition to the AT and the Pinhoti, there are two other long trails here. The aforementioned Benton MacKaye Trail heads north from Springer Mountain to reach the east side of the Great Smoky Mountains National Park after 250 miles. (Benton MacKaye was the man credited with the idea for the Appalachian Trail.) And the Bartram Trail, named for naturalist William Bartram, starts near the Chattooga River and meanders north into North Carolina. It is hoped that one day the Pinhoti will be a bridge between the Florida Trail to the south and the Benton MacKaye Trail to the north, creating a network of marked footpaths that traverse the entire eastern United States.

5

Fort Mountain

Total distance: 2 miles of interconnected trails

Hiking time: 1¾ hours

Vertical rise: 200 feet

Rating: Easy

Map: USGS 7.5' Crandall, Fort Mountain State Park

One of the greatest historical mysteries in the Southeast stands atop Fort Mountain. This mystery is the rock wall that runs in an east-west line near the summit of the mountain. No one can say with any certainty who built it or when. Was it the native Cherokee or was it, according to Indian lore passed down by word of mouth through the ages, a mysterious race of "moon-eyed" light-skinned people. Or was it Hernando de Soto, who passed this way during his ill-fated sojourn through the Southeast. We may never know for sure. . . .

One thing *is* for sure, though: the wall and its 29 parapets led to Fort Mountain becoming a Georgia state park. The land for the park was donated in the 1930s by Ivan Allen, and since then has been developed into a great destination, where the camping, mountain biking, swimming, fishing, and hiking are first-rate. Your adventure atop Fort Mountain includes wandering amid several short but interconnected trails that explore the mysterious walls, a more recently built stone fort at the crest, and a fantastic lookout that's as good as they get in Georgia.

HOW TO GET THERE

From the intersection of GA 52 and US 411 in Chatsworth, take GA 52 east for 7.1 miles to the state park, on your left. The Fort Mountain Trails start 2 miles beyond the park office, at the Old Fort Picnic Area.

THE HIKE

There are 2 miles of interconnected trails atop Fort Mountain if you hike them all. But

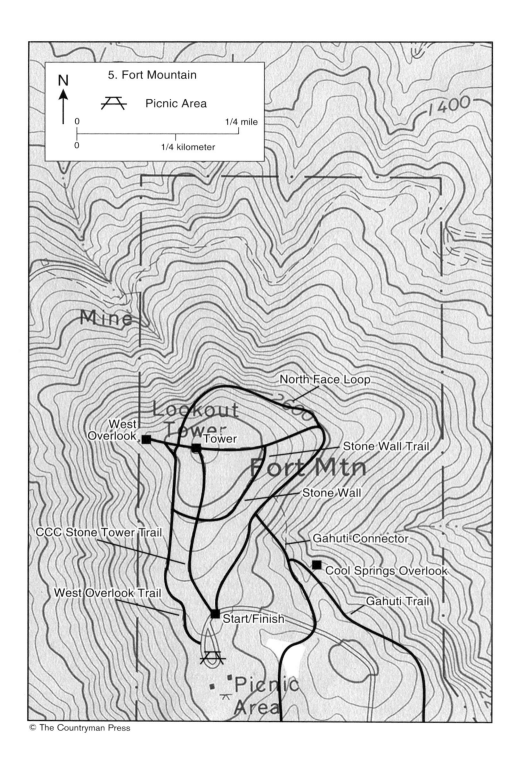

5. Fort Mountain

Picnic Area

N

0   1/4 mile

0   1/4 kilometer

1400

Mine

North Face Loop

Lookout Tower

West Overlook

Tower

Stone Wall Trail

Fort Mtn

Stone Wall

CCC Stone Tower Trail

Gahuti Connector

Cool Springs Overlook

West Overlook Trail

Gahuti Trail

Start/Finish

Picnic Area

© The Countryman Press

to hike them all you have to backtrack and rewalk parts of some paths, resulting in more total mileage. That is no problem up here, as the trails are fun and not too steep. Get a trail map at the park office so you can keep track of your whereabouts. If you are really patient and diligent, then you will hike the North Face Loop all the way around the perimeter of Fort Mountain. This trail is marked with yellow blazes and bounces among the rocks along the edge of the mountain, using stone steps that were difficult to place. Short spur trails lead to outcrops with partial views to the north.

The north face of the mountain is very steep. If the mysterious wall was built for defensive purposes, the defenders didn't bother to go all the way around the mountain because the unwalled portion formed a natural barrier to attack. The wall is 855 feet long and runs east to west, facing the more gently sloped side of the mountain, so maybe it really was made for defensive purposes. But why an east-west line? Perhaps it was religious or ritualistic. The parapets along the wall could've been places to track the sun across the sky throughout the day.

And just think of the labor necessary to actually build the wall. It couldn't have been easy, no matter why it was done. And there is the matter of time. Hernando de Soto stopped in the area, but was purportedly only here for around two weeks. It would've taken far more than two weeks for a band of traveling Spaniards to build this wall. And the wall you see today isn't nearly as high as it once was. Archaeologists believe that the original wall was higher and better shaped. Over time, visitors, vandals, and the elements have taken their toll. Former wall visitors were known to take a rock or two home with them as a souvenir. An early 20th-century theory was that the circular parapets were "Cherokee honeymoon suites," but this has been widely discounted as a trick to dupe tourists into coming to the mountain.

The CCC Stone Tower Trail is another worth walking. After this park was given over to the state by Mr. Allen, the Civilian Conservation Corps—a work project instituted by Franklin Roosevelt during the Great Depression—began developing the park, building this stone-lined trail over the stone wall to the top of the mountain. They also built the stone tower that stands on the peak. A plaque on the tower honors the landowner.

Look at the handiwork of the "CCC boys" on this trail. These workers were not local; a tenet of the program was to ship the workers far from home to discourage their running away. For their labor they were paid a dollar per day, and most of that was sent home to help their families. But this salary gave rise to the still-used phrase, "Another day, another dollar."

The stone tower atop the fort is several stories high, but you can't get to the top these days. Your best views atop Fort Mountain are from the West Overlook, reached by a short path down from the tower. An elaborate set of metal and wooden stairs leads down to an outcrop on the west side of the mountain. The views from the deck on the edge of the outcrop are among the best in North Georgia. Sitting benches allow for extended contemplation of the farm and town country of the Conasauga River valley below. To your south is the other end of Fort Mountain. Chatsworth is below you. Grassy Mountain and the Cohuttas are to the north.

While you are ambling around, try to walk every trail with the least amount of backtracking. No matter what route you take, you will be forced to cover a few of the same segments twice. But think how easy walking around here is now compared to when Prince Madoc supposedly did it.

The rocky wall at Fort Mountain

Madoc was an early Welshman who some historians believe brought 200 settlers in 11 ships to Mobile Bay in the year 1170. Yes, well before Columbus.

Madoc and company were driven inland by hostile Indians. This group was the fair-skinned, blue-eyed, "blond hairs" of Cherokee legend. They eventually ended up in North Georgia and made a home here. Hostilities ensued and the "moon-eyes" made a last stand against area tribes, likely building the mysterious fort wall as part of their defense. The Welsh were defeated and the remaining survivors intermarried with the Cherokee, disappearing as a culture. However, some historians contend that Madoc never even made it across the Atlantic.

The Old Fort Picnic Area is adjacent to this set of trails and has shelters in case the weather is inclement. Other pursuits at the park include more hiking trails, mountain biking, horseback riding, swimming, fishing, camping, and cabins for overnighting. So when you come up here, make an event out of it. After all, you will need the extra time to figure out the mystery of Fort Mountain.

6

Gahuti Loop at Fort Mountain State Park

Total distance: 8.2 miles

Hiking time: 5 hours

Vertical rise: 500 feet

Rating: Moderate to difficult

Maps: USGS 7.5' Crandall, Fort Mountain State Park

The Gahuti Backcountry Loop is one of the finest state park trails in Georgia. Why, you ask? For starters, it circumnavigates the entire crest of Fort Mountain, one of Georgia's most distinctive peaks. It stands on the western perimeter of the Cohutta Mountains, and drops sharply off to the west, down to the Conasauga River valley. When you look up Fort Mountain, it really looks like a mountain, rising steeply from the lowlands.

The *Gahuti* (a Cherokee word meaning "Mother Mountain") takes you through a variety of environments, from rhododendron-choked creeks and rocky overlooks to pine and oak forests and cool waterfalls. Elevations range from 2,100 to 2,600 feet. However, the many ups and downs aggregate to much more elevation change than 500 feet. Backcountry campsites are scattered along the path for those interested in overnighting at Fort Mountain State Park, which has a fine drive-up campground and cabins, too. There are also 30 miles of mountain biking trails and 18 miles of equestrian trails. The Gahuti Backcountry Trail is foot-only, save for a couple of very short stretches where bike or equestrian trails cross or share treadway for a brief period.

HOW TO GET THERE

From the intersection of GA 52 and US 411 in Chatsworth, take GA 52 east for 7.1 miles to the state park, on your left. The Gahuti Trail starts 1.8 miles beyond the park office, at the Cool Springs Overlook parking area, on your right.

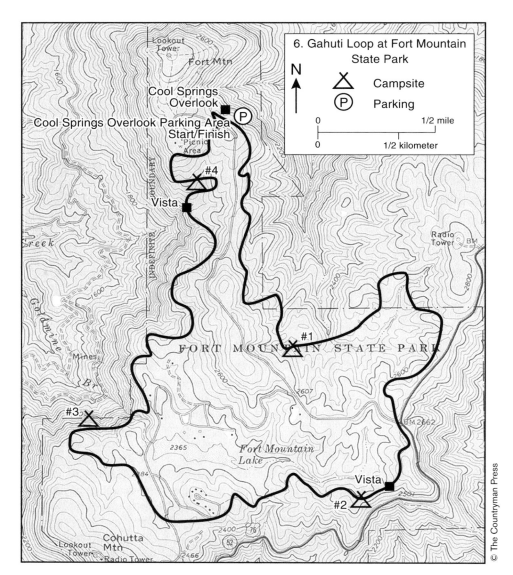

6. Gahuti Loop at Fort Mountain State Park

Hikers and backpackers using the Gahuti Trail need to register at the park office before departing.

THE HIKE

This description of the Gahuti Trail loop starts clockwise. Leave the trailhead and follow the orange blazes beneath pines and oaks. The path parallels the main park road before joining an old roadbed at a left turn. Trace the old roadbed as it dips to a rocky hollow, then ascends. The track becomes a narrow foot trail coursing southward along the east slope of the mountain. Rhododendron, mountain laurel, and young trees crowd the path. Trailside brush will trouble

The Conasauga Valley from Fort Mountain

backpackers even more. The path seemingly heads for every dip and hill it can find, tiring the hiker, who may complain about the ups and downs, but not about the fine scenery. Reach backcountry campsite No. 1, Hogpen, at 1.5 miles, just after stepping over a stream. This campsite, like the others, is merely a designated level spot with a fire ring.

The trail turns to bridge a bigger stream, Mill Creek, which it follows uphill, sharing trailbed with one of the park's many mountain bike trails. This is a beautiful hollow, a green Southern Appalachian cathedral in the summer. Climb from the drainage to circle rich groves of tulip trees. GA 52 is above the trail.

Cross the main park road near the park entrance at 2.7 miles. The Gahuti Trail soon joins an old road and is easy walking. This wide grassy path under sculpted hardwoods contrasts mightily with tangled tight woods through which the trail passed earlier. Reach an overlook on your left. The view is to the south. Reach the spur trail to campsite No. 2 at 3.4 miles. The white-blazed Goldmine Creek Trail leaves right here. The upper part of Goldmine Creek was dammed to create the 17-acre park lake, which also has a swimming beach. Shortly you pass the second junction with the Goldmine Creek Trail. An extended climb follows this junction. After leveling off, the Gahuti Trail leaves the old roadbed and winds away from the park cottages. The trailbed becomes very rocky after crossing a narrow old park road at 4.6 miles.

The track curves around to the west side of Fort Mountain, which is generally rocky. The stone-laden woods through which the path travels are among the finest in the park. The light boulders contrast nicely with bronze pine needles, green mountain laurel, and brown tree trunks. Gain the western edge of the mountain, getting glimpses of Chatsworth and the Conasauga River valley below.

Gahuti Loop at Fort Mountain State Park

Reach campsite No. 3, Moonshine, at 5.3 miles. This one is my personal favorite, as it's on the rim of the ridge. It is especially nice when the sun reflects off the ponds and lakes below, then sinks through the pines. Beyond the camp, the path descends to cross the first of a series of streams. The second one is bigger and is crossed via footbridge.

Soon you reach a trail junction. The Gahuti Trail leaves left and the Big Rock Trail heads up and to the right. Partial views open through the pines before you cross the boldest stream yet, Goldmine Branch. Turn up this stream, ascending beside numerous cascades that drop into small pools and then continue the relentless whitewater-splashed reach for the valley below. You can hear Goldmine Branch falling off the mountain and echoing in the distance all the way from near campsite No. 3.

Reach the other end of the Big Rock Trail at the top of the cascades. The Gahuti crosses the stream by footbridge, then climbs to rejoin the western rim of the mountain. Unless it dips to span a hollow, the trail stays along the rim. Pass the two ends of the white-blazed Campers Loop at 6.1 miles. Be careful at the second junction,

as the Gahuti abruptly leaves left from an old roadbed. The path changes character almost instantaneously here. One minute it is on a boulder-strewn slope pocked with pine, and the next minute it's winding along the steep side slopes of a moist cove with a continuous green floor of herbs and brush.

Watch for a spur trail leading left in piney woods at 7.1 miles. The path drops 50 or so feet to a rock outcrop where expansive views open to the west. To the southwest is the knob of Fort Mountain where campsite No. 3 stands. Step over a small stream, then come to the spur trail for campsite No. 4, Rock Creek, at 7.3 miles. The Gahuti Trail keeps climbing along the small stream and continues in dry woods. You are climbing toward the fort part of Fort Mountain. The Gahuti crosses the road to the Old Fort Picnic Area and Fort Mountain Trails. Just ahead, a spur trail leads left to the Fort Mountain Trail. The Gahuti turns east here, crosses a bike trail, and pops out on the Cool Springs Overlook observation deck. The northeasterly views into the Cohutta Mountains are impressive. Trace a paved path a short distance back to the Cool Springs parking area, completing the loop at 8.2 miles.

7

Grassy Mountain Tower via Songbird Trail

Total distance: 4.6 miles there and back

Hiking time: 3½ hours

Vertical rise: 480 feet

Rating: Moderate

Maps: USGS 7.5' Crandall, Chattahoochee National Forest

It is a wonder why this hike isn't more popular. Grassy Mountain is on the western edge of the Cohutta Mountains but is outside the bounds of the popular Cohutta Wilderness. So it receives less use than some Cohutta Wilderness trails, despite being near Georgia's highest-elevation lakeside campground, Lake Conasauga. The hike starts out at high elevation—above 3,000 feet—on the Songbird Trail, which is a pathway enhanced by the Forest Service for avian life, then joins the Tower Trail for a not-too-difficult climb to a fire tower where views open in nearly all directions.

It may be the drive that deters some hikers. There is a lot of gravel to cover between the lowlands and the trailhead, which is why it's wise to consider camping at Lake Conasauga while you're up there. The campground features a 19-acre lake with trout fishing and a swim area. It is a nice campground in an attractive setting, and it's a great weekend getaway, especially during the heat of a Georgia summer.

Lake Conasauga was dammed in 1940 by the Civilian Conservation Corps. The 0.8-mile Lakeshore Trail, also worth your time, courses through hemlock and rhododendron along the water's edge. A grassy glade with benches covers the dam. Sit down, relax, and absorb the atmosphere. Or use a canoe or small johnboat to fish for bream, bass, or trout. (Only electric motors are allowed.) Want to take a dip after your hike? A ringed-off swimming beach is across the lake from the campground. You

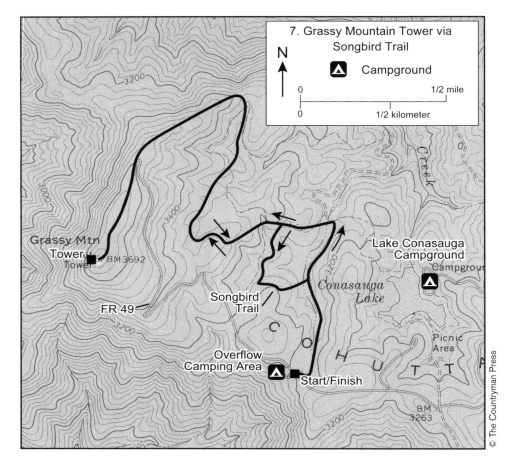

can reach it from the picnic area, which is the last right turn before you reach the Songbird Trail junction.

HOW TO GET THERE

From the intersection of US 411 and GA 52 in Chatsworth, drive north on US 411 for 4.1 miles to Eton. Turn right at the traffic light in Eton onto CCC Camp Road and follow it 10 miles to Forest Road 68, Old CCC Camp Road. Veer left on FR 68, reaching Holly Creek Gap at 2.4 miles. Stay left with FR 68 toward Lake Conasauga. At 5.9 miles, stay left again, still on FR 68.

(FR 64 goes right here.) Keep with FR 68, passing Lake Conasauga Campground on your right. At 11.1 miles, stay left with Forest Road 49, Grassy Mountain Road. Follow FR 49 for 0.3 mile to the Lake Conasauga Overflow camping area and the Songbird Trailhead. Parking is on the left side of the road.

THE HIKE

The trail starts in the overflow camping area. Cross the road from the trailhead parking area and pass through the campground toward campsite No. 3. Follow old Forest

Road 49-C, now closed and gated. The Songbird Trail descends gently, with uppermost Mill Creek to your left and young woods to your right. The upper reaches of Mill Creek are cloaked in rhododendron. Interpretive signs inform hikers about bird management and other information. At 0.4 mile, your return route on the Songbird Trail leaves left across a little footbridge. Keep forward and soon come to a deck extending into a high-elevation beaver pond.

Beavers have made quite a comeback in Georgia and the Southern Appalachians. They were nearly eliminated here by the 1940s, but the Georgia Department of Natural Resources implemented a restocking program, and beavers are once again common throughout the state. These industrious creatures are best known for their ability to down trees with their teeth; their unique front teeth never stop growing. They fell trees for two reasons: to get at the inner bark, which they consume along with young aquatic and land plants in summer, and to help with dam and lodge building. Their dams create shallow ponds, which attract other wildlife, especially waterfowl, and are generally a boon to any ecosystem. The dams slow watercourses, settling sediment and filtering waters to make them cleaner, primarily in lower elevations. Of course, Georgia's mountain streams are clear to start with.

Gray snags stand above the swamp, and wooded hills rise scenically behind the backed-up waters. More beaver dams downstream further slow the waters of Mill Creek.

Leave the deck and continue north on the Songbird Trail. At 0.7 mile, the Tower Trail comes in on the right from Lake Conasauga Campground. Stay left here and soon cross Mill Creek on a footbridge. Beaver dams are evident here, too. At this point the Tower Trail and the Songbird Trail share the same treadway, which tunnels beneath rhododendron. Leave the rhododendron and climb into a more open area of shrubby woods. These woods, resulting from fire, actually enhance the habitat for songbirds. At 0.9 mile, the Songbird Trail leaves left, and the Tower Trail splits right. Stay with the Tower Trail, which rises in a thick forest with a small branch flowing off the slopes of Grassy Mountain to your left. The trail leaves the creek and climbs through a small gap. The climb appears to begin in earnest but, surprisingly, the Tower Trail actually descends along an intermittent stream, which falls away to your right.

As trails to towers should, the climbing resumes on a rib ridge of Grassy Mountain. Galax thrives here. The track heads directly up the nose of the ridgeline into fern-floored woodland. When the mountain becomes too steep the trail slips off to the right, keeping a gentle uptick to make the crest of Grassy Mountain. Keep ascending on a singletrack, rocky tail. Flame azaleas brighten the woods here. Open onto Forest Road 49 at 1.9 miles. This forest road is closed to public access. The canopy opens overhead as you keep forward on the roadbed. The climb is negligible until one last jump up to the tower, reached at 2.3 miles.

Grassy Mountain Tower stands atop the 3,692-foot peak. It's a squat metal structure not more than 100 feet high, just enough to see over most of the wind-stunted oaks that stand on the western precipice above the Conasauga Valley to the west and north. The bulk of the Cohutta Mountains lie to the east, specifically Bald Mountain and East Cowpen Mountain. Fort Mountain stands clearly in the south and Big Frog and Tennessee are to the northeast. To the southeast are waves of mountains stretching across the northern end of the state. The

The Cohutta Wilderness from Grassy Mountain

room atop the tower can't be accessed, but a great view can be had from the uppermost metal stairwell.

After climbing the tower you could quickly return to the trailhead by following Forest Road 49 downhill, but then you would miss the second half of the Songbird Loop. Instead, backtrack 1.4 miles down the Tower Trail to the last intersection with the Songbird Trail. This time, veer right and wind through the rhododendron growing on the slopes of Grassy Mountain. Cross a footbridge over a wide, rocky, low-flow branch. You are now cruising along the far side of the beaver pond. Traverse a second branch, then follow it downstream.

In a short span, you find beaver swamp, rhododendron thickets, and open shrubby woods. Each of these environments help birds thrive in their own way. The open shrubby woods are favorable for bears as well. Don't be surprised if you see bear scat along the path. Soon you cross Mill Creek on a footbridge and reach a junction at 4.2 miles. Turn right here and backtrack 0.4 mile to the trailhead, completing the hike.

8

Wild Rivers Route

Total distance: 21.9 miles end to end

Hiking time: 14 hours; 3 days minimum for maximum pleasure

Vertical rise: 700 feet

Rating: Very difficult

Maps: USGS 7.5' Tennga, Hemp Top, Cohutta and Big Frog Wilderness, Chattahoochee National Forest

The Cohutta Wilderness is the setting for this one-way adventure—the toughest hike in the entire guidebook—that includes 55 wet-footed fords, 21 crossings of Conasauga River, 12 crossings of Rice Camp Branch and its tributaries, and 21 crossings of Jacks River! The distance mandates this trip be a backpack outing. The Cohutta's rivers were made even more rugged by 2004's Hurricane Ivan. Waterways were scoured, deepening fords, making huge debris piles, and obliterating parts of the old railroad grades that the trails followed. Even after trail maintenance, these watersheds will take years and years to return to their "normal" state. Though Ivan washed away many campsites, there are still plenty of places to overnight along both rivers. If you are looking for solitude, consider camping along the small streams of the Hickory Creek Trail.

Hikers should come prepared with a relatively light backpack, trekking poles or fording sticks, and shoes that can stay wet the entire trek. Also, this hike is recommended from the beginning of August through mid-October, when the rivers are typically at their lowest, yet the air and water temperatures are reasonable for wet hikers. Despite the above warnings/advice, I find this trek to be worth every step, as it shows off the extreme beauty of these two rivers, North Georgia's wildest watery destinations.

HOW TO GET THERE

To reach the trailhead from the intersection of GA 52 and US 411 near the courthouse

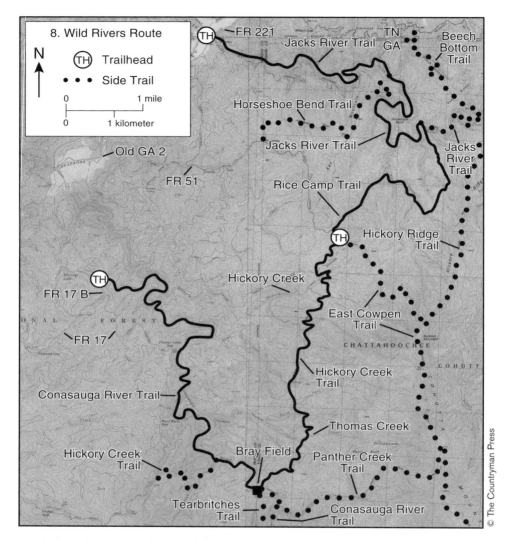

8. Wild Rivers Route

(TH) Trailhead
• • • Side Trail

N

0   1 mile
0   1 kilometer

FR 221

Jacks River Trail

TN
GA

Beech Bottom Trail

Horseshoe Bend Trail

Old GA 2

Jacks River Trail

Jacks River Trail

FR 51

Rice Camp Trail

Hickory Ridge Trail

FR 17 B

Hickory Creek

East Cowpen Trail

CHATTAHOOCHEE

COHUTT

FR 17

Hickory Creek Trail

Conasauga River Trail

Thomas Creek

Hickory Creek Trail

Bray Field

Panther Creek Trail

Tearbritches Trail

Conasauga River Trail

© The Countryman Press

in Chatsworth, keep north on US 411 for 13.1 miles to the hamlet of Cisco. Turn right onto Old GA 2, near the Cisco Baptist Church. Follow Old GA 2, which turns into Forest Road 16, for 8.5 miles, crossing Jacks River on an iron bridge. (On the way, take note of FR 17, which you pass after 3 miles.) Just after crossing the iron bridge, turn right onto FR 221 and follow it 100

yards to the Jacks River Trailhead. This is the end point of the Wild Rivers Route, where you must leave a shuttle car.

To get to the beginning of the Wild Rivers Route, backtrack over the iron bridge and follow Old GA 2 for 5 miles back to FR 17, very near the hunter check-in station you passed on the way in. Turn left up the steep hill on FR 17 and follow it 3.5 miles to

FR 17B. Turn left and go 0.2 mile to the Conasauga River Trailhead. The parking area is on your left, and the trail is to the right of FR 17B.

THE HIKE
Leave the Conasauga River Trailhead on a grassy roadbed. The level track continues as the trail makes an abrupt right turn off the grassy roadbed into full-blown woodland. Wind through low piney hills, entering the Cohutta Wilderness, then descend to the Conasauga River at 1.1 miles. Immediately make the first ford of the trip. Enter the lush world of the Conasauga River valley, where hemlock and rhododendron reign. The trailbed alternates between sand, pine and hemlock needles, rocks, and roots.

Shortly pass Hickory Creek, which was blown wide open by flooding after the hurricane. In places like this, where the trail was destroyed, remember to keep upstream. Also, know that fords generally angle upstream. Be prepared to scout around for both the trail and fords ahead. Trail-finding is part of the Wild Rivers Route challenge.

The second crossing is deep, as the old railroad trestle drops to a shale bank. The fourth crossing takes you over to the right bank (as you face upstream). When rain is threatening, I recommend camping on this side. If the river floods, you can escape up the ridge to your right, which leads out of the wilderness and on to Forest Road 17, without your having to cross the Conasauga.

Make the sixth crossing at 2.1 miles. (Even-numbered crossings put you on the right bank, heading upstream.) Begin passing many ledge-type cascades in the river, with much of the streamside rock exposed to the sun. The trail is hemmed in by a blasted rock wall that drips from the ridge above. There is only one crossing between

mile 2.1 and 3.6. The fords then resume fast and furious, with five crossings in a half mile.

The 16th crossing is tough, with many big boulders. Ahead, at 5 miles, across the river from the trail, Thomas Creek forms a waterfall as it flows into the Conasauga. After crossing No. 17, the trail climbs above the river, which has many falls. Just after crossing No. 18, the trail shortcuts a big bend in the river and slices through blasted rock. After ford No. 20, at 5.9 miles, Rough Creek enters on your right.

The Hickory Creek Trail comes in from Forest Road 17. From this point, the Conasauga River Trail makes no more fords and becomes much more open and well traveled. The walking is easy as it traces an old roadbed, gently winding around some beaver ponds before reaching Bray Field at 7 miles. This is a large, heavily used camping area. It was once a farm, then served the logging community before reverting to wilderness.

Follow the Hickory Creek Trail as it leaves left, making the final ford of the Conasauga, and heads north for Jacks River. Just upriver, the Tearbritches Trail and Panther Creek Trail leave the Conasauga River Trail. The Hickory Creek Trail immediately falls into the pattern of climbing hills, dropping to streams flowing west into the Conasauga, and then climbing again to make the next drainage north. You may notice the lack of white noise from continual rapids, and more birdsong.

Reach Thomas Creek at 8.1 miles, where the trail turns upstream before rising to a gap and a major tributary, Thomas Creek, at 8.7 miles. The scenic trail has its ups and downs before reaching a branch of Hickory Creek at 10.1 miles, then winds to a second branch. The path then joins an obvious roadbed and spans Hickory Creek

Fording Jacks River

by road culvert at 11.5 miles. Wind through moist coves, then briefly leave the Cohutta Wilderness, staying right as the roadbed widens. Join the East Cowpen Trail before drifting into the Rice Camp Trailhead at 12.5 miles.

The Wild Rivers Route then follows the Rice Camp Trail back into the wilderness as it descends into a damp valley. Small feeder branches join the main watercourse, which you are following downstream. Make the first wet crossing at 13.2 miles. The creek flows clear over long rock slabs. Ahead, the path is forced directly into the stream, which flows through a particularly narrow section of the hollow. After a third crossing, the trail traces Rice Camp Branch upstream. Look for the sliding waterfall here.

Begin the first of nine fords of Rice Camp Branch before the trail switchbacks left, uphill, and climbs along a small stream. Gorgeous white pines tower over the forest here. Keep uphill to cross this small stream at a campsite with the remains of a field behind it. This may have been an old homesite or woods cabin site at one time. Ascend to reach a gap at 14.9 miles.

The Rice Camp Trail undulates along a ridgeline running north toward Jacks River. Drop along a streamlet on your right to meet the Jacks River Trail at 16 miles. Turn left, heading downstream along the Jacks River,

tracing a railroad grade. The first ford comes soon, with 20 more beyond this one. The lower river was heavily damaged by Ivan in 2004. The river has scoured rock edges that make the fords harder to see and more complicated. If you are wondering whether or not to make a ford, look up- or downstream and see if you think a railroad could have continued on that side of the river or would have needed to cross.

Ahead are large gravel bars and boulders ripped bare by the power of water. The trail curves around what is known as Horseshoe Bend, where the river nearly doubles back on itself, though this is unnoticeable while on the hike. Occasional rock bluffs rise from the river's edge. By the 11th ford, the river breaks free of the bend and straightens out somewhat.

After the 13th ford, at 18.6 miles, the Jacks River Trail meets the hard-to-find Horseshoe Bend Trail. Sandbars, gravel bars, and debris piles border the river in spots. The pools in the river are getting quite large. At 20 miles, after the 21st ford of Jacks River, you are on the right bank. The walking may be drier, but it can still be tough, as the flood wiped the trailbed away, forcing you to walk over and around riverside rocks to make your way downstream. At 21.9 miles, the Wild Rivers Route ends at Forest Road 221. Good luck drying your boots and socks.

9

Tearbritches Wilderness Loop

Total distance: 10.1 miles

Hiking time: 6 hours

Vertical rise: 2,000 feet

Rating: Difficult

Maps: USGS 7.5' Crandall, Dyer Gap, Hemp Top, Cohutta and Big Frog Wilderness, Chattahoochee National Forest

This loop combines two of the least-used trails in the Cohutta Wilderness with one of the finest backcountry rivers in the Southeast. Take the Tearbritches Trail into the Cohutta Wilderness to climb Bald Mountain. Once on top, you have a 2,000-foot descent into the Conasauga River valley. Turn upstream here and make many wet-footed fords up the valley; trekking poles or a fording stick will be useful here. Beautiful scenes pop up around every corner and the crystalline river flows over boulders into surprisingly deep pools. This loop leaves the valley at low-use Chestnut Lead Trail, which goes up a smaller, yet no less attractive, valley of its own, where waterfalls form between steep drops on the upper portions of the creek it follows. The path then leaves the creek for a little ridge-running to crest out. The hike concludes with a short but necessary walk on a gravel forest road.

This hike also has a few more highlights, such as climbing a high mountain where yellow birch trees—more prevalent in northerly, colder climates—hang on up top. It can be a great one-night backpack or a challenging day hike. Be aware that the many fords on Conasauga River are unavoidable, and you will get your feet wet. Don't attempt this loop if the river is running high.

HOW TO GET THERE

From the intersection of US 411 and GA 52 in Chatsworth, keep north on US 411 for 4.1 miles to Eton. Turn right at the traffic light in Eton onto CCC Camp Road and go 10 miles to Forest Road 68. Veer left on

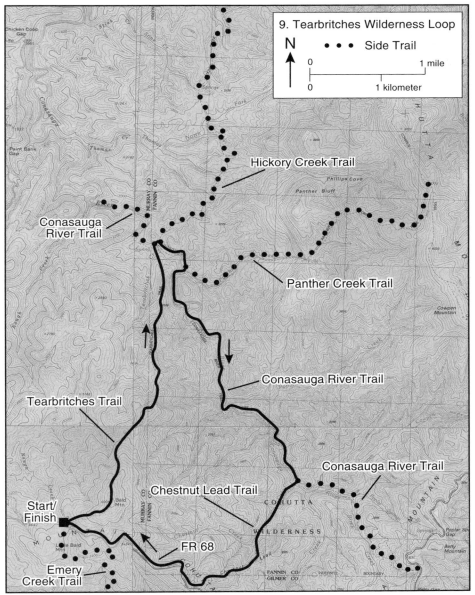

9. Tearbritches Wilderness Loop

N

• • • Side Trail

0   1 mile
0   1 kilometer

Hickory Creek Trail

Conasauga
River Trail

Panther Creek Trail

Conasauga River Trail

Tearbritches Trail

Conasauga River Trail

Chestnut Lead Trail

Start/
Finish

FR 68

Emery
Creek Trail

© The Countryman Press

FR 68, reaching Holly Creek Gap at 2.4 miles. Stay left with FR 68 toward Lake Conasauga. At 5.9 miles, stay left again, still on FR 68. At 9.3 miles, reach the Tearbritches and upper Emery Creek Trailhead. The Tearbritches Trail leaves right, behind the wooden posts and away from the Ball Field Group Camping Area.

THE HIKE

The Tearbritches Trail immediately ascends as it enters the Cohutta Wilderness in an open oak forest with a light understory. Bald Mountain has long since grown over. Near the crest of the mountain, look for non-native balsam trees. These evergreens were planted here years ago. Crest out at 0.4 mile, and begin a moderate descent on the north slope of Bald Mountain. Look in the woods for yellow birch trees, an indicator of a cool climate. Also note the black birches, known as sweet birches, which are prevalent here.

The descent sharpens as it heads straight down the mountainside. Wooden waterbars have been placed across the trail to prevent erosion. Many dead or dying locust and cherry trees tell the story of a forest in transition. These trees grew up in open fields and are now being replaced by more shade-tolerant trees. Step over a streamlet at 1.1 miles. These are the uppermost headwaters of Tearbritches Creek. A small campsite lies off to your right. The Tearbritches Trail climbs a bit away from the creek and levels off, giving your feet a respite from the downgrade. The steep slopes allow for views of East Cowpen Mountain to the northeast.

Descend steeply again to reach a gap, then level off. White pines become more common on the ridgeline, which narrows into a thin backbone. Mountain laurel and rhododendron border the spindly path. At 2.2 miles, you begin to hear Tearbritches Creek off to your left. You know you are getting close when you can hear the Conasauga River on your right and Tearbritches Creek on your left. Suddenly, the path makes a sharp left to reach Tearbritches Creek at 3.2 miles. Begin following the creek on a welcome level track in the narrow valley. Cross Tearbritches Creek and then reach a trail intersection at 3.4 miles. Dead ahead is the Conasauga River. This area is known as Bray Field. What remains of the field is to your left, downstream, where the Hickory Ridge Trail comes in. There are several campsites in the vicinity.

Turn right onto the Conasauga River Trail and cross Tearbritches Creek. The path immediately climbs sharply and you begin to wonder if you're on the trail. You are—the Conasauga River is to your left and you're heading upstream. Drop down to join the old railroad grade that once ran up the valley. The path generally stays along the grade, but in spots it has been washed out and continues along sandbars or an old stream meander, or it leaves the grade entirely.

Round a bend to reach the Panther Creek Trail at 3.9 miles. The Conasauga River Trail keeps forward to make the first of many fords of the Conasauga River. On each ford you will appreciate the beauty of the river valley, whether it is the deep, quiet pools, rushing shoals, or gray bluffs. Trekking poles or a fording stick are helpful in crossing. Some of the return points on the crossings are not evident, as Hurricane Ivan damaged the trail and rerouted and gouged out the river, but generally angle upstream if you are unsure.

The trail is banked primarily by rhododendron and hemlock. Large white pines tower over the river in places. A big pool is just upstream of the fourth crossing. Look for the regular pattern of bumps as you walk

Upper Conasauga River

on the trail. These were the locations of crossties on the logging railroad. In wet places, you can still see them preserved in the muck.

The waters of the Conasauga are clear enough that people scuba dive in the river just outside the wilderness boundary below where the Conasauga meets Jacks River. The waters are clear here, as well. The crossings continue and are hard to keep up with, even if you're an outdoor writer. At 5.5 miles, you are on the left bank and a side falls comes in on the right. These falls from the feeder branch are somewhat hard to see and are easier to locate with your ears. At 5.8 miles, the trail is still on the left bank. Instead of fording here, you stay on the left bank and climb along a steep slope on a singletrack path. But it isn't long before you drop to rejoin the railroad grade.

The Conasauga River is becoming decidedly smaller as you move upstream of feeder branches. Deep pools persist, however. At 6.3 miles, the trail crosses a side creek coming in from the right. Two more Conasauga crossings put you back on the right bank, and the walking becomes easy as the path continues on a mild grade for a relatively long period. All good things must come to an end, though, and the grade is pushed into the river at a boulder-strewn area. Make this crossing and come to an overused camping flat and a trail junction at 6.9 miles. The Chestnut Lead Trail leaves right.

Take the Chestnut Lead Trail and immediately make your final crossing of the Conasauga River. To your left, Chestnut Creek flows clear in this deep valley. This small stream supports trout, especially in the deep pools below the bigger drops. Cross the creek twice in a short span. The climbing picks up, but wait; there is a very steep section just after the third crossing, at 7.4 miles. Look to your right at Chestnut Creek after this third crossing to view a noisy rockslide cascade.

The trail levels off briefly before veering left up a side hollow. The roar of nearby falling water finally leaves your ears. The side hollow has many white quartz rocks brightening the woods. Turn again up a dry draw in gorgeous woodland. The understory is low among the scattered trees. Keep straight up the draw, then make a right to top out on Chestnut Lead. ("Lead" is another name for ridge, or ridgeline.) The American chestnut was decimated by a blight in the 1930s that spread through the Southern Appalachians. Turn right up the lead, and begin to climb in fits and starts. Just when you think you're topping out, the path levels off and then makes another jump uphill.

But soon enough, after one last climb, the trail pops out on Forest Road 68 at 8.6 miles. Turn right here and begin to enjoy some level, easy walking on the gravel track. The road curves around a knob to your left. To your right, the bulk of Bald Mountain is visible. Reach a gap at 9.2 miles, then make the final climb back to reach the trailhead at 10.1 miles, completing your loop.

10

Jacks River Falls via Rice Camp Trail

Total distance: 11.2-mile loop

Hiking time: 5¾ hours

Vertical rise: 1,600 feet

Rating: Difficult

Maps: USGS 7.5' Hemp Top, Cohutta and Big Frog Wilderness, Chattahoochee National Forest

Jacks River Falls is likely the busiest single destination in the entire Cohutta Wilderness. It is certainly worth seeing; but why not make a great loop hike out of it on lesser-traveled trails that not only display the beauty of the Cohutta, but also challenge the hiker?

This loop begins on Rice Camp Trail, which winds through intimate, thickly wooded hollows that deliver a real impression of remoteness. Rocky ridges run down to pounding Jacks River, which was scoured by torrential rains from Hurricane Ivan in 2004. Make the first of two mandatory fords of Jacks River before reaching Jacks River Falls, an impressive and voluminous cascade pouring over irregular rock ledges. Beyond the falls the trail courses up the rich valley before making its second crossing of the Jacks River to reach the Hickory Ridge Trail. It's a long climb up this path, but you are likely to have it to yourself. Finally, reach the East Cowpen Trail, where you take a well-earned extended downgrade all the way back to the trailhead.

HOW TO GET THERE

Reaching this trailhead requires two car fords of Jigger Creek. A high-clearance vehicle is mandatory for these car fords in all but the driest of times. From the intersection of GA 52 and US 411 near the courthouse in Chatsworth, keep forward on US 411 north for 13.1 miles to the hamlet of Cisco. Turn right onto Old GA 2, near the Cisco Baptist Church. Continue 7.7 miles to Forest Road 51. (Pass the Hopewell Baptist Church 1.7 miles before the turn and cross the

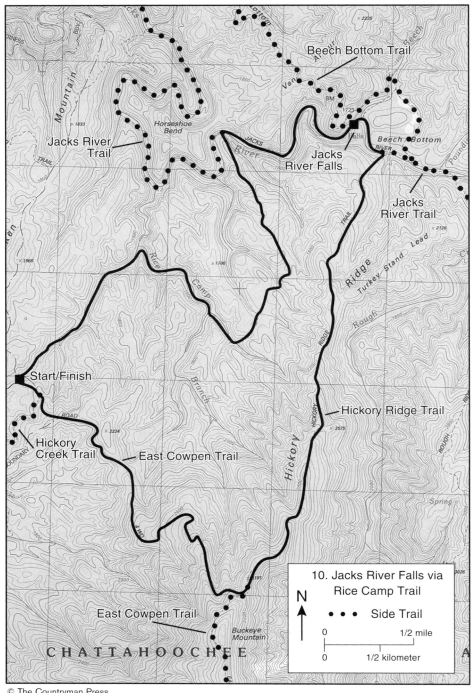

Beech Bottom Trail

Jacks River
Trail

Horseshoe
Bend

Jacks
River Falls

Beech Bottom

Jacks
River Trail

Start/Finish

Hickory Ridge Trail

Hickory
Creek Trail

East Cowpen Trail

East Cowpen Trail

Buckeye
Mountain

C H A T T A H O O C H E E

10. Jacks River Falls via
Rice Camp Trail

N

• • • Side Trail

0   1/2 mile

0   1/2 kilometer

© The Countryman Press

Conasauga River 0.6 mile before it.) Turn right and follow FR 51, making the two car fords at 1.9 miles.

If the auto fords are too high you should probably avoid this hike because the Jacks River foot fords will be high, too. Instead, go to nearby Fort Mountain State Park, where there are two good hikes to try (see Hikes 5 and 6). Continue on FR 51 beyond the fords to dead-end at 4.9 miles. The Rice Camp Trail is to your left.

THE HIKE

The Rice Camp Trail begins as a single-track path on an old woods road. Descend into a rich wooded valley. Small feeder branches join the main watercourse, which you are following downstream. The trail can be mucky in winter, spring, and after summer rains. Make the first crossing at 0.7 mile. You may as well walk through the creek because wet fords lie ahead. The creek flows clear over long rock slabs. Ahead, the trail is forced directly into the stream, which flows through a particularly narrow section of the hollow.

After a third crossing you may be perplexed by the trailside stream flowing against you. Here, at 0.9 mile, the trail begins tracing Rice Camp Branch upstream. Look for the sliding waterfall below and to your left on Rice Camp Branch. Soon cross Rice Camp Branch the first of nine times. This creek also has long, clean rock slabs beneath the water. After the ninth crossing a small stream comes in from the left at 1.9 miles. The trail switchbacks left, uphill, and climbs along the small stream. Gorgeous white pines tower over the forest here. Keep climbing to cross this small stream at a campsite with what remains of a field behind it. This may have been an old homesite or woods cabin site at one time. Ascend to reach a gap at 2.4 miles.

The trail now winds through low-slung hills with sluggish streams. With all its twists and turns, it is hard to figure out where the trail is going next. Join a ridgeline running north toward Jacks River. The Rice Camp Trail undulates along the ridge, tricking you into thinking the river is near. Eventually the river sounds will reveal its location. Drop along a streamlet on your right to meet the Jacks River Trail at 3.5 miles. Turn right, heading upstream along the Jacks River and tracing a railroad grade. A glance along the river reveals the scoured banks and piles of uprooted trees left by flooding in 2004. Over time, the debris piles will decay and vegetation will again overhang the river, but rerouting and island-building will last for a while. Nature sometimes works slowly, such as when wearing a river rock smooth. Other times the changes are cataclysmic. Both methods are demonstrated here on the Jacks.

Shortly make your first ford of Jacks River. This is a wide, fairly deep ford with many gray rock slabs. Continue upstream on the old railroad grade beneath thickets of rhododendron and mountain laurel. Watch for the evenly spaced bumps of the old crossties, which are sometimes exposed in wet areas. Also notice how often the exposed tree roots run perpendicular to the trail. These roots were forced to grow parallel to the crossties. Jacks River has big pools and rocky runs. The exposed rocks in the river make for great summertime sunning spots.

The trail climbs well above the river as it curves to the right. A series of falls crashes down below. The trail is open overhead when you reach Jacks River Falls at 4.7 miles. The roar of the water is unmistakable. Just ahead you can drop down to open rock slabs beside the falls. It is more difficult to reach the base of the falls, but there are erosive,

Jacks River Falls

user-created paths heading straight down the hill. Jacks River Falls plunges at an angle and finally reaches a pool. Another wide waterfall with a big pool lies just above here.

The trail scrambles past the falls before rejoining the storm-scoured and now rocky railroad grade. Curve with the river to reach Beech Creek. This is a heavily used camping area. A long pool stretches upstream of Beech Creek. Continue ahead on the level, easy trail through hemlock woods.

Intersect the Beech Bottom Trail at 5.4 miles. It leads left into Tennessee, just north of the state line. Pay close attention here. Keep forward just a bit, then drop into a camping flat on your right beside the river. There may be a sign for the Hickory Ridge Trail here. In any event, angle downstream and ford Jacks River. This is your second and last ford. After crossing the river, keep downstream along a gravel bar on the left bank. The storm damage makes this area confusing. Look left for a small stream that

creates a narrow, tight hollow. This is where the Hickory Ridge Trail leaves left, away from the river. If you reach the end of the gravel bar and haven't found the trail, backtrack.

This little stream is your last chance for water on the rest of the loop. Ascend the hollow, crossing the streamlet at a rock-slab cascade. Climb steadily away from the river to join a rib ridge of Hickory Ridge in pine-oak-hickory woods. Pass through a prominent gap and keep up the ridge to join Hickory Ridge. This lesser-used path continues to stair-step up the ridgeline. At 6.9 miles, reach a gap where you can clearly hear Rough Creek flowing to your left. It's a rough and steep 200-plus feet down to Rough Creek.

The trail climbs steadily from this gap. You are probably beginning to wonder why you didn't return the way you came. The ridgeline stays narrow and drops off sharply on either side. Come to a tough short pitch at 7.7 miles, the first of two short but brutal climbs. Break the 3,000-foot mark on the second climb and reach a trail junction and a level gap shaded by a large oak at 8.8 miles.

The East Cowpen Trail keeps forward and climbs more. You, however, turn right, also on the East Cowpen Trail. The bed of the East Cowpen Trail is very wide. It is the old Georgia Highway 2, and it's downhill almost the whole way back to the Rice Camp Trailhead. Work downhill around wide, rich coves with tall tulip and cherry trees. Sporadic views of the Jacks River valley open between the trees. The descent is fast and steady, and mountain laurel crowds the trail.

Make a couple of big turns at 9.3 miles. Keep descending; notice where rock was blasted from the side of the track. These locales look almost natural now, covered in ferns and moss. The trail leaves the Cohutta Wilderness at 10.9 miles. The downgrade sharpens as you roll over earth berms. The Hickory Creek Trail comes in on the left, just before the East Cowpen Trail ends at a pole gate and the Rice Camp Trailhead.

11

Emery Creek Falls and Overlook

Total distance: 7.4 miles there and back

Hiking time: 4¾ hours

Vertical rise: 2,200 feet

Rating: Difficult

Maps: USGS 7.5' Crandall, Dyer Gap, Chattahoochee National Forest

This hike takes a top-down approach to the many features along the Emery Creek Trail. You start by leaving the high country of the Cohutta Mountains, heading away from the Cohutta Wilderness. After passing through a historic Cherokee gathering place, the hike takes you to a precipice along Little Bald Mountain, the Emery Creek Overlook, where waves of North Georgia mountains meld into the distance. Beyond this point, the secluded trail descends into the Emery Creek watershed, passing an unnamed triple-tier fall. After reaching the depths of the creek valley, the forest changes to lush and dark classic Southern Appalachian hemlock woodland. Emery Creek gathers in pools and foams white over rocks. The rush of falling water is audible as you pass a little-visited series of falls before reaching Emery Creek Falls via a short spur trail.

Make no mistake about it—this is a tough hike. It involves a 2,200-foot descent, which is easy. It's the return trip that tests your lung power. But the visual rewards and the solitude make the hike worthwhile. One effect of the reduced foot traffic is an overgrown path. So consider wearing long pants here during the summer to protect against briars and stinging nettle, which grow on the upper half of the path.

HOW TO GET THERE

From the intersection of US 411 and GA 52 in Chatsworth, near the courthouse, keep north on US 411 for 4.1 miles to Eton. Turn right onto CCC Camp Road at the traffic

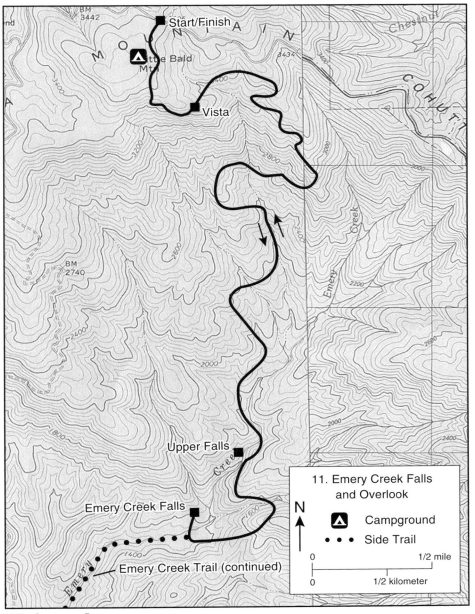

BM
3442

Start/Finish

M
O
U
N
T
A
I
N

Little Bald
Mt.

Vista

Chestnut

COHUTTA

3434

Emery Creek

BM
2740

Upper Falls

Creek

Emery Creek Falls

Emery Creek Trail (continued)

Emery

11. Emery Creek Falls
and Overlook

N

△ Campground

● ● ● Side Trail

0   1/2 mile

0   1/2 kilometer

© The Countryman Press

The Emery Creek Trail

light and go 10 miles to Forest Road 68, Old CCC Camp Road. Veer left on FR 68, reaching Holly Creek Gap at 2.4 miles. Stay left with FR 68 toward Lake Conasauga. At 5.9 miles, stay left again, still on FR 68. At 9.3 miles, reach the Tearbritches and upper Emery Creek Trailheads. The Emery Creek Trail leaves left up and through the Ball Field Group Camping Area. It is best to park near the entrance to the group area, on FR 68.

THE HIKE

Leave the trailhead on Forest Road 68 and walk uphill beyond the pole gate for the Ball Field Group Camp. Follow the road that centers the field, heading up Little Bald Mountain. This field was once a ball field and gathering spot for Cherokee Indians. Today it is a gathering spot for all groups who enjoy the mountain woods. Group campers primarily set up on the wooded perimeter of the field.

The road stops at the upper end of the field. Look for a wide track in the upper left corner of the field. Walk this track just a few feet, then veer left onto a singletrack path. Painted blazes mark the trail. The roadbed continues straight uphill. The forest is beautiful here—ferns and brush grow beneath scattered trees. Gray rocks add more color to the shades of green. The Emery Creek Trail comes alongside the southeast edge of Little Bald Mountain. Soon a cleared overlook opens to the right of the trail at 0.4 mile. You can see Fort Mountain, the Emery Creek valley, and other points to the east.

Beyond the overlook, the path descends along the edge of the mountain before turning left and dipping into the Emery Creek watershed, passing a small branch. Continue descending to pass a second branch, flowing off the south side of Cohutta Mountain. From here, the woods open again, with scattered trees and low brush that allow long in-forest views. Begin descending by switchbacks along the south slope of Cohutta Mountain, eventually joining the top of a ridge covered in white pine. Bronze needles carpet the trailbed. In places, this ridgeline descent is moderated by switchbacks; in other places it goes steeply down the nose of the ridge. You will remember this part of the hike on the return trip.

Leave the white pine ridge with a hard turn to the right. Partial views extend beyond the mountainside. Pass beneath a slope of exposed rock to reach a trickling creek. Dip sharply but briefly along this branch and resume a moderate descent to reach a more voluminous stream at 2.2 miles. Look upstream here. A small waterfall is in front of you, and two more cascades are farther up. Emery Creek Trail now leaves the branch and circles around a steep, moist, shallow cove with more towering trees, such as tulip trees.

The hike soon changes as you return to the creek. The watercourse is now enveloped in hemlocks and rhododendron, a deep, dark forest contrasting with the woods through which you've been walking so far. Pick up an old roadbed after stepping over the creek. The footing improves here, but the descent continues and your concern may begin to rise about the return trip. Deep woods shade the path and the crashing creek beside you. Note the plethora of dwarf crested iris along the trail. Look also for big boulders beside the track.

The descent moderates in a cove that was decimated by Hurricane Ivan in 2004. Scores of downed trees line the path. Cross back over the creek amid these blowdowns. At 3.6 miles, the trail reaches closed Forest Road 78E. Pay attention here. The Emery Creek Trail turns left along the forest road and follows it just a few feet before veering off and shortly crossing Emery Creek, which has come in from the left. The path continues through the storm-damaged area to cross back over to the right bank of Emery Creek. The pools are now larger, as feeder branches add water volume.

The path cuts a deep, dark hollow here. Soon you make another crossing. At this point, the creek drops steeply below to the right and the trail actually climbs a bit. The valley widens considerably. You will soon hear the upper falls crashing below. Save that cascade for the return trip and continue along the old roadbed, which surprisingly turns away from Emery Creek and slips over to a feeder branch. The path then follows the feeder branch to meet the spur trail to Emery Creek Falls at 4.7 miles, just before crossing Emery Creek again. The signed spur trail leads right, upstream along Emery Creek for about 100 yards to reach the falls. This is a multitiered cascade that makes numerous drops into small pools before ending at a deep pool and great swimming spot. The spur trail continues to a little hemlock flat above Emery Creek Falls and below a shorter, wider single-drop fall.

Most folks come the 2 miles upstream from the lower Emery Creek Trailhead, which is easier, but busier, and doesn't have the overlooks. To reach the upper set of falls you passed earlier, backtrack up the Emery Creek Falls Trail to the point where you can see and hear the upper falls, just before your first crossing of Emery Creek on the return trip. You will notice that there is no direct trail to these falls, even though many people have scrambled over to clear the way. Be careful here, however.

12

Panther Creek Falls and Overlook

Total distance: 8.2 miles there and back

Hiking time: 4 hours

Vertical rise: 1,275 feet

Rating: Moderate to difficult

Maps: USGS 7.5' Hemp Top, Cohutta and Big Frog Wilderness, Chattahoochee National Forest

Some hikes include a waterfall and an overlook on the same trek, but it isn't often that a hike takes you to a waterfall and vista from the same spot. This one does, and it's among the finest destinations in all of North Georgia. Better still, it takes place in the famed Cohutta Wilderness.

The hike leaves the East Cowpen Trailhead and climbs over East Cowpen Mountain, breaking the 4,000-foot barrier before descending to the Panther Creek Trail. This path wanders along a wooded ridge and then drops to the upper section of Panther Creek, essentially a hanging valley, to arrive at the top of Panther Creek Falls, where a rocky rim allows an unobstructed view into the Cohuttas. A look down at the falls reveals an open rock face, laid bare by the torrential rains of Hurricane Ivan in 2004. The Panther Creek Falls Trail leads down by the base of the falls, where you can get the bottom-up perspective to complement your top-down view.

This is a great hike if you want to go to the Cohuttas, but high water on the Jacks and Conasauga Rivers makes fording impractical.

HOW TO GET THERE

To reach the trailhead from the town square in Ellijay, take GA 52 east, Dalton Street, for 5.1 miles to Gates Chapel Road. Turn right and continue 5.4 miles. The pavement ends on Gates Chapel Road. Veer right here, joining Wilderness Trail (Forest Road 90). Keep on FR 90 for 1.6 miles to Holly Gap and FR 68. Turn right onto FR 68, passing Barnes Creek at 1.1 miles. After 3.4 miles

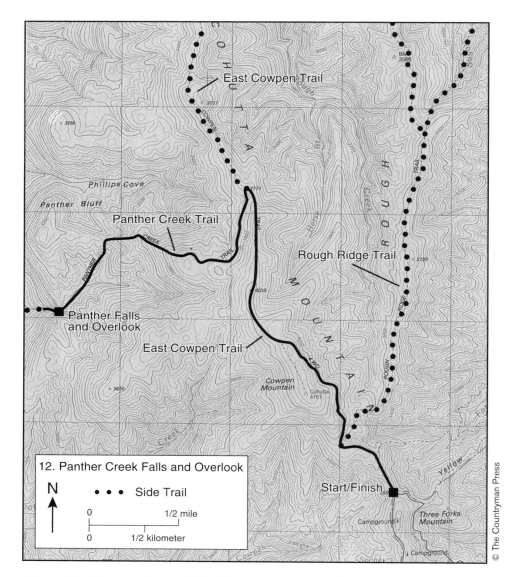

12. Panther Creek Falls and Overlook

N

• • • Side Trail

0   1/2 mile

0   1/2 kilometer

total on FR 68, veer right onto FR 64. Continue 4.2 miles to the Three Forks Trailhead and the East Cowpen Trail.

THE HIKE

Leave the parking area on FR 64 and begin to climb on the East Cowpen Trail. This was once a highway, Old GA 2, and it remained

open for a while after the Cohutta Wilderness designation in 1975. The wide track makes for easy walking, and at 0.4 mile you are already at the junction with the Rough Ridge Trail, which leaves right. Keep forward, still ascending. The mountaintop to your left is rising faster than the trail. Ferns become more prominent in the understory.

View from the outcrop atop Panther Creek Falls

In places the canopy is somewhat open, but the old roadbed is also being shaded by witch hazel, a small tree that can barely reach over the trail. The leaves make this tree easy to identify because they are wavy and almost as wide as they are long. Another key identifier for this tree is its multiple trunks. Witch hazel grows in moist soil throughout Georgia. Mountain folk made divining rods from witch hazel limbs to find water underground.

The trail reaches its high point at 4,100-plus feet. Travel an azalea-lined pathway along the ridgetop, then begin a descent broken with level spots. The walking is easy. Reach the Panther Creek Trail at 2.3 miles. Turn acutely left here on a narrower trailbed. The path heads south, in nearly the opposite direction you were traveling on the East Cowpen Trail. The footing is good as you wind through a cove hardwood forest rife with tulip, birch, and maple trees. The path becomes rougher as it turns west on a rib ridge emanating from East Cowpen

Mountain. The trail begins to drop faster here, entering better terrain for a waterfall. But at this point you can't even hear water running yet.

Pines, galax, and mountain laurel flank the track as its pitch increases. Reach a piney gap at 3.5 miles. The Panther Creek Trail splits left and nosedives into a cove. Ramrod-straight tulip trees grow in the cove, along with a few wobbly locusts. The rill at the cove's low point finally musters up enough water to begin flowing off to your right, just as you meet Panther Creek, which flows wide and shallow here. Panther Creek flows through a beautiful little valley, perched high in the Cohutta Wilderness. Campsites lie in the most level locations.

Cross over Panther Creek a second time. You are now on the right bank as the path tunnels beneath rhododendron and hemlock trees. Follow Panther Creek until it reaches Panther Creek Falls at 4 miles. The watercourse dives off Panther Bluff, a westward-oriented mountain face. The bare rock face allows for both a vista and a waterfall view. Be careful here, as you are literally on the edge of the falls.

To your west is the Conasauga River valley, backed by the ridgeline that forms the western boundary of the Cohuttas. Before you there is nothing but nature. Below you, Panther Creek is spilling onto the rock face, stripped bare of vegetation by the rains from Ivan. Those who saw the falls before that storm will be in for a surprise when they see this change. The water runs where it always did, but now it is bordered by nothing but rock. Uprooted trees lie in a tangled pile at the base of the falls. These trees will decay long before the bare face along Panther Bluff is revegetated.

To reach the base of the falls, stay with the Panther Creek Trail as it curves beneath the steep wall of Panther Bluff, to the right of the falls as you are looking out. The trail runs along the base of the bluff before zigzagging down near the bottom of the falls at 4.1 miles. A little scrambling will take you from the trail to the base of the falls and the bare rock alongside it.

13

Cascades of Crenshaw

Total distance: 7.2 miles there and back

Hiking time: 4½ hours

Vertical rise: 1,280 feet

Rating: Difficult

*Maps: USGS 7.5' Dyer Gap,
Chattahoochee National Forest*

This hike follows the infrequently used upper section of the Mountaintown Creek Trail, and heads down to see two sets of impressive cascades on Crenshaw Branch. The trail ends in pretty flat flanked by two creeks, Crenshaw Branch and Heddy Creek, which together form Mountaintown Creek. The flat where this hike ends is not only a good picnic spot and turnaround point, but it also makes for a good campsite. The three creeks at the flat—Mountaintown, Heddy, and Crenshaw—all offer quality trout fishing, as well. I caught my biggest trout in the Southeast backcountry in this watershed. You may find the falls along the creek more impressive than my trout-catching prowess, especially the second set of continuous whitewater that shoots down a bare rock chute, careening and ricocheting toward its confluence with Heddy Creek.

The Mountaintown Creek Trail is not often hiked for two reasons. First, it is very near the more popular Cohutta Wilderness trails, and second, control of the access road on its lower end has been a source of controversy among private property owners in the area. Therefore, you will likely be enjoying this pretty path by yourself.

HOW TO GET THERE

From Blue Ridge, where US 76 and GA 5 diverge, drive north on US 76 for 3.7 miles to Old State Road 2. A sign there reads OLD S. R. 2. Turn left here and go 10.6 miles to Watson Gap, located at the intersection with Forest Roads 64 and 22. Turn left on FR 64 and follow it 5.7 miles, passing Jacks

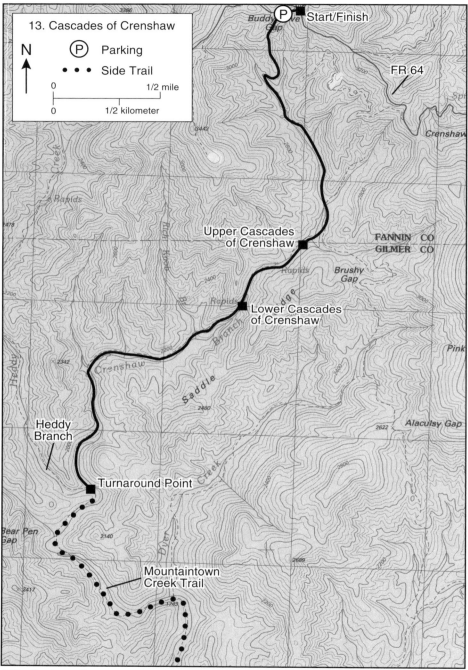

River Fields Campground at 4 miles. The trailhead is on your left and the Buddy Cove Gap parking area is on your right, just beyond the trailhead.

THE HIKE

The Mountaintown Creek Trail, which shares treadway with the Pinhoti Trail, leaves south from Forest Road 64, angling down toward Crenshaw Branch. A singletrack, white-blazed path overlies an old woods road, and a south-facing slope of pine and deciduous trees provides shade. Make a quick, steep drop in quiet woods, then level off in hemlocks. At 0.5 mile, make a big switchback to the left as you come to the uppermost part of Crenshaw Branch. A sign reminds anglers that this watershed allows artificial lures only.

The sound of rushing water accompanies your descent and will be with you the rest of the hike. Pass through a clearing that has almost disappeared. The forest changes in both type and thickness. Moisture-loving trees such as birch, hemlock, and Fraser magnolia rise above tangles of rhododendron. Make your first crossing of Crenshaw Branch at 1.2 miles. You can get across this one dry-footed, but wet fords likely lie ahead.

The creek flows clear but not too fast in this hanging valley, bordered on the east by Saddle Ridge and on the west by Rich Knob. Mosses, mushrooms, snails, and slugs like the cool, damp hemlock woods in this high-elevation hollow. Make the second crossing of Crenshaw Branch just above a feeder stream at 1.5 miles. Crenshaw Branch is gaining volume and momentum. Just ahead are the Upper Cascades of Crenshaw. On your right, a short waterfall creates a nice deep pool sure to harbor secretive trout. The second fall is more impressive. It widens after dropping 20 feet over a rock face, spreading its white froth as far as momentum and gravity will allow. This one is easily viewed from the trail, although a short path leads to its base. More narrow drops continue, heard but unseen.

There was once a relatively high bridge at the third crossing of Crenshaw Branch at 1.9 miles. This is a certain ford unless you are an accomplished fallen-tree crosser. Now come to the long Cascades of Crenshaw. You will hear them before you see them. To your left, Crenshaw Branch begins to drop steeply, sliding and crashing over a massive rock slide, made barren by the continuous pinballing froth of whitewater. The noise echoing in the constricted valley will fill your ears. Due to the deep cut in the creek and heavy vegetation, the cascades are hard to see, but every now and then you can glimpse the whitewater. The creek falls faster than the trail through this canyon, though your downgrade is significant.

Wild areas like this are great harborages for Georgia's black bears, which are common in the Cohutta Mountains. The bruin is thriving not only in the mountains but throughout the state, which counts over 2,200 bears in its population. The bears live in three distinct areas of the state: in the North Georgia Mountains, where Crenshaw Creek lies; in the center of the state in the Ocmulgee River basin; and in the swampy southeast, centered in the Okefenokee Swamp.

Wild black bears typically live 8 to 15 years. Bears that retain a healthy fear of man typically outlive food-habituated bears. You should never feed a bear. Human food is the drug that wild animals can't shake, and they will eventually do anything to get it. If they are lucky, such animals end up being relocated, but usually they end up shot or run over.

An adult bear may grow to 6 feet in length and around 3 feet high at the shoulder. Adult

One of the many cascades of Crenshaw

females weigh up to 300 pounds and attain breeding status at 3 or 4 years of age. The breeding season is in July, and cubs are born in the den in late January or February. Bear cubs weigh under a pound when born, are relatively undeveloped, and are entirely dependent on the mother. They stay with their mother throughout the first year, den with her during the following winter, and stay with her until she finally drives them away the following spring. Due to this extended level of care, females only produce a litter every two years.

Adult males can weigh over 500 pounds and may breed as early as 1.5 years of age. But these are exceptional. You are more likely to see a bear under 200 pounds. Bears have poor eyesight but an excellent sense of smell. They are good tree climbers, can swim well, and are able to run at speeds of up to 30 miles per hour.

Finally, the creek levels off and the trail catches up to the watery tumble. The path curves around a side creek coming in on

the right at 2.3 miles. More small streams add to the flow. Keep down alongside Crenshaw Branch to reach the fourth crossing at 3.2 miles. Be careful, as this is a deceptive crossing. The water is fast and the rock-slab creek bottom is slick; the crossing is just above a small falls. The creek has many plunge pools in this section. Make one more crossing.

At 3.6 miles, the trail comes to a flat at the turnaround point. Just ahead, the Mountaintown Creek Trail fords Heddy Creek, which has come in on your right. Crenshaw Branch and Heddy Creek meet to form Mountaintown Creek. Towering white pines shade the flat between the Crenshaw and Heddy. This setting is good for a picnic, a backpack campsite, or just for contemplation. If you wish to explore farther, you can continue down Mountaintown Creek Trail to its end at private property, or if you are feeling more adventurous, trace the old roadbed/fisherman's trail up Heddy Creek.

14

Penitentiary Loop

Total distance: 13.1 miles

Hiking time: 7 hours

Vertical rise: 820 feet

Rating: Difficult

Maps: USGS 7.5' Hemp Top, Cohutta and Big Frog Wilderness, Chattahoochee National Forest

The name "penitentiary" may make you wonder about taking this hike, which completes a circuit on the east side of the Cohutta Wilderness. The story goes like this: In the 1930s, when the Jacks River basin was being logged, the Great Depression was on. The loggers were very appreciative of having a job, knowing there were many men behind them to take their jobs if they quit. The hours were long and so was the work week—six days on, one off. During the week they had to live in the logging camp, but they could go anywhere they wanted on their day off. The problem was that there was nowhere nearby where they could go in one day and still be back when the work bell rang the next morning. So the men were stuck at the logging camp on a feeder branch of Jacks River seven days a week—like being stuck in the penitentiary. That feeder branch on the Jacks River got stuck with the name Penitentiary Branch, and the trail up that creek met the same fate.

This hike heads north along the Hemp Top Trail, tramping through the high country before turning onto Penitentiary Branch Trail, where it winds along the edge of Penitentiary Ridge with views into the Jacks River valley open between the pines. Once on Jacks River, the 18 fords make for a challenging and intimate way to get to know this clear and picturesque river. The upper Jacks River has numerous crashing rapids that add to the scenery. This section is also challenging due to damage from Hurricane Ivan, which scoured the river, washed away trees, and created slides along the trail.

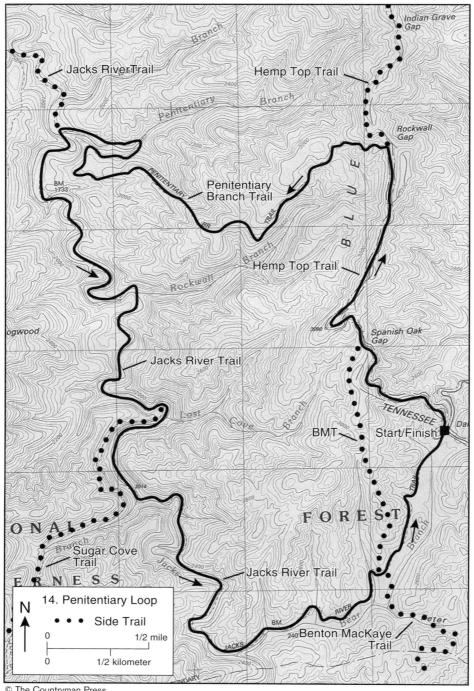

Jacks River Trail

Hemp Top Trail

Penitentiary
Branch Trail

Hemp Top Trail

Rockwall

Jacks River Trail

Spanish Oak
Gap

TENNESSEE

BMT

Start/Finish

FOREST

Sugar Cove
Trail

ONAL

ERNESS

Jacks River Trail

Benton MacKaye
Trail

N

14. Penitentiary Loop

• • • Side Trail

0   1/2 mile

0   1/2 kilometer

© The Countryman Press

The path then leaves Jacks River, heading up quieter Bear Branch for a surprisingly easy end. Making the loop counterclockwise keeps your feet dry for the longest period, because once you're on the Jacks River the fords are inevitable. Also, consider taking this trek in late summer or early fall, when the river is at its lowest. This loop is a long but very doable day hike or an easy overnight backpack. It starts at Dally Gap, a lesser-used trailhead in the Cohutta Wilderness. I was once stuck there with a dead car battery on a weekday for 24 hours before a car came by.

HOW TO GET THERE

To reach the trailhead from Blue Ridge, where US 76 and GA 5 diverge, drive north on US 76 for 3.7 miles to Old State Road 2. A sign reads OLD S. R. 2. Turn left here and continue 10.6 miles to Watson Gap, located at the intersection with Forest Roads 64 and 22. Turn right on FR 22 and follow it 3.4 miles to the Dally Gap Trailhead.

THE HIKE

Dally Gap has two trails emanating from it, and you will leave on one and return on the other. Head around the pole gate on the Hemp Top Trail and curve uphill, entering the Cohutta Wilderness. Make a gentle but steady climb on this old woods road that was closed two decades ago. Pine and locust trees are filling the margins, making it look ever less roadlike. The adjacent forests grow much taller. At 0.7 mile, the trail passes a big mudslide that has made the going more tenuous and opened a view to the east.

At 0.9 mile, the Benton MacKaye Trail (BMT) meets the Hemp Top Trail. Together they leave the gap and share treadway into Tennessee, where the BMT heads to the Smoky Mountains. At this point, the path

switches to the inside of a hollow, the uppermost part of the Bear Creek drainage. It circles around the upper end of the hollow, gaining elevation to curve back around to the top of the ridge. The trail resumes its northbound ways. Climb a bit more to reach a high point at 1.5 miles. The trailside vegetation now includes more low brush.

Cruise through the high country, slipping over to the west side of Hemp Top. A good ear can hear Jacks River frothing far below. Oaks, pines, mountain laurel, and grasses grow on this west slope, where rock was blasted to make the trail. Reach the Penitentiary Branch Trail at 2.3 miles. Veer left here and descend on a more slender track. Chestnut oaks, sourwood, and hickory trees enjoy this drier slope of Penitentiary Ridge. The path is rockier and more uneven than Hemp Top.

Pass through an obvious gap along the ridge at 2.8 miles. The trail then shifts to the south-facing edge of the ridge, where you can look into the valley below between the pines. The low, dull roar of the Jacks remains, as the trail occasionally curves into a cove or two. Turn into Penitentiary Branch at 5 miles. It has a different sound than the bigger Jacks. A hemlock-birch-rhododendron complex covers the valley. Cross the stream at 5.4 miles, just below where Penitentiary Branch and a smaller stream meet. Continue down the narrow valley. This creek, falling in cascades between pools, was scoured by Ivan, which also left piles of trees pinned against other trees.

Intersect Jacks River Trail at 5.8 miles. This area, with campsites and attendant social trails, can be confusing. This may be the location of the "Penitentiary Logging Camp." Immediately ford Jacks River, angling upstream. This is the first of 18 fords. Some are easy, some more difficult. They come fast and furious, sometimes one after another.

A turtle on the Jacks River Trail

And to think, a railroad once followed this route! In places the railroad bed is obvious, and you can even see the homemade ties. Elsewhere, the bed was scoured, or washed away, and the Jacks River Trail makes its way along sandbars and twists among hemlocks, moving upstream in a dark moist valley where the sound of rapids echo skyward.

Ivan piled debris, moved rocks, deepened the fords in places, and created new stream meanders. As you ascend, Jacks River falls at a steeper gradient, becoming a frothy whitewater ribbon dashing over gray boulders in a green cathedral. The trail curves around the nose of the ridge, which Sugar Cove Trail descends. At 8.7 miles, the Sugar Cove Trail comes in from the right. You are on the left bank. At 9.3 miles, across the water, Sugar Cove Creek creates a falls as it meets Jacks River.

The trail steepens and rises well above the river, then reaches a bare rock slide that extends all the way down to the water, which you can see below. Be careful crossing this section. Keep winding around a big curve; a good view opens down the Jacks River valley. The trail descends to the river just as a side stream slides over a rock face. Come to a second, smaller slide that is easily negotiated before you pass through a low gap at 10 miles. The Jacks River makes a bend that the trail shortcuts. There is a tough ford here, the first one in a while. Keep upstream as the river quiets down. Moss grows on anything that doesn't move in the shade of this valley.

Make a last ford over to the left bank. The trail is much improved, as you join an old roadbed and curve into the Bear Creek basin. Head up this rich valley. The walking is easy as you step over small creeks flowing into Bear Creek. The path heads away from Bear Creek, meandering along the mid-slope in lush woods where creek noise is conspicuously absent. At 12.1 miles, the Benton MacKaye Trail comes in from the right and shares treadway with the Jacks River Trail for a few hundred yards before leaving left again.

Keep forward in gently rolling terrain and reach Dally Gap, completing the loop at 13.1 miles.

15

Gennett Poplar on Bear Creek

Total distance: 2.9 miles loop

Hiking time: 1¾ hours

Vertical rise: 400 feet

Rating: Moderate

Maps: USGS 7.5' Dyer Gap, Chattahoochee National Forest

The mountains of North Georgia are full of superlative views, mountains, watercourses— and some big trees. And the Gennett Poplar may be the biggest of them all. This massive tulip tree was spared the logger's ax by Andrew and N. W. Gennett, who owned this land before it was purchased for the Chattahoochee National Forest. You can see this colossal tree in the green cathedral of Bear Creek.

Your gateway to the Gennett Poplar is the Bear Creek Loop Trail, which is actually two loops, plus a spur to a picnic area. This adds up to over 7 miles of paths, which were built in part as a service project sponsored by the outdoor gear store REI in 1992. The Bear Creek trail system is popular with mountain bikers, but also hikers who want to see this tree and the area where it thrives up close. The loop described here is the lowermost loop, which makes a 2.9-mile circuit, heading up Bear Creek before joining a closed and seeded woods road along the upper slopes of the Bear Creek valley. Wildlife clearings have been constructed that enhance your chances for seeing deer, turkey, and other critters that roam these woods.

HOW TO GET THERE

From the town square in Ellijay, take GA 52 east, Dalton Street, for 5.1 miles to Gates Chapel Road. Turn right and go 5 miles to the bridge over Bear Creek, which is immediately followed by a right turn onto Forest Road 241. Continue 2 miles to dead-end at the trailhead. After 1 mile on FR 241, you pass the Bear Creek Primitive

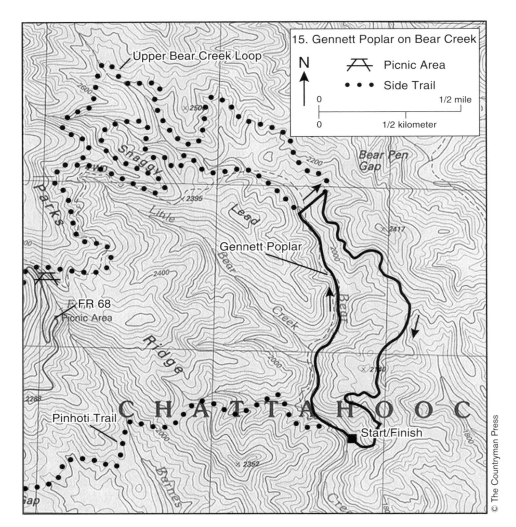

15. Gennett Poplar on Bear Creek

N

Picnic Area

• • • Side Trail

0   1/2 mile

0   1/2 kilometer

Upper Bear Creek Loop

Shaggy

Parks

Little

Lead

Gennett Poplar

FR 68
Picnic Area

Bear Creek

Ridge

CHATTAHOOC

Pinhoti Trail

Start/Finish

Gap

Barnes Creek

© The Countryman Press

Camping Area, which is accessed by a short vehicle ford and then a footbridge to an attractive creekside camping flat beneath white pines. Vault toilets are the only amenity. Bear and Mountaintown Creeks at the camping area are stocked with trout during the warm season.

THE HIKE

The Bear Creek Trail leaves the parking area and passes around some large earth berms.

Small, clear Bear Creek flows to your right. Just ahead is a large plunge pool on the watercourse. Rhododendron crowds the stream. The foot bed is dirt and rock. The luxuriously wooded sides of the valley rise tall, crowding out all but the midday sun, which still has to fight its way through the hemlock, maple, and birch trees. Begin climbing above the creek. At 0.2 mile the Bear Creek Trail reaches a junction; here, the Pinhoti Trail joins the Bear Creek Trail as it continues upstream. This part of the Georgia Pinhoti connects the nearby Benton MacKaye Trail with the Alabama Pinhoti Trail. Just ahead, cross a branch of Bear Creek.

The moist valley is a real haven for hemlocks. Unfortunately, Georgia's hemlocks are imperiled by an invasive bug known as the hemlock wooly adelgid. This Asian critter somehow reached the United States and made its way down the Appalachian Chain. It is in Tennessee as of this writing, devastating the evergreens in the Smoky Mountains, among other places. This bug's signature is the tiny white round "golf balls" it leaves on the undersides of hemlock needles. Trees die within three to five years of infestation. There is hope, however, as another insect, which kills the adelgid, is being propagated and let loose to eliminate it. The verdict is still out on the long-term viability of the hemlock, a staple tree in moist creekside hollows such as this. While researching this book, I traveled trails from the west side of North Georgia to the east and saw only healthy hemlocks.

At 0.5 mile, cross Little Bear Creek at its confluence with Bear Creek. Occasionally a gap opens in the dense woods, and these areas seem very bright. It makes you realize just how dark it is in here. This moist hollow can be especially thick after a summer thunderstorm. Cross Bear Creek to reach the Gennett Poplar at 0.8 mile.

This tree is truly a giant, and worth saving. It is 18 feet in circumference, measured 4 feet off the ground, and its massive trunk rises high into the sky. Many ancient trees such as this have broken off trunks, from lightning or decay, yet the Gennett Poplar stands tall and proud. But the name is actually a misnomer, for it is not a true poplar at all. It is actually a tulip tree, the modern and scientifically correct name for this species. The tulip tree, also known as yellow poplar or tulip poplar, is recognized for its arrow-straight trunk, and is one of the largest growing hardwoods in the eastern U.S. Its large, showy orange and yellow flowers, which bloom in May in North Georgia, do resemble a tulip somewhat. However, the tree's leaves—which turn yellow in the fall—are shaped exactly like the outline of a tulip, making it easy to identify.

Tulip trees prefer moist valleys like Bear Creek and north-facing slopes and coves. The Gennett Poplar is just one of many giant tulip trees in the Southern Appalachians. North Carolina's Joyce Kilmer Memorial Forest features many old-growth tulip trees, as does the Albright Grove Nature Trail on the Tennessee side of the Great Smoky Mountains National Park.

Beyond the Gennett Poplar, the trail continues forward to reach a trail junction at 1 mile. The shorter loop turns right, along with the Pinhoti Trail. If you wish to extend the loop to 6-plus miles, keep forward on the Bear Creek Trail, then go right at the next trail junction. The left fork leads to Barnes Creek Picnic Area and the upper Bear Creek Trailhead on FR 68. The shorter loop turns right here and climbs along a trickling branch before meeting up with a closed forest road at 1.1 miles. The longer loop of Bear Creek comes in here.

Turn right on the grassy track with a small path overlain down its middle. This former road was intentionally seeded and closed to create what is known as a linear clearing. This type of trail combines scenic beauty with man-made wildlife openings, enabling you to see the Forest Service's efforts to create a better habitat for the region's fauna. Wildlife openings contain highly nutritious plants and grasses that are planted for the benefit of birds, turkey, deer, and other animals. Forest and grassland interface in these openings, producing

The author at the Gennett Poplar

"edges" where vegetation from both environments mix to attract wildlife. Wildlife management is a key element of the Forest Service's multiple-use concept for our national forests.

The walking is easy on this part of the trail. The canopy is open overhead but the path is bordered by young tulip trees, among other species. It is hard to imagine the Gennett Poplar being this young. White pines grow tallest in the surrounding forest. Their symmetrical evergreen crowns are easy to spot. The atmosphere on this part of the loop is quite different from the thick, dark, shady trail on Bear Creek, which is off to your right.

The roadbed opens into a wide grassy clearing that is more of a traditional wildlife clearing. Beyond this opening the path turns away from Bear Creek and passes through a second wildlife opening. After the third wide grassy clearing the trail reenters woods. This wooded section demonstrates the positive difference when an area is managed for wildlife. Reach the fourth wide wildlife clearing at 2.3 miles.

The Bear Creek Loop turns sharply right into shady woods, marked by a brown plastic post. The roadbed continues forward, but the Bear Creek Loop begins wending its way back to the trailhead. A surprising descent follows. The earlier elevation gain was hardly noticeable. Reach Bear Creek, then turn upstream to cross without the benefit of a bridge. This may be a wet-footed crossing. Climb a bit and complete the loop at 2.9 miles.

16

Benton MacKaye Trail near Aska

Total distance: 6.6 miles there and back

Hiking time: 3¾ hours

Vertical rise: 1,250 feet

Rating: Moderate

Maps: USGS 7.5' Blue Ridge, Chattahoochee National Forest

On most hikes, the highlight—maybe a vista or waterfall or other place of note—is at the end of the walk. In this case, the main feature, Fall Branch Falls, is near the hike's beginning, where it tumbles down alongside the Benton MacKaye Trail (BMT) in a remote section of the Chattahoochee National Forest. After passing the falls, the hike takes an uphill tack in an area forgotten by most other trail travelers, leaving it to all of nature's beasts—and anyone who chooses to walk to an unnamed knob where the BMT meets the Stanley Gap Trail. Obscured and winter views can be had along the way to the top.

HOW TO GET THERE

From the junction of the GA 52 overpass and GA 515/US 76, just north of Ellijay, keep north on GA 515/US 76 for 7.8 miles to Rock Creek Connector. Turn right and go 0.1 mile to Rock Creek Road. Turn right again and continue 5.9 miles to the Fall Branch trailhead on your left. (Rock Creek Road turns to gravel after 2 miles and passes the Stanley Gap Trailhead at 5 miles.) Look for the double-diamond blazes on the trail heading upstream along Fall Branch.

THE HIKE

This hike takes place in the Rich Mountain Wildlife Management Area, a disjointed tract of the Chattahoochee National Forest located northeast of Ellijay and southeast of Blue Ridge. The trailless Rich Mountain

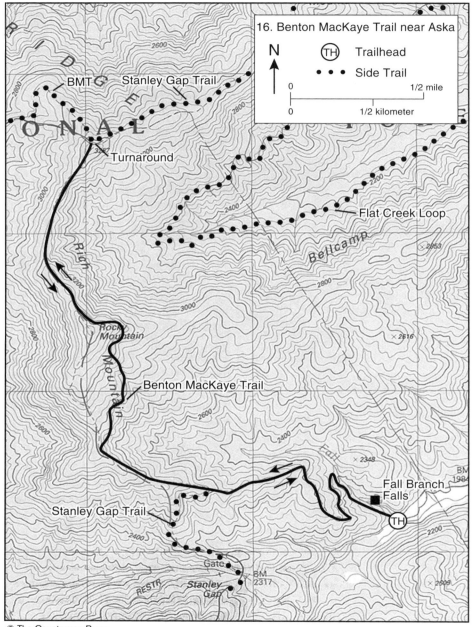

16. Benton MacKaye Trail near Aska

N

(TH) Trailhead
• • • Side Trail

0   1/2 mile
0   1/2 kilometer

BMT Stanley Gap Trail

Turnaround

Rich

Flat Creek Loop

Bellcamp

× 2853

Rocky
Mountain

3000

× 2616

Mountain

Benton MacKaye Trail

Fall

× 2348

BM
198

Fall Branch
Falls

Stanley Gap Trail

(TH)

2200

Gate

RESTR Stanley
Gap

BM
2317

× 2609

© The Countryman Press

An old chimney near Fall Branch

Wilderness occupies the southern half of the area. The Aska Trail System, located on the east side of the area, receives the most pressure (see Hike 17, Flat Creek Loop), relegating the Benton MacKaye Trail to its usual role as second fiddle. The BMT is normally overshadowed by the Appalachian Trail, which is nowhere in sight around here. Although both trails begin atop Springer Mountain, the AT heads northeast toward North Carolina and the Nantahala National Forest, while the BMT angles northwest for Tennessee and the Cherokee National Forest before reaching the Smokies.

Pick up the BMT just as it is reentering the national forest from a road walk through private land. On a recent backpacking trip on the BMT through Georgia, I was glad to see this particular stretch of trail as it turned up along Fall Branch and met woods. As a matter of convenience, Rich Mountain was the next stretch of public land through which to lay out the trail, but I believe it was

a stroke of luck for us hikers because here, the BMT traverses isolated forests where pleasant seclusion is guaranteed any day of the week.

Before you leave the trailhead, there is something to see. As you face upstream, look to your left in a hemlock copse. Notice the leveled-off land with a rock wall built into the hillside? Look a little closer and you may notice the fallen chimney, too. Here are the remains of a cabin built by a mountaineer who likely settled along Fall Branch—then the back of beyond—to harness some of that gravity-driven water power to push an old tub mill for grinding corn into cornmeal and to lighten the load of innumerable chores at a subsistence farm.

Leave the trailhead and walk around some boulder vehicle barriers. Ascend along Fall Branch, passing a pair of cabins located on a small slice of private land across the creek. Leave the inholdings behind and enter the cool, dark world of a Southern Appalachian streamside forest. The climb steepens, but before you know it you are at the spur trail leading right, down to an observation platform below Fall Branch Falls. The three-tiered drop makes a sort of "S" as it descends first as a curtain-type drop, then shifts to the left side of a second rock face, gathers together in a pool, and resumes its downgrade on the right side of the third rock face. This cascade gave Fall Branch its name.

Continue up along Fall Branch, gaining more glimpses of the waterfall. At 0.3 mile, the BMT leaves left, away from the old roadbed you have been following, and continues as a singletrack footpath. The sound of falling water becomes fainter as the BMT curves along a rib ridge of Rocky Mountain, one of many peaks named Rocky Mountain in these parts. Aromatic pines shade the path and deposit their needles upon the forest floor. Sourwoods, maples, and sassafras accompany the evergreens. The path shows significantly less use beyond Fall Branch as it turns onto the nose of the rib ridge, keeping uphill. A sense of solitude descends upon the lonely woods.

Reach a trail junction at 1.1 miles after entering young brushy woods, well on their way to recovery from a forest fire years back. The Stanley Gap Trail leaves left 0.5 mile to Stanley Gap and joins the BMT as it heads right, still working up the rib ridge in a dry forest. This was once known as the Rich Mountain Trail. Blueberries are abundant along the path, thanks in part to the forest fire. Locust and sourwood also compete for the increased light that falls on the low canopy. Some pines withstood the flames and rise above the rest of the trees, which are still open enough to allow south-facing views of the mountains across the Rock Creek drainage.

The climb levels off and makes a sharp turn to the right at 1.7 miles, on the south shoulder of Rocky Mountain. Keep working uphill. Boulders, bluffs, and rocks jut out above the path. Obscured views open to the east. The trail finally levels off again on the crest of the ridge, just north of Rocky Mountain's peak, at 2.6 miles. Here the BMT makes a pleasant cruise on a nearly level path around 3,200 feet in elevation. You get the sense that no one will cross your path in this area. The trail becomes quite rocky before reaching a junction just below an unnamed knob at 3.3 miles where the BMT and Stanley Gap Trail diverge.

The Stanley Gap Trail leaves right 3.7 miles for Deep Gap and the primary Aska area trailhead, while the Benton MacKaye Trail leaves left, shortly tops out on the knob, and then keeps northwest for Scroggin Knob before dropping down to US 76 near Cherry Log. This trail junction makes a good place to turn around. If you are in need of water, continue 0.9 mile down the BMT to a spur trail marked by stones that leads right 100 yards to a spring on a steep mountainside.

17

Flat Creek Loop

Total distance: 5.7 miles

Hiking time: 3 hours

Vertical rise: 500 feet

Rating: Moderate

Maps: USGS 7.5' Blue Ridge, Chattahoochee National Forest, Aska Area Trails

This is a classic loop day hike. The Flat Creek Trail is about the right length at 5.8 miles and travels some varied terrain with no overly rugged climbs. However, there is no single feature to see; rather, it is simply a good trail to walk and enjoy some beautiful North Georgia Mountain woodlands and streams. It leaves the Aska trailhead, which is popular with both hikers and mountain bikers, and travels old forest roads before looping into the Flat Creek drainage, crossing the creek by bridge, and returning to the trailhead. The loop is best enjoyed in spring, fall, or winter, since elevations are relatively low. Winter is an especially good time to hike here due to those low elevations, and you can keep your feet dry the entire way.

HOW TO GET THERE

From Blue Ridge, at the intersection where GA 5 and GA 515/US 76 diverge, take US 76 east for 0.7 mile to Windy Ridge Road (just after an overpass). Turn right and continue 0.2 mile to dead-end at First Street/ Old US 76. Turn left and go 0.2 mile to Aska Road. Turn right and continue 4.4 miles to reach the campground, on your left. The Deep Gap parking area is on the right side of the road, shortly after the actual Deep Gap.

THE HIKE

Be prepared to share the trail with mountain bikers, though the path is well used by hikers as well. The ranger station in Blue Ridge has a good area map, titled "Aska Area Trails," that you may find helpful. You

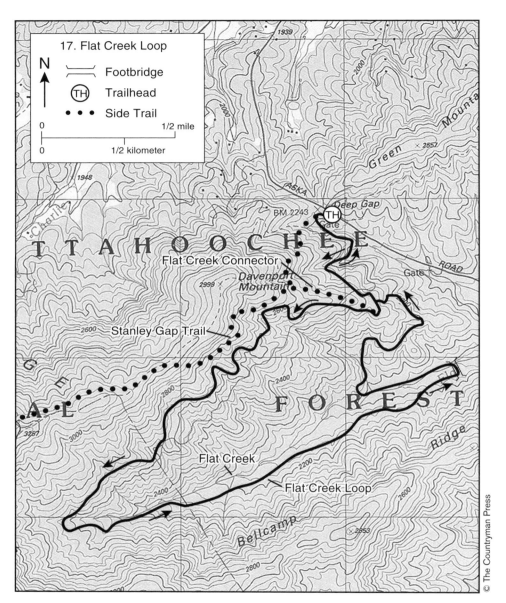

will see that the Flat Creek Loop is but one of several marked and maintained paths in the area.

The hike starts at the Aska Trailhead, immediately enters woods on a gravel track, and curves to the left. Soon the Stanley Gap Trail leaves right to meet the Benton MacKaye Trail near Rocky Mountain. The Flat Creek Loop Trail continues up an old forest road. Spindly trees growing tightly together border the old roadbed. This is an early stage of forest competition. Over time,

Fern-floored woodlands near Flat Creek

the healthiest trees will begin to tower over the weaker ones, which will die and return to the soil. This allows the best trees to co-opt the energy left from their fallen brethren, which assures a vigorous forest.

Span a stream by a culvert left over from the days when logging vehicles drove the trail. The young forest is heavy with straight gray-trunked tulip trees. These young trees have smooth bark, and when the lower branches fall off they leave mustache-like scars. Look for the branch scars on the trailside tulips. Reach the loop portion of the Flat Creek Trail at 0.6 mile. Keep forward on the old roadbed, as the return route splits down to the left. Notice the green and white circular blazes marking the trail.

The term "blaze" for the marking of a trail comes from the old days, when woodsmen would hack a mark into a tree with an ax or hatchet. The resulting scar would indicate the direction of travel along a path, "blazing" the trail. Among some woodsmen, two

blazes meant going toward camp, and a single blaze meant going away from camp. Today, forest personnel mark trails with paint blazes, such as those on this trail, or metal markers of various shapes and sizes nailed into a tree. Interestingly, when metal markers are nailed on, the blazes and nails are not driven entirely into the tree; instead, room is left for the tree to grow toward the nailed marker.

Ahead, on a right curve, the Flat Creek Connector Trail leaves right to meet the Stanley Gap Trail. The red Georgia clay path continues to rise along the mid-slope of Davenport Mountain, rising to your right. Flat Creek flows more than 500 feet below you.

Mid-slopes, especially south-facing ones such as this, are notoriously dry and harbor oaks, hickories, and pines, as well as huckleberries and mountain laurel. Squirrels, deer, and black bears depend on the acorns, nuts, and berries produced on these mid-slopes. This food of the woods is collectively known as *mast*. More bear cubs are born in the spring following a good mast year, and fewer in years of little mast production, usually the result of drought and other natural occurrences. Some adult bears and deer may not survive the winter following a poor mast season, since it's difficult to put on the necessary pounds to make it through the lean, cold months.

Moister species grow in the small coves indented into the mountain slope, where tiny streams sometimes flow beneath culverts. Other than an occasional muddy spot, the trailbed is dry.

At 2.3 miles, the trail descends to cross uppermost Flat Creek by culvert. The path then curves into the Flat Creek valley, where many tributaries gather to further feed Flat Creek, which is anything but flat in this basin bordered by Rocky Mountain and Bellcamp Ridge. The creek tumbles over rocks and crashes noisily downward. The creek probably receives its name from the gentle lower stretches near its terminus at the Toccoa River. In spite of being named Toccoa here in Georgia, this river is named the Ocoee in Tennessee, where it was the site of whitewater events when Atlanta hosted the 1996 Summer Olympic Games.

Begin working downstream along Flat Creek. Fern-floored woods border the path, and sweet birch, hemlock, and rhododendron populate the valley. The now-rocky path continues circling wide around the hollow, which soon tightens. Old roadbeds spur off the main trail. More tributaries feed Flat Creek, sometimes turning the trailbed into a creekbed.

At 3.3 miles, the trail enters a spindly, narrow-trunked thicket. Flat Creek lies off in the woods to your left. The trail's descent is mild, but it doesn't catch up with Flat Creek until the path reaches an abrupt left turn at 4.1 miles. It heads toward a bridge spanning the creek. The old trail continued on to ford the stream, and many hikers miss this turn. The path remains confusing after the footbridge. Turn left, upstream, along Flat Creek, which is now on your left. The path eventually turns away from Flat Creek and climbs along a feeder branch, then keeps uphill as a singletrack path. The moist stream environment is left behind and piney woods take over again.

Finally, the Flat Creek Loop curves back into a cool, moist cove, rejoining the front leg at 5.1 miles. Backtrack 0.6 mile to the trailhead.

18

Amicalola Falls Loop

Total distance: 2.2 miles

Hiking time: 2 hours

Vertical rise: 750 feet

Rating: Moderate

Maps: USGS 7.5' Nimblewill, Amicalola, Amicalola Falls State Park

Amicalola Falls State Park is one of North Georgia's special places. It is quite popular for numerous reasons, including the fine hiking trails that course through its mountain lands. This particular hike climbs alongside 729-foot Amicalola Falls on a footpath with hundreds of steps that are an engineering marvel. At one point, the bridge crosses the falls, availing an excellent view.

The return route for this hike uses the famous Approach Trail to the master path of the East, the Appalachian Trail, where it begins atop nearby Springer Mountain. Hikers intent on following the AT all the way from Springer Mountain to Mount Katahdin in Maine, a months-long endeavor, often spend their last days before starting here at Amicalola Falls State Park. The final mile of this hike is on the AT Approach Trail, and you may see someone beginning the quest to hike the entire 2,100 miles of the Appalachian Trail.

HOW TO GET THERE

From the town square in Dawsonville, take GA 53 west for 3 miles to GA 183. Turn right and go 10 miles to GA 52. Turn right again and continue 1.5 miles to the state park, on your left. Start this loop on the Creek Trail, in the parking area across from the visitor center. Do not park in front of the visitor center, as there is a 30-minute limit.

THE HIKE

Start this loop on the Creek Trail, which is one of the park's many interconnected paths. Immediately cross Little Amicalola Creek on

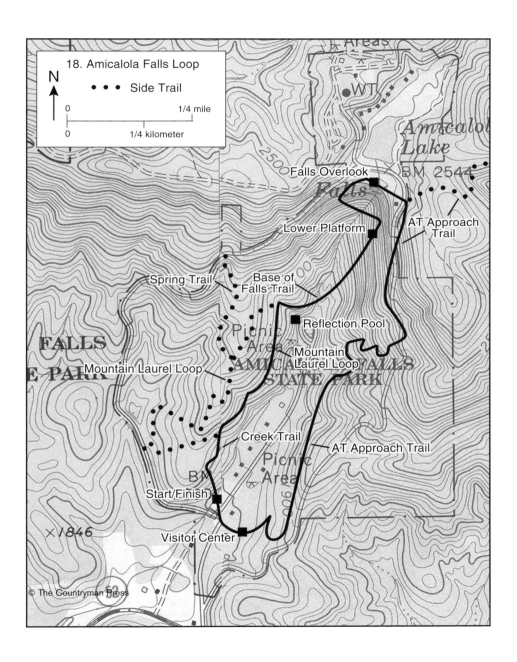

18. Amicalola Falls Loop

• • • Side Trail

0   1/4 mile

0   1/4 kilometer

N

Falls Overlook

BM 2544

Amicalola Lake

AT Approach Trail

Lower Platform

Spring Trail

Base of Falls Trail

Reflection Pool

Picnic Area

Mountain Laurel Loop

FALLS

E PARK

Mountain Laurel Loop

AMICALOLA FALLS STATE PARK

Creek Trail

AT Approach Trail

Picnic Area

BM

Start/Finish

×1846

Visitor Center

© The Countryman Press

Top-down view of Amicalola Falls

a footbridge. It is but a mere babbling brook here, completely belying its wild nature upstream in the tumble off the edge of a steep escarpment, the centerpiece of this park. The yellow-blazed path ascends, then turns up the stream. Stone steps aid your climb, which takes you well above the creek in pine-laurel woods. Soon you reach a trail junction. The Mountain Laurel Loop heads in both directions. Turn right toward the base of the falls and keep upstream, passing another junction. Stay right again toward the base of the falls. The Mountain Laurel Loop leaves left here.

Drop down to a man-made trout pond, the Reflection Pool, where anglers and water lovers gather. There is a parking area here that some people use to begin their trek to the falls. This part of the hike, the Base of Falls Trail, can be very busy on nice weekends. Cross Little Amicalola Creek on a footbridge and join a paved path leading up to the falls. Watch for a massive tulip tree to the right of the trail. To the left, Little Amicalola Creek is tumbling more loudly, reflecting the terrain's steeper uptick. A switchback takes you up toward the lower observation platform, where you can look up at the high falls.

Amicalola Falls is so high that it's hard to gain a perfect vantage point. However, from here you will see steeply tumbling water crashing down, and you will continue to see the falls as you climb the 785 stairs, broken by resting/observation decks. Just as you hit the stairs notice the fender and other remains of an old jalopy that was evidently pushed off the steep escarpment above you a long time ago. The steps were built by laborers from the Georgia state prison system. Their handiwork is amazing, and it offers continual vistas from one of the most unusual paths in the state. The roar from the cascades is loud. Just about every form of waterfall can be found along this continuous drop.

Amicalola is Cherokee for "tumbling waters." Amicalola Falls, at 729 feet, is reputed to be the tallest waterfall in the East, and while walking this path you will come to believe it. Reach the bridge across the falls. People stop here for another unique aspect of this path: a bridge midway across a falls. After you look up at the waterfall, don't forget to look back as the elevation you have gained allows for a good vista.

Beyond the bridge, the West Ridge Staircase leads you to the top of the falls, another spot where easy auto access allows less-fit folks to enjoy the falling water. You will be sweating up a storm. Turn right here and look out from the top of the falls, which drop over a ledge and can't be seen further. But what can be seen is a landscape extending miles beyond the state park boundaries. Exit this area on a paved path and leave the crowds and the roar of rushing water behind.

Reach a parking area and rest room. The park lodge is above you. Turn right here, joining the AT Approach Trail as it descends along a wide old road. The views really open up to the south and west and are as good as they get in Georgia. The sky is open overhead, which can be a problem on a sunny day. The views end as the roadbed becomes canopied. Leave right from the old road and enter a pine-oak-mountain laurel woodland.

The AT Approach Trail descends by switchbacks. Often the path winds beneath laurel, with its irregular limbs twisting in odd forms, as if part of a scene from a scary fairy tale. Pass the spur trail to the Max Epperson Trail Shelter, where late-arriving AT Approach Trail hikers spend the night. This shelter is similar to others spaced roughly a day's hike apart all the way from here to Maine. Many thru-hikers choose to over-night in these shelters, while others tent camp, sleep out in the open, or stay at more developed hostels, which are generally located near towns. Most AT thru-hikers overnight using a combination of the above.

Just ahead is the park visitor center. Pass through a stone arch and complete the hike. Before you leave, however, check out the displays inside the visitor center about the Appalachian Trail, its evolution, and early thru-hikers. The gear has changed quite a bit through the years.

You will also see that this state park is much more than a waterfall. Part of a scenic mountainscape, the park offers other hiking trails, a good campground, some of the best interpretive programs anywhere in the country, and a lodge where you can stuff yourself silly after your hike.

19

AT Benton MacKaye Legacy Loop

Total distance: 4.5 miles

Hiking time: 2½ hours

Vertical rise: 400 feet

Rating: Moderate

Maps: USGS 7.5' Noontoola, Chattahoochee National Forest

This hike rolls three holy grails in the world of hiking into one trip: the southern terminus of the Appalachian Trail, the southern terminus of the Benton MacKaye Trail, and the top of the most famous mountain in Georgia—the place where these long trails begin—Springer Mountain. The hike makes a loop, giving trekkers a sample of each path on the way through some of the most southerly high country in the North Georgia Mountains.

HOW TO GET THERE

From the point where US 76 and GA 52 cross near East Ellijay (76 crosses 52 on an overpass), take GA 52 east for 4.8 miles to Big Creek Road. Turn left and go 12.5 miles to Forest Road 42. Mount Pleasant Baptist Church is at the junction of FR 42 and Big Creek Road. Turn right on gravel FR 42 and follow it 6.8 miles to the Springer Mountain parking area on the left.

Alternate directions from Dahlonega: Take GA 52 west for 5 miles to the split of GA 52 and GA 9. Stay right on GA 52 west for 4.6 more miles to Nimblewill Church Road. Turn right and continue to Forest Road 28-1. Turn right on FR 28-1 and follow it 2.1 miles to FR 77. Veer left onto FR 77. Follow it 5.1 miles to Winding Stair Gap, where you make a hard left onto FR 42 and go 2.7 miles to the trailhead.

THE HIKE

This loop starts by crossing FR 42 from the parking area, southbound on the Appalachian Trail. Imagine you are a thru-hiker

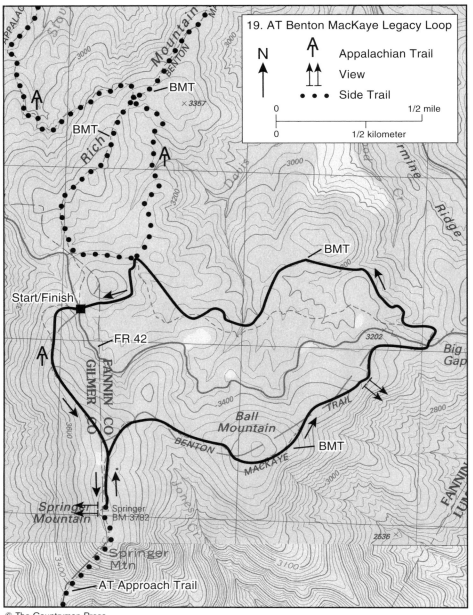

19. AT Benton MacKaye Legacy Loop

N

Appalachian Trail

View

Side Trail

0   1/2 mile

0   1/2 kilometer

BMT

BMT

× 3357

BMT

Start/Finish

FR 42

Big
Gap

3202

Ball
Mountain

BENTON

MACKAYE   TRAIL

BMT

2800

GILMER   CO.

FANNIN   CO.

3600

Jones   Cr.

3000

FANNIN

Springer
Mountain

Springer
BM 3782

2536 ×

Springer
Mtn

3100

AT Approach Trail

3400

Rich

Mountain

BENTON

Stou

APPALAC

3000

3000

Dalus

3000

rming   Cr

Ridge

© The Countryman Press

heading from Maine to Georgia and that you are on your last mile. What a feeling that must be! Begin to climb away from FR 42. The path is open bedrock along with smaller stones, and brush lines the way. This hike stays above 3,000 feet its entire length, keeping it relatively cool, even in summer.

The rocky track travels beneath wind-stunted oaks growing on the margin of Springer Mountain. At 0.7 mile you reach a trail junction; the Benton MacKaye Trail leaves left. Go ahead and walk 0.2 mile farther on the AT to the top of Springer. On the way up, you pass the side trail to the Springer Mountain shelter and water source. This shelter has a loft, picnic table, and fire grate. A spring flows nearby. Other campsites are dispersed atop the mountain, but keep in mind that bears are active here, so hang your food high.

At 0.9 mile, reach the top of Springer Mountain and the official southern terminus of the Appalachian Trail. This is where many hikers have begun adventures and disappointments, and where others have ended thru-hikes or ended their hopes for taking on the AT. There are two plaques up here. One, erected in 1934 by the Georgia Appalachian Trail Club, marks the spot where the AT begins with the words that have greeted all those who come here: THE APPALACHIAN TRAIL, GEORGIA TO MAINE, A FOOTPATH FOR THOSE WHO SEEK FELLOWSHIP WITH THE WILDERNESS. The Georgia Appalachian Trail Club was founded in 1930 in nearby Dahlonega, and is still actively promoting the Appalachian Trail.

A 1992 Forest Service marker maps the AT on its path through the East. There is also the last white blaze, or the first, depending on your perspective. Additionally, a view awaits at the top of the 3,782-foot mountain. The vista opens to the west, ironically the opposite direction from the one in which the AT heads for the first several miles. This is one of the most often photographed vistas on the AT.

The AT Approach Trail runs south from the top of Springer for 8 miles down to Amicalola Falls State Park.

The Appalachian Trail extends roughly 2,100 miles to Maine. The mileage changes yearly because portions of the path are rerouted. About 20 percent of the two thousand or so hikers who attempt the AT make it the whole way. Thru-hikers generally take around six months to complete the trail. Other people "section hike" the AT; that is, they hike one section at a time, taking years to complete the entire path. Of the thru-hikers, 20 percent have quit after the first 30 miles, 50 percent after the first 160 miles, and 60 percent after the first 1,000 miles.

The Benton MacKaye Trail, completed in 2005, is 290 miles long. It also travels the Appalachian corridor, but its terminus is at Davenport Gap on the Tennessee/North Carolina state line, at the eastern end of the Great Smoky Mountains National Park. Far fewer people have hiked the entire BMT, despite its much shorter length, because it's less known, less "glamorous," and seemingly easier. But mile-for-mile, the BMT is every bit as challenging as the AT, maybe more so, due to steeper ups and downs, fewer resupply locations, and no hiker hostels. No reliable statistics have been compiled on the number of BMT thru-hikers.

Backtrack down the AT and begin the Benton MacKaye Trail. I think Benton Mac-Kaye, who came up with the idea for the Appalachian Trail, deserved to have his trail start atop Springer; instead, it's a little down the mountain. The BMT is marked with diamond-shaped white blazes as it courses among young oaks growing over rock outcrops and ferns. You will immediately notice how much

The southern terminus of the Appalachian Trail

more slender and less used is the BMT. At 1.1 miles, on the right, a plaque commemorates Benton MacKaye.

Descend away from Springer Mountain as the bulk of the mountainside drops sharply to your right. Ferns carpet the forest floor. Reach a low point, then make a short climb over Ball Mountain to resume the downgrade. The track atop Ball Mountain is bordered by grass and mountain laurel. At mile 2.4, a sign marks a side trail leading right, to a view. On the edge of a steep rock face you can look east toward Little Sal Mountain.

The BMT continues its descent to Forest Road 42 and Big Stamp Gap at 2.8 miles. Cross the forest road and keep descending to a forest heavy with white pines. The trail curves back westward to cross a high country stream cloaked in rhododendron at 3.3 miles. It picks up an old roadbed and the

walking becomes easier. Just past the crossing, on the right, is a small campsite. The fist-sized aromatic green plant lining the trail is galax, which grows tall white flower clusters in May and June around these parts. It was once heavily harvested for flower arrangements. The leaves turn a deep reddish-purple in fall.

Ascend away from the stream over a small gap, then drop down and step over Underwood Creek and one of its feeder branches to meet the Appalachian Trail at mile 4.1. Again, notice the difference in the trail treads—the AT is much more heavily used. Turn left here, going south on the AT on level ground to reach the parking area on FR 42 and the end of the loop at 4.5 miles. If you wish to extend your hike a couple of miles, you can keep forward on the BMT, which intersects the AT again in a mile. Turn right (south) on the AT to get back to the parking area.

20

Long Creek Falls

Total distance: 2.4 miles there and back

Hiking time: 1¼ hours

Vertical rise: 280 feet

Rating: Easy

Maps: USGS 7.5' Noontoola, Chattahoochee National Forest

The Appalachian Trail and the Benton MacKaye Trail are both known for being ridge-running, high-country paths with mountain-top vistas, and for the most part this is true. However, these long-distance trails also travel through lower country, sometimes to features like this particular destination, Long Creek Falls. This waterfall lies along a stretch of pathway shared by both the AT and the BMT.

HOW TO GET THERE

From Dahlonega, take GA 52 west for 5 miles to the split with GA 9. Stay right on GA 52 west for 4.6 more miles, to Nimblewill Church Road. Turn right and continue to Forest Road 28-1. Turn right on FR 28-1 and follow it 2.1 miles to FR 77. Veer left onto FR 77, and follow it for 5.1 miles to Winding Stair Gap. Veer slightly left onto FR 58 (not the sharp left to FR 42). This is a confusing road junction. Descend along FR 58 for 2.6 miles to a signed spot where the Appalachian Trail and the Benton MacKaye Trail cross FR 58. Parking is on either side of the road.

THE HIKE

This hike leads from a place known as Three Forks, just a few miles north of Springer Mountain. Here, Chester Fork, Stover Creek, and Long Creek meet to form Noontoola Creek. At Three Forks the Benton MacKaye Trail and the Appalachian Trail are marked and running conjunctively. You can see a bridge spanning Chester Creek at the trailhead. This bridge takes you south on both

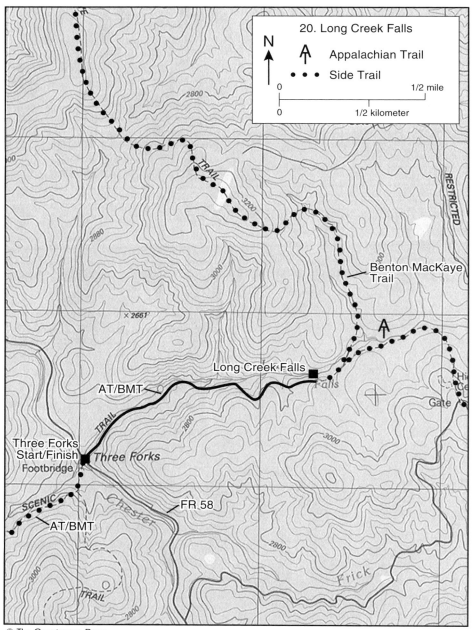

20. Long Creek Falls

N

Appalachian Trail

••• Side Trail

0   1/2 mile

0   1/2 kilometer

2800

3200

TRAIL

Benton MacKaye
Trail

RESTRICTED

2880

3000

× 2661'

Long Creek Falls

Falls

Hi
Ge

Gate

AT/BMT

TRAIL

2800

3000

Three Forks
Start/Finish
Footbridge

Three Forks

Chester

FR 58

SCENIC

AT/BMT

2800

3000

Frick

TRAIL

2800

© The Countryman Press

Long Creek Falls

the AT and BMT, the wrong way for this hike. Instead, head north on the twin trails from Forest Road 58. You are heading upstream along Long Creek, which is to your left. The blazes representing both paths are painted on the trees. The diamond is for the Benton MacKaye Trail and the classic white 2-by-6-inch rectangle is for the Appalachian Trail.

The wide level track passes a small clearing to your left that is growing up in white pines. The forest here is typical of what you would expect in such a rich mountain hollow where three creeks meet. Rhododendron covers much of the ground. The next vegetational layer is occupied by birch, tulip, and hemlock trees. And over this towers the white pine. It is hard to believe that less than a century ago much of North Georgia's forests were cut over, logged with little afterthought. When the valuable timber was removed, the leftover trees and brush burned

in forest fires, destabilizing the soil and leading to erosion and siltation of streams. The landowners were eager to sell these "wastelands" to the U.S. Forest Service, which established the system of national forests we see today.

Of course, North Georgia's national forest is known as the Chattahoochee, which began to take shape in 1911 when the Forest Service purchased 31,000 acres in Fannin, Gilmer, Lumpkin, and Union Counties from the Gennett family for $7 per acre. Back then, this fledgling forest was part of the Nantahala and Cherokee National Forests, lands where the AT travels to this day. The BMT travels through the Cherokee but not the Nantahala.

The Forest Service continued acquiring more land, doing fire duty, and managing their areas for wildlife. The Civilian Conservation Corps gave the Chattahoochee a leg-up with manpower—planting trees; building fire towers, roads, ranger stations, and recreation areas; laying communication lines; and doing erosion-control work. You can still see the stone handiwork of the CCC workers at recreation sites. In 1936, the forest was organized into two ranger districts, the Blue Ridge and the Tallulah. Today, the Chattahoochee contains over 750,000 acres, has 8 ranger districts, and employs over 200 people.

The public has indicated it no longer wants national forests as only timbering havens. So today the Forest Service primarily manages the Chattahoochee for wildlife enhancement and preservation, as well as recreation use. Destinations such as Long Creek Falls, the Chattooga Wild and Scenic River, and the Cohutta and Ellicott Rock wildernesses are now places where forest visitors go to recharge their batteries and enjoy nature's offerings. A good example of forest managers reacting to public wishes is right below Three Forks off FR 58, where primitive car camping is available along Noontoola Creek. The Forest Service has installed tent pads at designated streamside sites, fostering recreation yet minimizing erosion.

Many campsites lie along the trail near Three Forks, as AT and BMT thru-hikers overnight here. The pathway begins to climb a bit, and you can hear Long Creek dropping over other, lower, falls that missed getting a moniker because they were overshadowed by the larger and more powerful Long Creek Falls.

At 1.1 miles, you reach a three-way trail junction. To your right, the Appalachian Trail heads to Maine. Ahead, the Benton MacKaye Trail runs to its end point in the Smokies. And to your left is the spur trail to Long Creek Falls. Take this blue-blazed spur trail, passing campsites. The roar of Long Creek Falls grows louder, and soon you are looking dead-on at one of North Georgia's lesser-known watery destinations.

I can't help but wonder how many thru-hikers on these long trails arrive at the spur trail to Long Creek Falls and pass it by in their eagerness to get on with their journey. (Springer Mountain, the beginning point for both trails, is but a few miles back.) But anyone determined to see the best of the Appalachian Mountains should stop to view this beautiful waterfall.

There is a two-tiered drop framed in thick woods. The upper drop is shorter and set back from the viewing area, but the lower drop is steep, wide, and quite dramatic. The falls roar after a summer thunderstorm, enveloped in a roof of tree leaves. Sitting rocks that face the falls add to the appeal of the destination. On your way back, you will be southbound on the AT and BMT, and be much closer to their end points atop Springer.

21

Cooper Creek Scenic Area Loop

Total distance: 4.8 miles

Hiking time: 2¾ hours

Vertical rise: 500 feet

Rating: Moderate

Maps: USGS 7.5' Mulky Gap, Chattahoochee National Forest

Cooper Creek Scenic Area is the setting for this classic woods walk with that everywhere-you-look beauty. Most paths in North Georgia's mountains follow old wagon tracks or logging grades, but this area is an exception, utilizing slender singletrack trails almost entirely. This makes for an intimate woodland experience in the 1,240-acre scenic area. Unlike most hikes in this book, there is no singular feature, or set of features, to enjoy here. Rather, the hiker traveling in this neck of the woods will enjoy the solitude of mature white pine stands and thick creekside woods, and maybe combine the trip here with a camping outing at Cooper Creek Campground, a fine national forest venue.

HOW TO GET THERE

From Blue Ridge, take US 76 east for 4 miles to GA 60. Turn right and go south for 18 miles to Cooper Creek Road. Turn left here and continue 5.2 miles to Forest Road 236. Turn right and go 0.2 mile to the campground.

From Dahlonega, take US 19/GA 60 for 24 miles to Cooper Creek Road. Turn right and continue on to Forest Road 236. Turn left and continue to the campground entrance on your right. Enter the campground and follow the main road a short distance to where the lower campground loop road exits. The Mill Shoals Trail begins just beyond where the lower campground loop road exit meets FR 236.

THE HIKE

The loop hike follows several interconnected trails that course through the Cooper Creek

21. Cooper Creek Scenic Area Loop

▲ Campground

••••• Side Trail

N

0   1/2 mile

0   1/2 kilometer

Spencer Knob

Rhod... Creek

Spencer Creek

Hickory Knob

3205

2979 ×

3000

FR 39

Shope Gap

Shøpe

DUNG...

Shope Gap Trail

Harkins Cem

2280

2600

FR 39

Creek

Mitchy

Millshoal

Yellow

Mountain

2963

2800

Yellow Mountain Trail

Mill Shoals Trail

Cooper Creek Recreation Area

Cooper Creek Trail

2800

▲ Campground

Start/Finish

Yellow Mountain Trail

Horse Knob

2600

2200

2600

× 2701

© The Countryman Press

Scenic Area, part of the Chattahoochee National Forest. The trek begins on the Mill Shoals Trail, which leaves near the end of the lower loop at Cooper Creek Campground. The singletrack trailbed is a carpet of white pine needles. White pines dominate the forest here. Holly, laurel, maple, and other trees form the understory beneath the tall pines.

Eastern white pines are near their southerly limit here in the North Georgia Mountains. They range up the spine of the Southern Appalachians and become widespread from New England west to Minnesota. The white pine is easily the largest and most valuable of the evergreens in the East. These trees grow straight and tall, reaching massive proportions. Their trunks were used for masts in early America.

The white pine grows in well-drained, sometimes sandy soils. Here, this rich slope is the habitat, but the white pine often grows in mountain creek valleys, where it towers above the other trees. White pines have horizontal branches emanating from the trunk, and one row of branches is added each year, making the trees somewhat easy to age. However, in the crown of taller trees it's difficult to see and count the branch rows. The lower limbs fall off taller trees, but the notches where the limbs once grew are easy to spot. Areas with thick white pines can be quite fragrant.

Spur paths leave left to campsites in the upper loop of Cooper Creek Campground. The path climbs the nose of a ridge emanating from Yellow Mountain. The climb continues to a gap in the ridge and a trail junction at 0.6 mile. The Cooper Creek Trail, which doesn't get near water, leaves right and shortcuts the loop. The Mill Shoals Trail descends from the gap into the upper part of a pretty cove, briefly crossing an old forest road to enter a rhododendron thicket with a pair of streamlets. Hemlock trees also grow here.

Woodland wonders can be large or small.

Young white pines form nearly pure stands along the trail. Step across a bigger creek before descending to Mill Shoals Creek. The Mill Shoals Trail crosses the stream, then begins ascending upstream on an old roadbed before making a hard switchback to the left, heading uphill to reach Forest Road 39 at 1.2 miles. To continue the loop, turn right on FR 39 and follow it gradually uphill. You may notice the blazes on the trees here. These remind hikers that even though they are on a gravel forest road, FR 39 is part of the Cooper Creek Trail system.

Tall white pines dominate the forest here, too. And small streams pass under the roadbed by culvert to feed Mill Shoals Creek, which runs to your right. The track continues its upward tick to reach Shope Gap at 2.3 miles. The loop leaves FR 39 and joins the Shope Gap Trail, a lightly used, narrow footpath heading south. This trail climbs a knob, then levels off to enter a wildlife clearing. Be careful here, as an overgrown old road goes right and left. Keep forward, crossing the old road, then turn left near a pile of rocks, still on a singletrack path.

The walking is pleasant, a ridge ramble through the North Georgia woods. Make a jump to reach an intersection and meet the Yellow Mountain Trail at 3 miles. This is the end of the Shope Gap Trail. The Yellow

Mountain Trail keeps forward to reach Addie Gap and also turns right to return to Cooper Creek Campground. Go right here, and continue the ridgeline walking, drifting off to the west side. Cooper Creek is audible well below. Partial views can be gained to the left of the trail. Persimmon, oaks, sourwood, hickory, and blueberries thrive in the dry, south-facing woods.

Seemingly just for contrast, the trail turns into a watershed and comes near a branch flowing off Yellow Mountain. The forest changes to dark hemlocks. This rich slope is a great place to see the Indian ghost pipe, one of North America's strangest wildflowers. This white plant, with a flowerlike end, has no chlorophyll and resembles the white clay pipes used by Indians for smoking tobacco. It can be seen in summer in the North Georgia Mountains. Ghost pipe obtains its nutrients from other plants in a complex relationship with fungi that is not completely understood. Do not pick the ghost pipe—not that you would want it for a bouquet—because its flesh soon blackens when cut or even bruised, and oozes a clear, gelatinous substance. Its natural white color and tendency to "melt" on picking also give it the moniker "ice plant."

Leave the dark hemlock woods as the creek drops sharply away. You are well into the Cooper Creek valley. The path reaches Forest Road 4 at 4.7 miles. Turn right here and follow it a short piece to complete your loop.

Consider a stay at Cooper Creek Campground while you're in the area. It is located on the edge of the scenic area, allowing easy access to the creek and its surrounding ridges. This locale features a quintessential mountain stream flowing beneath a richly wooded valley where white pines tower over hemlocks, rhododendron, and hardwoods aplenty; where wildflowers bloom in spring and the high country air stays crisp in summer; where fall colors contrast with the clear green water frothing white over gray boulders before slowing in opaque pools, only to gather speed again on its inevitable course toward the sea. This pretty creek is a popular trout-fishing venue.

Also, you can walk the Eyes on Wildlife Interpretive Trail, starting where FR 236 crosses Cooper Creek. It makes a 1.3-mile loop, traversing many habitats, including a couple of wildlife openings, grassy plots in the forest designed to increase food for nature's animals.

22

Preaching Rock via Dockery Lake

Total distance: 10.2 miles there and back

Hiking time: 5½ hours

Vertical rise: 1,550 feet

Rating: Difficult

Maps: USGS 7.5' Neels Gap, Chattahoochee National Forest

The view from Preaching Rock may be good enough to cause a religious conversion. A stone slab extends down the side of Big Cedar Mountain in the Blood Mountain Wilderness, providing vistas of the mountains and beyond. The Dockery Lake Trail only improves upon this by offering an early vista before coursing through several scenic creeks and making its way to the high country and the Appalachian Trail, where Preaching Rock stands.

HOW TO GET THERE

From Dahlonega, take GA 60 north for 12 miles. Turn right at the sign for Dockery Lake on Forest Road 654 for 1 mile. Pass through the campground, then stay right to reach the day-use parking area. The Dockery Lake Trail starts on the right side of the parking area.

THE HIKE

Though the hike starts on the Dockery Lake Trail, only a small portion of the path passes along Dockery Lake. The rest wanders along mountainsides, through dark hemlock-enshrouded creeks, and up into the high country, where it meets the Appalachian Trail at Miller Gap. From here, the hike heads south on the AT, climbing to the top of Big Cedar Mountain, where a blue-blazed spur trail leads to Preaching Rock.

The Dockery Lake Trail is underused and underappreciated, though it emanates from Dockery Lake Recreation Area, which is a nice but rustic campground beside a trout-filled lake. The lake is fed from the chilly

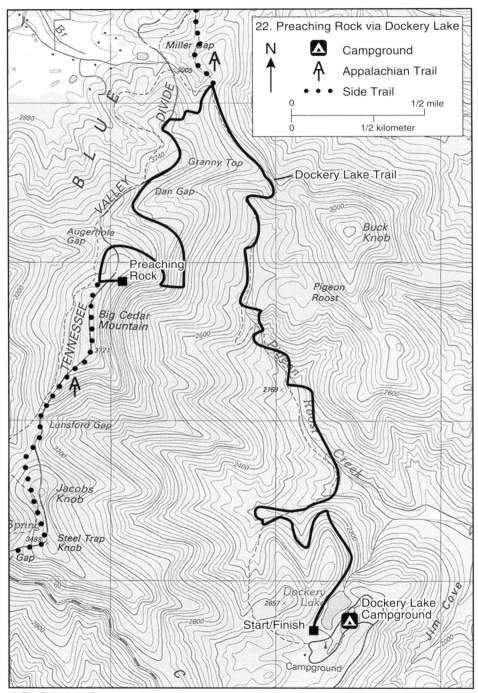

22. Preaching Rock via Dockery Lake

N

△ Campground

Ⱥ Appalachian Trail

• • • Side Trail

0   1/2 mile
0   1/2 kilometer

Miller Gap

3005

BLUE

DIVIDE

Granny Top

3240

Dan Gap

Dockery Lake Trail

VALLEY

2880

Augerhole Gap

Buck Knob

3000

Preaching Rock

3200

Pigeon Roost

Big Cedar Mountain

TENNESSEE

3721

2600

2169

Ⱥ

Pigeon

Roost

Lunsford Gap

3200

2600

Creek

2400

Jacobs Knob

Spring

3488

Steel Trap Knob

Gap

2200

Dockery Lake

2657

Dockery Lake Campground

△

Start/Finish

2800

Jim Cove

2000

2900

Campground

© The Countryman Press

Dockery Lake

headwaters of Waters Creek, tumbling off the slopes of Jacobs Knob along the Appalachian Trail. You will cross other feeder branches of Waters Creek. Fishing is a popular pastime here.

Leave the parking area on the Dockery Lake Trail and descend a short piece, passing through a pretty picnic area, then veer left along the thickly wooded shore of Dockery Lake on a gravel track. Short spur paths leading to platforms at the water's edge provide good fishing or lake-viewing spots. The lake is clear, cool, and alluring. Soon you reach the lake dam. A wooden platform with handrails sits over the small barrier. It's a good vantage point to take in the crystalline body of water. A waterfall tumbles below the dam, and a short trail continues across the dam to the camping area.

At this point, the Dockery Lake Trail turns left, passes through a little muddy section, then becomes a singletrack path curving left toward Waters Creek. Crashing water

can be heard in the valley below. The trail winds along the side of a knob, gently descending. Watch for a large rock face below the trail. The rock slab, absent the heavy tree cover present in the rest of the woods, opens views to the east across the lower Waters Creek valley. Other rock outcrops and boulders add a rugged aspect to the forest of oak, pine, and mountain laurel.

Soon the trail leaves the steep mountainside and reaches a few streams. Here, the forest changes; hemlocks dominate and darken the woodland. The terrain has changed too, and is more level. Step over a small creek and join a wagon track. Rock piles and low rock fences beneath the evergreens indicate this area wasn't always closed to the sun. Long ago, this mountain flat was farm- or pastureland, open overhead where an early Georgian tilled the earth here in the back of beyond. Today it is once again backwoods, and a fitting place for a hike.

Preaching Rock via Dockery Lake

The descent sharpens beyond the farm site, and the trail crosses a third branch and enters the Blood Mountain Wilderness at 1.2 miles. This third creek, the actual Waters Creek, is the biggest so far, but it's still an easy rock hop. You may wonder how a downhill path is going to reach the ridge-running AT. The trail now turns left and begins the expected climb, heading up Pigeon Roost Branch, which flows in the hollow to your right. The old wagon track is quite rocky, despite the removal of stones and boulders that line the way. The deep dark prevails here, and the stream echoes off the canopy.

Step over small branches and keep climbing to make a hard right. You can hear a dramatic waterfall on Pigeon Roost Branch, but it's only partially visible in winter and not at all in summer. Just ahead, a long, angled slide cascade is easy to see. Keep uphill along this stream to cross it on a wooden bridge. Just ahead, the Dockery Lake Trail leaves the old wagon track for higher ground, as the track is quite muddy. The trail still roughly parallels the creek below, passing beneath fragrant white pines. You may begin to notice that this area was burned. The tree cover is relatively sparse, and the underbrush is all evenly aged. Look across the creek, where the woods are much thicker. It is obvious that the creek itself acted as a barrier to the forest fire.

Briefly return to the creek, joining the wagon track as it turns to leave Pigeon Roost Branch for good at 2.1 miles. The trail climbs through oak-dominated woods to reach a gap at 3 miles. Buck Knob rises to your right. At this point, the path turns left

and joins a long-abandoned logging road. Make an easy trek toward the AT, climbing now and then but not often. Big Cedar Mountain rises to your left. At 3.4 miles, a small spring branch crosses the trail.

Ahead, at 3.6 miles, the Dockery Lake Trail meets the Appalachian Trail near Miller Gap. This hike turns left on the AT, southbound, and begins to climb Granny Top. The dirt track of the AT winds through fern-floored woods to reach the ridge crest, then turns left, still ascending. Round out over Granny Top and then drop to Dan Gap at 4.1 miles. The walking is not bad as the AT contours up the south side of Big Cedar Mountain, which is rising much faster than the trail.

Pass a high-elevation stream before making a sharp switchback to the right. You are obliviously below Preaching Rock at this point. The AT begins to level off on the north shoulder of Big Cedar Mountain. At 4.9 miles, a blue-blazed spur trail leads left, just after another trail leads right down to a campsite. Take the blue-blazed side path and follow it through low oak woods to reach the opening of Preaching Rock, your North Georgia Mountains cathedral.

Here, at 3,600 feet, wind-stunted oaks and soft grass frame the southern and easterly views. You will immediately notice that the views of Preaching Rock are not made by a rock extension, but rather a long sloping rock face that prevents tree cover and opens the mountainside to the sky. Hardy lichens and mosses cling to the massive slab. The Waters Creek valley is below and mountains surround the valley. The grassy area near the rock is a great place to linger.

23

Bear Hair Gap Loop

Total distance: 4.3 miles

Hiking time: 2¾ hours

Vertical rise: 830 feet

Rating: Moderate

Maps: USGS 7.5' Coosa Bald, Vogel State Park, Chattahoochee National Forest

This loop hike begins and ends at Vogel State Park. Make a winding trek among Burnett Branch and its feeder streams, climb the unnamed knob with the vista, and then drop down to Wolf Creek and its tributaries before descending back to the state park. Along the way you enter the Chattahoochee National Forest and the Blood Mountain Wilderness. Though the path has some elevation changes, they are never severe or too long, making this hike ideal for anyone who wants to see classic Southern Appalachian woods without getting completely whipped or investing a full day.

HOW TO GET THERE

From Dahlonega, follow US 19 north for 25 miles to Vogel State Park. Park near the visitor center and walk uphill on the road to the right (as you face the visitor center) for about 200 yards to the trailhead, near cabin No. 7.

THE HIKE

The Bear Hair Gap Trail underwent rerouting and rehabilitation in 2004 and 2005, making a good trail even better. There is a small stone building at the trailhead with a drink machine and pay phones. Climb the stone steps away from the park road and pass the stone building, entering lush woods in the greater Burnett Branch valley. Start a slight uptick, passing the Reece Nature Trail at 0.2 mile. This trail is a fine walk in its own right, traveling a mile through the forest, with interpretive signs informing hikers about various aspects of the park flora and fauna.

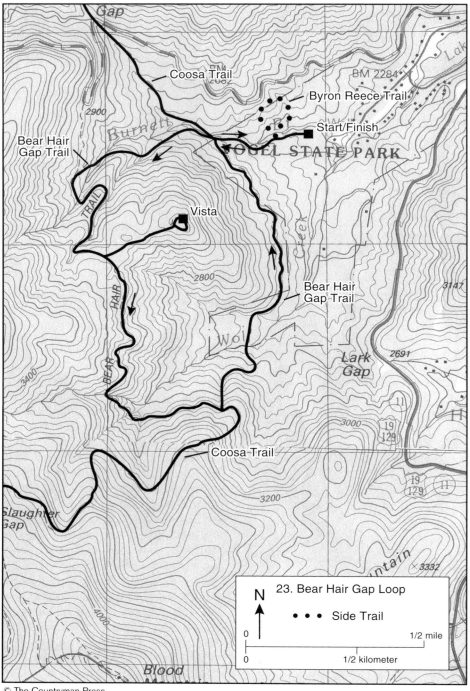

Coosa Trail

Byron Reece Trail

Start/Finish

VOGEL STATE PARK

BM 2284

Bear Hair
Gap Trail

Vista

Bear Hair
Gap Trail

Coosa Trail

Lark
Gap

Slaughter
Gap

Blood

N   23. Bear Hair Gap Loop

• • • Side Trail

0   1/2 mile

0   1/2 kilometer

© The Countryman Press

A tight spot on the Bear Hair Gap Trail

Ahead, cross Burnett Branch on a footbridge. Stay right here, as spur trails lead to campsites in the park campground. Keep upstream to reach another trail junction at 0.4 mile. This is the beginning of the actual Bear Hair Gap Trail. You can also see the return route of the orange-blazed Bear Hair Gap Trail, which shares treadway down here with the yellow-blazed Coosa Backcountry Trail (see Hike 25). Follow a wide track that heads right to begin your loop. Another trail junction is just ahead. The Coosa Backcountry Trail leaves right over a wooden footbridge, while the Bear Hair Gap Trail veers left, crossing a feeder branch by culvert. A steady ascent follows beneath shaded woods.

Water flows on both sides of the path, really an old roadbed. The trail bridges the left branch by culvert twice and then ascends to enter the valley of the right branch, Burnett Branch. At first, you are well above the creek, which is soon crossed on a wooden footbridge at 0.9 mile, part of the 2004 reroute. Continue uphill, switchback left, cross Burnett Branch for the final time. The trail nearly doubles back on itself, gaining elevation. Cross yet another branch by culvert. All these creek crossings and turns may seem confusing, but the path is well marked, especially in potentially troublesome areas. At 1.3 miles, the path cuts between some wooden posts and enters the Chattahoochee National Forest and the Blood Mountain Wilderness.

Curve onto a dry, laurel-dominated mountainside and leave the old roadbed, climbing by switchbacks with many erosion-preventing wooden waterbars. Reach the 0.2-mile Vogel Overlook spur trail at 1.6 miles. This spur trail makes a mini-loop of its own. Take this path left as it climbs to the top of a knob. You have broken the 3,000-foot barrier. A cleared view opens to the northeast. The park lake, Lake Trahlyta, lies in the lowlands below. You were there not long ago. If the day is clear you can see Georgia's highest point, Brasstown Bald, in the distance among other mountains to the north. This is an unusual vista, as most views in the North Georgia Mountains open in a southerly direction.

Complete the loop of the spur trail, passing the top of the knob in white pines before returning to the Bear Hair Gap Trail. The southbound track makes for glorious walking, nearly level and simply cruising through the forest. Just when you get used to the quiet uplands, the trail curves right and enters a noisy watershed. The creek, Wolf Branch, makes quite a literal splash as it dashes downward to feed Lake Trahlyta. Cross the stream, which flows off the eastern slopes of Slaughter Mountain. A series of switchbacks and rock steps ease the descent on this ultrasteep slope, more rerouting work. Go slow here. The Bear Hair Gap Trail slices between massive boulders. This scenic spot makes for a good lunch or contemplation location.

Reach the stream just beyond the boulders and keep the downgrade to make a trail junction at 2.8 miles. The Coosa Trail comes in from the right and joins the Bear Hair Gap Trail. The path continues forward, immediately spanning a tumbling branch. There is a nice waterfall about 50 yards upstream. Continue a steep descent in hemlock-tulip tree woods. At 3.1 miles, the trail leaves the Blood Mountain Wilderness. A spur trail loops down to a shelter and returns to the main path. The trail wanders back toward Burnett Branch, completing the loop portion of the Bear Hair Gap Trail at 3.9 miles. Backtrack to the stone shelter and the trailhead to finish the hike.

There is much more to see and do at Vogel State Park in addition to hiking the Bear Hair Gap Trail. Located amid the Chattahoochee National Forest on land donated by Fred Vogel, the park makes the most of its mountain environs. This is the second-oldest state park in Georgia. The campground is great for tent campers, due to the 18 walk-in campsites and a loop made exclusively for tents, vans, and popup campers. Folks with RVs also enjoy camping here, and don't forget about the park cabins.

There is also some watery action on Lake Trahlyta, named for a Cherokee princess. This mountain impoundment offers a swim beach and paddleboats for tooling around the lake or fishing for trout in spring, and bass or bream in summer. The Civilian Conservation Corps Museum is located near the lake and details the story of the young men who developed this park during the Great Depression. A miniature golf course is located beside the park office. You can also follow trails around the lake and to the falls below, or travel the Coosa Backcountry Trail (see Hike 25).

24

Sosebee Cove Nature Trail

Total distance: 0.5 mile double loop

Hiking time: 1 hour

Vertical rise: 150 feet

Rating: Easy

Maps: USGS 7.5' Coosa Bald,
Chattahoochee National Forest

This short trek through the uppermost part of Sosebee Cove offers a chance to see some big trees and wildflowers in season. The trail was dedicated to Arthur W. Woody, a native of nearby Suches, and the cove is a designated 175-acre scenic area due to its rich concentration of plant life.

Since this is such a short hike, you can combine a visit here with nearby hikes like the Bear Hair Gap Loop (see Hike 23) or the Coosa Backcountry Loop (see Hike 25), which encircles this hike. Or you can enjoy the shorter paths at Vogel State Park, which it passes along the way, such as the Trahlyta Lake Trail or the Byron Reece Nature Trail. That being said, this little loop has plenty to see in every season, so stop by whenever you are in the area. In spring and summer, you can admire the big tulip and buckeye trees and the extensive wildflower display in this high-elevation, north-facing cove. In fall, the diversity of tree species makes for a colorful walk. And in winter, you can just sit on a contemplation bench and see how cold you get.

HOW TO GET THERE

From Dahlonega, follow US 19 north for 25 miles to Vogel State Park. A short distance past the state park entrance, GA 180 is on your left. Turn left on GA 180 and follow it for 3 miles to a parking area, on the right side of the winding road. The Sosebee Cove Trail starts here.

THE HIKE

This path makes two loops, but even if you hike both you will soon be finished. As short

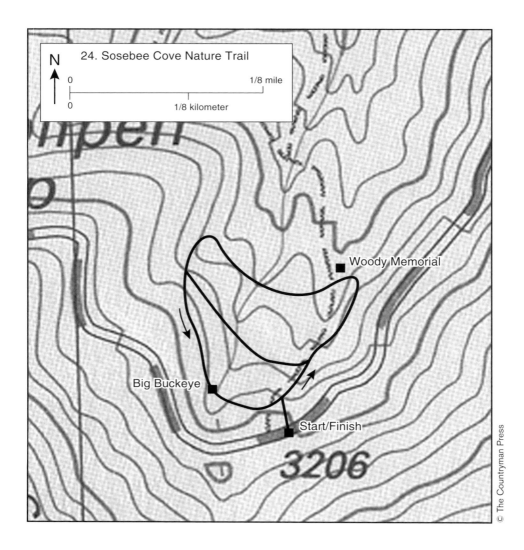

© The Countryman Press

as it is, though, the Sosebee Cove Trail definitely deserves your full attention because it provides a rare chance to see one of the biggest buckeye trees around—certainly one of the largest I have seen anywhere in the Southern Appalachians. This is a yellow buckeye, the largest species in the buckeye family.

It thrives in moist coves and along streams of the Southern Appalachians and reaches its greatest concentrations in the Smoky Mountains National Park and west to the Cumberland Mountains in Tennessee. Buckeyes are easily identified by their leaves. A set of five to seven evenly saw-toothed, yellow-green leaves extend outward from a single stalk. The bark of the tree is brown to gray and becomes fissured in large scaly plates on older trees. Georgia's Indians ate the seeds of the buckeye; while naturally poisonous, soaking and roasting makes them edible. The yellow buckeye is near the southern limit of its range here, and it extends northeast up the Appalachian Chain and west to Indiana.

This cove also has many large tulip trees. They are not old growth, mind you; however, their girth and height will impress. These are second-growth stands of tulip trees, and are around a century old. Imagine the giants that were logged from here in the 1800s. Other trees include red and white oaks, basswood, ash, and cherry. Yet what most people find impressive about Sosebee Cove are its wildflowers: trillium, bloodroot, violets, and very showy ones such as Dutchman's breeches and lady's slipper. Bring a wildflower guidebook along if you come in spring.

Leave GA 180 and walk down stone steps to begin the loop. Buckeye trees dominate the cove, along with tulip trees, and cherry and birch trees have fair representation, as well. The right path leads downhill, cutting into a power-line clearing before reaching some interpretive signs. The middle loop trail leaves left here. On one sign, you can read about the dedication of Sosebee Cove to one of the Chattahoochee National Forest's most beloved employees, Arthur W. Woody. He was a ranger in the North Georgia Mountains from 1911 to 1945. Many area landmarks bear Ranger Woody's name in tribute to his stewardship. It was Woody who negotiated the purchase of Sosebee Cove for the Forest Service, just a part of the 250,000 acres he helped acquire for wildlife and forest visitors to use.

Ranger Woody also promoted conservation. Unwise land and resource use had caused the deer and trout populations to virtually disappear. The woods and waters were devoid of wildlife. Woody brought trout and deer back to North Georgia. The trout were shipped to Gainesville and hauled across narrow, dirt, mountain roads and released in the streams. Woody also purchased fawns with his own money, and fed them until they could be released on what became the Blue Ridge Wildlife Management Area.

Behind the signs, an unmaintained path continues along West Fork Wolf Creek down Sosebee Cove to reach Forest Road 107. A walk down here will increase your wildflower count in spring and also get your lungs pumping on the way back up.

Continue on the outer loop to drop to West Fork Wolf Creek. Many large gray-trunked tulip trees grow here. In summer the trunks contrast with the green ground cover of already bloomed flowers such as Solomon's seal. During the spring blooming season, the ground is still covered with the brown decay of fallen leaves. In the dark, moist nether regions below the leaves and near the stream are salamanders. The Southern Appalachians are rich in the number and variety of salamanders, and a moist, north-facing cove like Sosebee has plenty, ranging from small pygmy salamanders to the notorious hellbender. In Georgia's mountain streams, hellbenders can reach an amazing 2 feet or more in length. Being so strange and ugly, hellbenders were historically killed on sight, but no longer. Part of the Southern Appalachian web of life, they prey upon minnows, worms, crawdads, and small fish.

You will likely see much smaller salamanders up here in Sosebee Cove. Pick one up and it may try a harmless little bite on your finger, but biting is not the only defense mechanism these amphibians use. Anatomy is their best survival tool. If they lose a tail to a predator, they simply grow another one. And if their toxic skin doesn't work, they play

The Sosebee Cove Trailhead

dead. Sometimes a nontoxic salamander will even fool its enemies by looking like a toxic one. Usually, they'll combine one or more of these techniques, often against their own kind. But these are only generalities; it would take a whole book to describe the individual characteristics of each of the more than 25 species of salamanders that inhabit the mountains of the South.

Contemplation benches are scattered along the trails here. The outer loop climbs toward the upper part of the cove, reaching the big buckeye. The trunk of this tree is amazing. There should be a separate contemplation bench solely for this giant. Just ahead the outer loop returns to the trailhead. Feel free to loop around a second or third time.

25

Coosa Backcountry Loop

Total distance: 12.7 miles

Hiking time: 8 hours

Vertical rise: 2,100 feet

Rating: Difficult

*Maps: USGS 7.5' Coosa Bald,
Neels Gap, Vogel State Park,
Chattahoochee National Forest*

The Coosa Backcountry Loop is a long and strenuous trek, especially as a day hike. It leaves Vogel State Park and climbs to Burnett Gap. From here, the trail circles the Sosebee Creek valley, where it reaches a low point. From Sosebee Creek, the path makes a long climb to wooded Coosa Bald, breaking the 4,000-foot elevation mark. Some serious ups and downs follow as the path enters the Blood Mountain Wilderness and reaches Slaughter Mountain before making its way back down to the state park. There are many campsites along the trail for anyone who wants to make this loop an overnighter.

HOW TO GET THERE

From Dahlonega, follow US 19 north for 25 miles to Vogel State Park. Park near the visitor center and walk uphill on the right road (as you face the visitor center) for about 200 yards to the trailhead, near cabin No. 7.

THE HIKE

Make sure to register and receive a hiking permit at the state park visitor center before beginning the hike. It is required on the Coosa Backcountry Trail whether you stay overnight or not. The park rangers want to know who is out there and, more importantly, who has returned. The approach trail to the actual loop begins at a stone building and shares treadway with the Bear Hair Gap Loop.

Start a slight uptick, passing the Reece Nature Trail at 0.2 mile. Span Burnett Branch on a footbridge. Stay right here, as

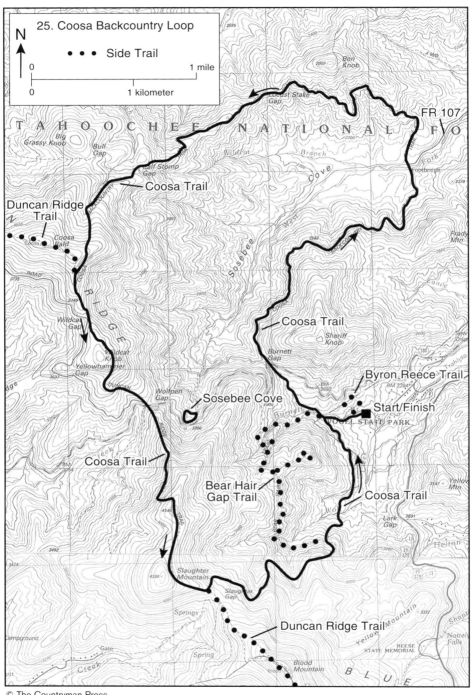

25. Coosa Backcountry Loop

••• Side Trail

N

0   1 mile
0   1 kilometer

Coosa Trail

Duncan Ridge Trail

Coosa Trail

FR 107

Coosa Trail

Byron Reece Trail

Start/Finish

Sosebee Cove

Coosa Trail

Coosa Trail

Bear Hair Gap Trail

Duncan Ridge Trail

© The Countryman Press

spur trails lead to campsites in the park campground. Keep upstream on Burnett Branch to reach another trail junction at 0.4 mile. You can see the return route of the yellow-blazed Coosa Backcountry Trail (CBT) and the orange-blazed Bear Hair Gap Trail. Make the loop counterclockwise as the climbs are gentler in this direction.

A wide track heads right; follow it to begin your loop. Another trail junction is just ahead. Here the Bear Hair Gap Trail and the Coosa Backcountry Trail go their separate ways. Turn right with the CBT, immediately crossing Burnett Branch on a wooden footbridge. The CBT now ascends the shallow valley formed by a feeder of Burnett Branch. The creek becomes more rock than water. Mixed woods shade the rocky path, which makes its way gently uphill to Burnett Gap at 0.9 mile.

Burnett Gap lies between Sheriff Knob to your right and Slaughter Mountain to your left. Cross GA 180 and Forest Road 107, which pass through the gap, and continue the CBT on a jeep track. Begin the long descent in cove hardwood forest. Pass an earthen berm at 1.3 miles; the trail becomes much narrower. As you continue north, deeper into Sosebee Cove, a small spring seeps across the trail. At 1.6 miles, the trail splits two tiers of a spring branch waterfall that flows over the path. Continue a gentle descent, passing around piney rib ridges and into moister coves.

The CBT turns left at 3 miles to follow a tributary creek as it beelines for West Fork Wolf Creek. Bottom out at a bridge over the creek. The trail then passes through a roadside campsite before crossing FR 107 at 3.4 miles and reentering woods. Get your mojo on here. You are at a low point, with a lot of climbing ahead. The path immediately jumps up in white pine woods on a bed of needles and red Georgia clay. Ramble

Fire pink wildflowers

through the woods and drop to cross a small creek at 3.7 miles. There is a campsite here.

The trail heads right and climbs along the gravelly branch before switchbacking away, trying to make elevation. Along the way the singletrack path passes two more branches in hickory-oak-pine woods. The red bands you see around the trees indicate the national forest boundary.

The ascent continues, and the trail finds itself atop a ridgeline at Locust Stake Gap at 4.9 miles. Now the CBT turns southwest and ascends toward Coosa Bald. Pass a dry campsite on the crest at 5.1 miles. Partial views open to the south of Sosebee Cove and Sheriff Knob, along with Frady Mountain. Young oaks cover the crest, the spindly trunks racing upward to compete for sunlight. The bulk of the mountainside rises to the left, and the CBT trail slips over to the right side of the ridge, then switchbacks uphill to rejoin the crest. You are now above 3,000 feet. Continue climbing in pine-azalea woods before making a final steep climb through a tunnel of mountain laurel to reach Calf Stomp Gap at 6 miles. There is a campsite here, as well as Forest Road 108. Long Branch flows within earshot.

Cross the forest road and continue the ascent of Coosa Bald on a singletrack path. This is part of the 7,100-acre Coosa Bald Scenic Area. Flame azaleas thrive on this mountain, lighting up the woods in mid-June. The path angles toward Long Branch, your last water source for some miles. You travel uphill along the branch before switchbacking away and ever upward to break the 4,000-foot barrier. The woods atop the mountain are somewhat open. Like many Southern Appalachian balds, Coosa Bald is now forested. At one time, fire and/or grazing kept these mountaintop fields completely open. However, without continued human intervention, the balds are giving way to forest and losing their vistas.

A dry campsite stands at the crest, at 7.1 miles, and a short path here leads left to an outcrop with partial views to the east. The CBT keeps forward to meet the Duncan Ridge Trail just ahead. The trail turns left, sharing a wide treadway with the Duncan Ridge Trail. Make an irregular but steep descent that gives credence to the idea of hiking this loop counterclockwise. Reach Wildcat Gap and Forest Road 39 at 7.6 miles. Keep forward and walk FR 39 just a short distance, then veer left back into the woods, climbing toward Wildcat Knob. The ascent is steady, but soon you are descending again, this time working around boulders.

The going is slow but scenic on the rocky track, and the CBT finally reaches Wolf Pen Gap (3,260 feet) and GA 180 at 8.5 miles. Cross the paved road and enter the Blood Mountain Wilderness. Work uphill by switchbacks and at other times by

nosing straight up the north shoulder of Slaughter Mountain. Reach the crest of the ridge, once again making 4,000 feet. The brush is high here in summer.

The CBT keeps along the east side of Slaughter Mountain, which rises higher. Begin working toward Slaughter Gap, although a reroute now takes the trail below the gap to allow the area to regenerate after excessive camping. On the descent, watch for a few very uncommon yellow birches directly beside the trail. The rerouted trail arrives at a junction at 10.2 miles. The Duncan Ridge Trail leaves right to meet the Appalachian Trail, while the CBT veers left and begins a steady descent into the Way Creek watershed.

You pass a piney flat and cross a wide, rocky rill before making a steep descent on a rugged, boulder-strewn track beneath rhododendron. Work deeper into a valley of several streams to meet the Bear Hair Gap Trail at 11.1 miles. The two trails share treadway, continuing forward to Wolf Creek. This branch has a nice waterfall about 50 yards upstream of the crossing.

Continue a steep descent past hemlocks and tulip trees, leaving the Blood Mountain Wilderness. A spur trail loops down to a shelter and then returns to the main track. The path wanders back toward Burnett Branch, completing the loop portion of Coosa Trail at 12.3 miles. From this point, you can backtrack to the stone shelter and the trailhead.

26

Jarrard Gap AT Loop

Total distance: 5.9 miles

Hiking time: 3½ hours

Vertical rise: 885 feet

Rating: Moderate

Maps: USGS 7.5' Neels Gap, Chattahoochee National Forest

This reasonable loop starts at Lake Winfield Scott, a great camping, swimming, and fishing destination, and explores sheltered mountain valleys divided by an Appalachian Trail ridge walk. It heads up Slaughter Creek, crossing streams galore on a moderate grade to meet a rerouted section of the AT. It then travels atop a lightly wooded ridgeline on the world's longest marked footpath to reach Jarrard Gap. You complete the hike with an easy descent on the Jarrard Gap Trail. This could be a one-night starter backpack or just a good initiation into the North Georgia Mountain country.

HOW TO GET THERE

From Dahlonega, take US 19 north for 9 miles to Stone Pile Gap and GA 60. Veer left on GA 60 and follow it 7 miles to GA 180, Wolf Pen Gap Road. Turn right and go 4.4 miles to Lake Winfield Scott Recreation Area, on your right. Enter the recreation area and continue 0.4 mile to a parking area on your left, just before the bridge over Slaughter Creek, where the creek enters Lake Winfield Scott.

THE HIKE

Leave the day-use parking area and cross the bridge over Slaughter Creek. Lake Winfield Scott is to your left. The Slaughter Creek Trail starts on your right. Begin walking up a grass-lined gravel track to reach a bridge over the creek. Veer left here into thick woods. The bridge leads to the campground.

Suddenly you are in rhododendron-hemlock woodlands sprinkled with Fraser

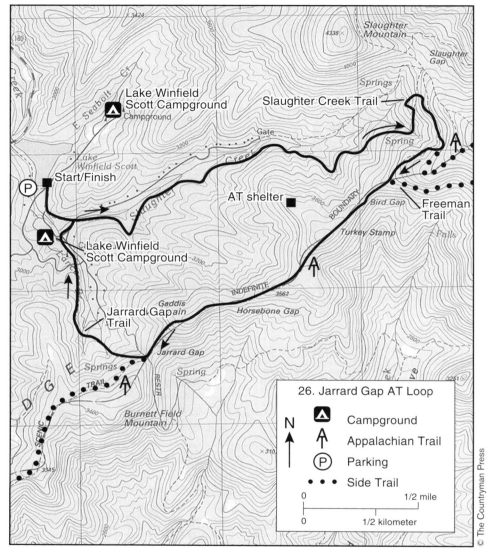

26. Jarrard Gap AT Loop

N

◭ Campground

Ⱥ Appalachian Trail

Ⓟ Parking

• • • Side Trail

| 0 | 1/2 mile |
| 0 | 1/2 kilometer |

© The Countryman Press

magnolia trees. The blue-blazed path crosses Slaughter Creek on a wood bridge to emerge onto a gravel road. Keep forward, crossing the gravel road, and begin the loop portion of your hike. Tunnel under rhododendron. Gaddis Mountain rises to your right. Cross the first of several branches of Slaughter Creek emanating from the ridge-line to your right, where the AT is and where you soon will be. Most of these crossings are bridged, and this well-maintained trail leaves and joins old roadbeds with regularity. Worry not, for the path is well marked.

Rise gently through laurel thickets. Slaughter Creek is within earshot, crashing below, making its way down to Lake Winfield

North Central Georgia Mountains

Lake Winfield Scott

Scott. Both mountain laurel and rhododen- dron grow here. Rhododendron, with bigger, leathery evergreen leaves, prefers shaded ravines and streamsides, but will also grow along moist slopes and on high-elevation, well-watered ridges. Mountain laurel, with smaller evergreen leaves, prefers dry, south- facing ridges and pine-oak forests. The two sometimes overlap habitats, as is the case here. Many mountain pioneers called moun- tain laurel "ivy." They called rhododendron "laurel," as well as calling hemlock trees "spruce." Botanists of the last century who were trying to catalog the vast array of plants in the Southern Appalachians must have been confounded by all the names the locals had given their flora.

At 1.7 miles, a trail comes in from the left. It leads down to a campsite by the water. Slaughter Creek is losing steam by this point and is more rock than water. Enter the Blood Mountain Wilderness at 1.8 miles. The stony track keeps a moderate

ascent, crossing ever-smaller branches. Judging by the crossings, it seems Slaugh- ter Creek has more tributaries than any other stream in Georgia. Finally, cross Slaughter itself and another tributary to enter oak woods, a sign of a drier forest. An- other common tree up here is goosefoot maple, also known as striped maple. As the name implies, this understory tree, which rarely grows higher than 25 feet, has verti- cal stripes on its trunk. The leaf resembles the webbed foot of a goose.

Reach the reroute of Slaughter Creek Trail at 2.6 miles. A keen eye will spot the old path heading up toward Slaughter Gap, which was a central trail junction and camp- ing spot that was overused through the years. Nowadays, no trails go through Slaughter Gap. Instead, the reroute veers to the right on a steep hillside, passing through a rugged boulder field seamed with small streams. Intersect the Appalachian Trail at 2.9 miles, beside the headwaters of

Slaughter Creek. You can see the old AT coming in, which was also rerouted.

If you are camping, head left, up stone steps on the AT to a camping area about 100 yards distant. Leveled tent sites are situated on a little loop off the AT. No fires are allowed in this tent camping area.

This particular hike, however, keeps forward, downhill and southbound on the AT. The walking is pleasant here, despite the rocky track. The Slaughter Creek valley is to your right. Oak, hickory, and white pine dominate the woods along with locust and birch, representing both moist and dry forest flora. It is a somewhat confusing mix, but it's really indicative of the biodiversity of the Southern Appalachians, which is rich in ecosystems with varying forest habitats. The technical term is an overlapping of ecotones.

Ahead, the tree cover becomes sparse as you descend toward Bird Gap. Intersect the Freeman Trail at 3.2 miles. There are campsites here, too. Also ahead is a spur trail leading right about a half mile to the Woods Hole Trail Shelter, a three-sided Adirondack-style shelter with a picnic table and bearproof food storage cables. Water can be had from a spring before you reach the shelter.

The AT keeps a gentle track, slightly ascending from Bird Gap but curving around the side of Turkey Stamp, a small knob. It then works its way downhill to Horsebone

Gap and curves around Gaddis Mountain. The walking is easy in the lightly wooded terrain. The trail avoids the mountaintops but does pass through the gaps.

After Gaddis Mountain, reach Jarrard Gap at 4.7 miles. The AT continues forward, and Jarrard Gap Road crosses the gap. To complete the loop, turn right down this gravel road and follow it just a short piece, looking for the blue-blazed Jarrard Gap Trail leaving left. The singletrack trail slips by a nice spring and continues downward to join an old jeep track. The woods thicken as you make your way down toward Lake Winfield Scott. Soon cross a rill, or small brook, on a footbridge. The descent picks up and more small seeps cross the path. The stream to your right, Lance Branch, is flowing well by the time you pass around some vehicle-barrier boulders to reach Slaughter Creek Road.

Keep forward, following Slaughter Creek Road around a curve to the left, then to the right. Reach the Slaughter Creek Trail just ahead and end the loop portion of your hike. You have been here before. Turn left to backtrack to the lake and the trailhead. Consider combining your loop hike with a camping trip at Lake Winfield Scott. This recreation area has a little bit of everything—a serene lake with fishing, boating (electric motors only), and a swim beach, and a quality campground, parts of which are open year-round.

27

Blood Mountain Loop

Total distance: 5.8 miles

Hiking time: 4 hours

Vertical rise: 1,390 feet

Rating: Moderate to difficult

Maps: USGS 7.5' Neels Gap, Chattahoochee National Forest

Blood Mountain is one of Georgia's legendary peaks, and deservedly so. The views from the rock faces and outcrops are simply stunning. It does involve some climbing, but how else do you get a well-earned view from a mountaintop? The trek starts with a climb to the Appalachian Trail on the Byron Reece Trail. Once on the AT, begin a rerouted direct approach to the rock faces, stunted trees, and brush atop 4,400-foot Blood before descending to meet the Freeman Trail at Bird Gap. The Freeman Trail makes a rocky return on the south side of Blood Mountain and has its own views and general rugged nature. By the way, this entire hike takes place within the Blood Mountain Wilderness.

HOW TO GET THERE

From Cleveland, head north on US 129 for 19.1 miles to the Byron Reece Trail and the Neels Gap Trailhead parking area. You actually pass through Neels Gap and begin a downgrade, reaching the left turn to the parking area 0.4 mile beyond Neels Gap.

THE HIKE

Leave the trailhead on a wide track, the Byron Reece Trail. Extended parking is non-existent at Neels Gap, due to Walyasi-Yi Center, the state-run Appalachian Trail gathering spot, so the Forest Service built this lower parking area and the Byron Reece Trail to connect with the AT. And they picked a scenic route. The trail enters the Blood Mountain Wilderness, then heads up a bold stream bordered by rhododendron.

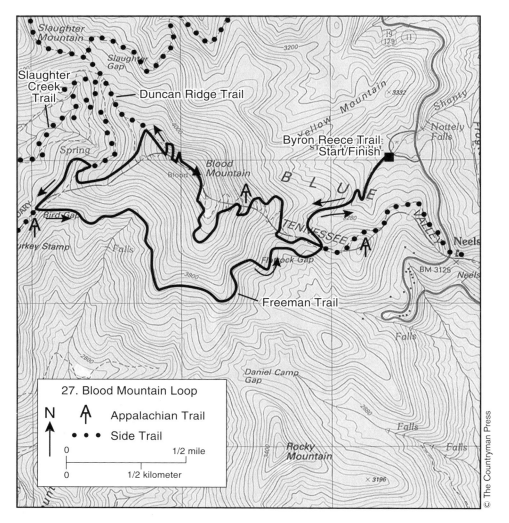

Slaughter Mountain

Slaughter Gap

Slaughter Creek Trail

Duncan Ridge Trail

Spring

Blood Mountain

Blood

Byron Reece Trail Start/Finish

Yellow Mountain

Shanty

Nottely Falls

B L U E

Bird Gap

Turkey Stamp

Falls

TENNESSEE

VALLEY

Neels

Neels

BM 3125

Freeman Trail

Flatrock Gap

Daniel Camp Gap

Falls

Rocky Mountain

Falls

Falls

27. Blood Mountain Loop

N

Ⱥ Appalachian Trail

• • • Side Trail

0   1/2 mile

0   1/2 kilometer

Step over Shanty Branch, passing some large hemlocks.

Climb away from the creek by switchbacks on well-placed steps, passing a waterfall. Then return to the creek and enter a fern-floored cove to meet the AT and Freeman Trail at 0.7 mile. The Freeman Trail is your return route. Turn right, southbound on the AT. Soon reach the first of many vistas on a rock slab that opens to the south. The trail also passes over rock slabs, often bordered by Virginia pines, which are able to grow in the shallow soil where other trees cannot.

Open rock bluffs and scattered oak tree cover provide more views. The path switchbacks over new rock faces, some of which have water seeping over them, so be careful. Stone steps have been added in certain places to make the ascent easier. The labor to install the steps must have been backbreaking. They make the hiking seem like a breeze, despite the uphill grade. This part of

Blooming mountain laurel atop Blood Mountain

the AT was rerouted, and it's one of the prettiest sections in Georgia. Watch for a tilted rock at 1.1 miles on trail right. You can be assured that many hikers have gotten under it during thunderstorms.

The AT levels out, then reaches a good vista at the crest of the mountain. Reenter woods and come out on a rock face with a grand vista that makes all previous views pale in comparison. Mountains sweep across the horizon to the south and east, ranging far and wide above the trees. And the expansive rock face adds to the dramatic effect. From this point, the AT weaves in and out of a stunted oak-pine-mountain laurel forest. Watch for blueberries here, as well.

More sporadic outcrops open as you climb, including some with views to the north, before you reach the top of Blood Mountain (4,461 feet) at 2 miles. A USGS survey marker is embedded in the rock. This is the AT's highest point in Georgia. The

path runs just a few feet more to reach the Blood Mountain shelter. This stone structure was built in the 1930s by the Civilian Conservation Corps. It is fully enclosed, but the windows are without glass and the fireplace has been rocked shut. Picnic Rock, an elevated outcrop, is next to the shelter and makes a good viewing and picnicking spot.

Blood Mountain was named after a particularly deadly battle between Cherokee and Creek Indians atop the peak. It was said that the mountain ran red with blood after the altercation, also giving rise to the name of nearby Slaughter Creek.

The AT leaves the rocky crest of Blood Mountain. Begin a descent by switchbacks, passing more rock outcrops and entering thick woods with azaleas aplenty. This part of the AT was rerouted to bypass Slaughter Gap, and it reaches the Duncan Ridge Trail at 2.5 miles. It has come some 31 miles from its beginning at Three Forks, where it diverges from the AT near Long Creek Falls.

Blood Mountain Loop

The reroute continues downhill to reach a spur loop and tent camping area at 2.8 miles. Leveled campsites and tent pads have been strung along the spur loop for AT backpackers. Just ahead, beside the gurgling headwaters of Slaughter Creek, you appropriately intersect the Slaughter Creek Trail, which has come 2.9 miles from Lake Winfield Scott.

The AT turns left here and rejoins its former route, heading downhill on an easy, but at times rocky track through sparse woods with a brushy understory to reach Bird Gap and the Freeman Trail at 3.3 miles. This loop heads left, but know that a spur trail leads right, just beyond the Freeman Trail, to reach water and head on to the Woods Hole Trail Shelter, an Adirondack-style shelter with a picnic table and bearproof food storage cables. The shelter is about a half mile from the AT.

Follow the Freeman Trail as it turns sharply left (east) in sporadic tree cover.

This lesser forest allows views to the south. More views open where the Freeman Trail crosses rock faces similar to the ones higher up on Blood Mountain. Since the trail is on the south slope of Blood Mountain and has limited tree cover, it can be warm in the summer. At your feet, the singletrack path is quite bouldery, making travel slow—but who is in a hurry to get through this beautiful scenery anyway?

You pass a few rocky rills, the upper branches of Blood Mountain Creek, starting at 3.7 miles. The tree cover thickens here and the trail undulates a bit, but it's mostly level, running generally around 3,500 feet. It roughly parallels the track of the AT atop Blood Mountain. More rock slabs lie ahead. Pass a second set of rocky streams, then a couple more rock slabs to meet the Appalachian Trail and the Byron Reece Trail at 5 miles. You have now completed the loop. Backtrack 0.7 mile down the Byron Reece Trail to the trailhead.

28

DeSoto Falls
Double-Decker Hike

Total distance: 2 miles there and back

Hiking time: 1¼ hours

Vertical rise: 200 feet

Rating: Easy

Maps: USGS 7.5' Neels Gap, Chattahoochee National Forest

This hike visits two waterfalls in one pretty place, the 650-acre DeSoto Falls Scenic Area. Both falls have an observation deck, hence the double-decker moniker, and both live up to their scenic billing. Located in the Frogtown Creek valley, this area also has a nice picnic area and campground, and a quality trout stream.

HOW TO GET THERE

From Cleveland, head north on US 129 for 15 miles to the DeSoto Falls Recreation Area. Turn left and keep left to enter the falls parking area. If you keep forward, you will enter DeSoto Falls Campground.

THE HIKE

It is strange, the pairing of the names DeSoto and Frogtown. According to North Georgia legend, local settlers found an odd piece of armor at the base of the falls here on Frogtown Creek. The armor was supposedly left behind by Hernando de Soto himself as he hunted for gold during his ill-fated odyssey through what became the American South. This story may have been invented by locals to increase visitation to the area, but such a pretty place needs no legend to augment its natural beauty. Frogtown Creek and its tributaries fall fast from the mountains to the north, where the Appalachian Trail rolls on the high ridges. Neither falls is actually on Frogtown Creek; they both drop on feeder branches.

The DeSoto Falls Trail leaves the parking area on a gravel path, passing rest rooms to

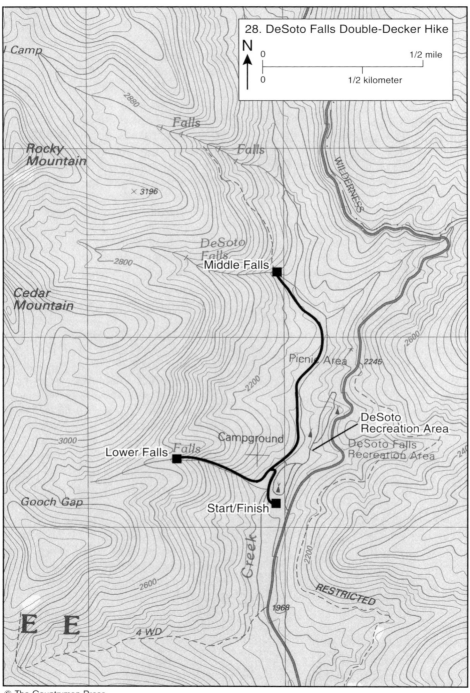

28. DeSoto Falls Double-Decker Hike

N

0   1/2 mile

0   1/2 kilometer

Camp

2880

Falls

Rocky
Mountain

Falls

WILDERNESS

× 3196

DeSoto
Falls

2800

Middle Falls

Cedar
Mountain

Picnic Area   2245

2600

2200

3000

Falls

Campground

DeSoto
Recreation Area

DeSoto Falls
Recreation Area

Lower Falls

240

Gooch Gap

Start/Finish

Creek

2200

2600

RESTRICTED

1968

E E

4 WD

© The Countryman Press

reach an attractive and well-shaded picnic area. Frogtown Creek flows in the background. Turn right here and travel upstream, passing more picnic sites to open into the lower loop of the DeSoto Falls Campground. Stay left on the paved loop road, coming near Frogtown Creek and along some campsites to reach a trailside kiosk and bridge across from the campground host's campsite.

Cross the wooden bridge over Frogtown Creek and enter the DeSoto Falls Scenic Area. Here, the trail splits. Turn right and head toward the upper falls. Doghobble borders the track, while birches, maples, and hemlocks shade it from above. Doghobble is a low, arching shrub that exists only in the Southern Appalachians. In late spring clusters of small, bell-shaped flowers droop from its arms. The waist-high thickets prove quite an impediment for most creatures, including humans and dogs. In pioneer days, hunted bears would plow through such thickets using their powerful bodies, losing the dogs that pursued them and eventually giving the plant its name.

You can see campsites across Frogtown Creek. Don't be surprised if a camper-turned-angler is vying for trout here. The creek and its tributaries offer quality trout fishing, and Georgia Game and Fish stocks the stream weekly during the summer. Nearby Waters Creek offers special-regulation trophy-trout fishing.

Georgia's mountain streams have three kinds of trout: brook, rainbow, and brown. The only native trout is the brookie, which is technically a char from Arctic waters, forced south by the last ice age. During the logging days at the beginning of the last century, many of North Georgia's streams became warm and silted, unfit for the finicky brookie. Some early naturalists noticed the absence and restocked many of Georgia's streams

with rainbows, natives of the West, and later, brown trout that were brought from Germany and Scotland. They were carried into the mountain streams by rail, mule, and foot, and expanded their range through the years. Now the rainbow is king in the North Georgia Mountains, and the native brook trout has been pushed back into remote headwater streams high in the mountains. In retrospect, of course, it would have been best to restock these streams with brook trout.

Georgia has over 4,000 miles of trout streams. However, many are seasonal, stocked only in winter when the waters are cool enough for trout to survive. In addition to cool temperatures, trout need clean water with minimal sedimentation. Stream sedimentation smothers both trout eggs and the aquatic insects upon which trout feed.

The path is nearly level as you pass over a bridge spanning a feeder branch of Frogtown Creek. The wide path begins to climb into laurel thickets. Resting benches have been placed beside the trail for the weary. Drop back down and cross another feeder branch on a footbridge. A now-closed trail led forward to the upper falls, but this path currently leads left to a viewing deck and the middle falls at 0.9 mile. Middle Falls, also simply known as DeSoto Falls, is quite loud. It drops 90 feet in four tiers. The uppermost tier is but a slender ribbon of white, followed by a wider cascade, followed by another cascade, followed by a final cascade. A border of rhododendron frames the multitiered drop on its way down from Rocky Mountain and Cedar Mountain.

Backtrack to the lower falls, returning to the bridge near the campground host site. The path heads downstream along Frogtown Creek just a short distance before climbing away from the water. It seems odd

DeSoto Falls

that the trail would climb to a downstream waterfall, yet the switchbacks continue uphill, and you soon realize that this falls is also on a feeder branch of Frogtown Creek.

The trail rises to the second viewing deck and the lower falls. This waterfall makes a 35-foot drop over a ragged cliff line, and the water bounces its way down amid a forest of thick trees. Do not forget to look back across the valley at Hogpen Mountain. Backtrack to the parking area.

While you are here, you may want to check out the DeSoto Campground. Twenty-four large campsites are split among two creekside loops arranged beneath a dense forest of deciduous and evergreen trees. It is just 2 miles from the DeSoto Recreation Area to the parking area for the Appalachian Trail. If you want to combine this DeSoto Falls Double-Decker Hike with another trek, the 5.8-mile Blood Mountain Loop starts here (see Hike 27).

29

Cowrock Mountain from Hogpen Gap

Total distance: 3.6 miles there and back

Hiking time: 2 hours

Vertical rise: 800 feet

Rating: Moderate

Maps: USGS 7.5' Cowrock, Chattahoochee National Forest

How could you not want to go on a hike that travels to a place called Cowrock Mountain from a place called Hogpen Gap? Names aside, this is a good hike on the Appalachian Trail to one of my favorite views in the North Georgia Mountains. The trek travels up from Hogpen Gap and over Wildcat Mountain, where a warm-up view awaits. From here, it's downhill to Tesnatee Gap and the historic Logan Turnpike. A final climb leads to the wide rock slab on the side of Cowrock Mountain, with views out over the Towns Creek valley and beyond. Every time I come here I wonder why this vista doesn't draw more visitors.

HOW TO GET THERE

From Cleveland, take US 129 north/GA 75 Alternate for 3 miles. Turn right on GA 75 Alternate and follow it for 5.1 miles to GA 348. Turn left and go 7 miles to the trailhead parking area in Hogpen Gap, on your right. Make sure to go south on the AT, crossing GA 348 from the parking area.

THE HIKE

At the parking area, take time to admire the inscribed-granite Appalachian Trail marker here at Hogpen Gap. The hike starts with a brief walk down GA 348, the way you came, heading into White County. Cross GA 348 and begin climbing the Appalachian Trail. A blue-blazed spur trail leads left and downhill to water. The AT begins angling up the side of Wildcat Mountain via switchbacks, entering the Raven

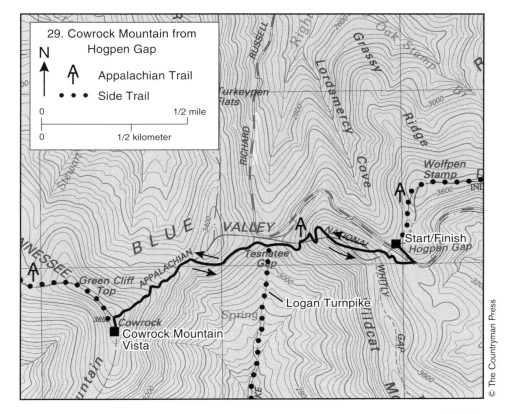

29. Cowrock Mountain from Hogpen Gap

N

⋔ Appalachian Trail

• • • Side Trail

0   1/2 mile

0   1/2 kilometer

Wolfpen Stamp

Start/Finish
Hogpen Gap

Logan Turnpike

Tesnatee Gap

Green Cliff Top

Cowrock Mountain Vista

© The Countryman Press

Cliff Wilderness. Sporadic, thin stands of oak rise above the thick brush.

At 0.5 mile reach the crest of the mountain and a trail junction. A spur trail leads left 1.2 miles to the Whitely Gap Trail Shelter, a three-sided Adirondack-style structure with a picnic table and bearproof food-storage cables. When the AT was first laid out it was supposed to continue out the string of mountains on the east side of Towns Creek, through Whitely Gap. The AT was instead routed north through Hogpen Gap and beyond, leaving the Whitely Gap shelter far off the main path. The huge majority of AT shelters are within a quarter mile of the trail itself. Nevertheless, this is a pretty spot with a good spring, and on the way back you can

stop by if you feel like extending your hike by 2.4 miles round-trip.

The Appalachian Trail has been rerouted in many places through the years, and continues to be rerouted today. Often, the master path of the East was moved to get around private property or to reach newly acquired public lands. Other times, it was rerouted toward particularly scenic areas or away from sensitive areas.

The AT turns east beyond the trail junction, cruising atop the mountain. The forest is denser up here. Partial views open out to the south, but soon you reach a rock outcrop and a view of Cowrock Mountain and the rock face where you are headed. It is neat to see your destination from such a

Cowrock Mountain from Hogpen Gap

Looking out from Cowrock Mountain

clear vantage point. The AT begins working off the mountain, passing through an interesting boulder field that lures you in for a walk. Many short and sharp switchbacks lead down toward Tesnatee Gap. The going is slow, so take your time and reach Tesnatee Gap at 0.9 mile, passing a monument to Richard B. Russell, for whom the scenic byway of GA 348 is named. To your left, the historic Logan Turnpike leads left and down steeply to Towns Creek.

The road that became Logan Turnpike helped open what was then remote and little-wanted Union County to markets. The county was established in 1832, carved from former Cherokee County, and was named Union for its founder John Thomas's pro-union stance. Most of Georgia's coastal residents were for states' rights.

Much of the land was disbursed in a land lottery, but only mountain people of Georgia had an interest in the area. The Union Turnpike Company received a state charter to build a toll road across Tesnatee Gap to connect two existing roads, thereby connecting Blairsville with Gainesville, Georgia, by way of Cleveland. The road was completed in 1840. In 1841 Major Francis Logan bought the rights to run the toll road from the company and built a home, a lodge, and the tollgate. In 1871 he purchased additional land in Union County, and the road became known as the Logan Turnpike. The tollgate was operated by his family until 1922, when work was completed across Neels Gap on a paved road—today's US 19/129—and the tollgate was abandoned.

A lot of traffic and produce has passed through Tesnatee Gap over the years. Now GA 348 carries tourists near the gap, but today it is primarily hikers that actually cross it. It is said that famous naturalist John Muir took the Logan Turnpike through Tesnatee Gap on his thousand-mile walk to the Gulf of Mexico in 1867. The Logan Turnpike is a steep, 2-mile hike down to Kellum Valley

Road. Access from the bottom requires a high-clearance vehicle and perhaps four-wheel drive during wetter times, as the uppermost section includes creek crossings.

Tesnatee Gap has a parking area off of GA 348, and if you want to shorten your hike you can start here—but you won't get full exercise credit. The AT crosses the parking area and begins rising at an angle on Cowrock Mountain. The path passes over small rock slabs and a neat little overhang before reaching a gap at 1.2 miles. You slip over to the east side of the mountain but quickly turn back, zigzagging to each side of the ridge you're climbing. Birches become more common up here, as does witch hazel.

Finally, at 1.8 miles, the trail opens to the rock face of Cowrock Mountain. Wide vistas open to the south of the Towns Creek valley below and the rest of Georgia as far as the eye can see. Wildcat Mountain, Adams Bald, and Rocky Mountain are across from Towns Creek valley, and that is where the Appalachian Trail would have gone through Whitely Gap in the original plans. If you poke around up here, you can find more outcrops that offer other vistas. Stunted oaks, and even a cedar tree, border the rock outcrop. If you want to extend your hike by 2.4 miles on the way back, take the trip out to the Whitley Gap shelter before dropping to Hogpen Gap.

30

Martin's Mine Meander at Smithgall Woods

Total distance: 6.5-mile double loop

Hiking time: 4 hours

Vertical rise: 240 feet

Rating: Moderate

Maps: USGS 7.5' Cowrock, Helen, Smithgall Woods Dukes Conservation Area

Martin's Mine was one of the most productive gold mines in North Georgia, the site of America's first gold rush. Here in White County, along the gorgeous Dukes Creek drainage, you can visit the Martin's Mine, which is located within the confines of the state's second-largest state park, Smithgall Woods Dukes Creek Conservation Area. Not only can you see a slice of mining history and an amazing recovery of nature, but you can also enjoy the clear waters of Dukes Creek and an additional interpretive path, Laurel Ridge Trail. And when you visit this Peach State treasure, you will realize that the suggested hike is but a sampling of the exploration opportunities available in the 5,600-acre preserve.

HOW TO GET THERE

From Cleveland, take US 129 north/GA 75 Alternate for 3 miles. Turn right on GA 75 Alternate and follow it for 5.7 miles to the gates of Smithgall Woods, on your right.

THE HIKE

Before taking off on your adventure, stop inside the Smithgall Woods Visitor Center and learn more about what this park used to be and what it currently offers. It is now a place managed for wildlife, yet laid out so nature lovers can enjoy the flora and fauna. The grounds of the entrance area and visitor center are attractive and well kept.

Leave the parking area on a paved road leading east that is closed to private vehicles but open to bicycles, should you choose to hike and bike here. The Martin's Mine Trail and the Laurel Ridge Trail are

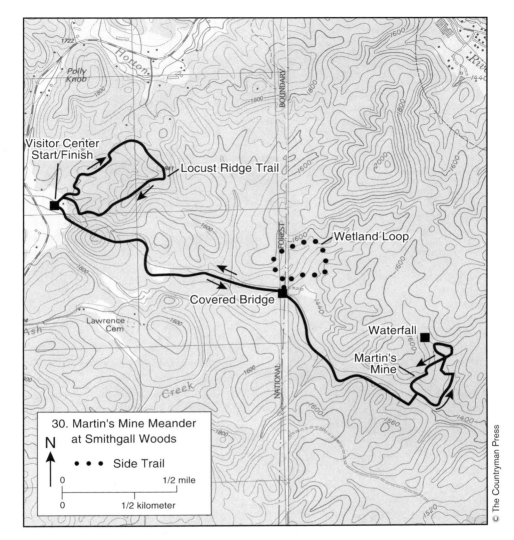

Map labels:
- 1722
- Polly Knob
- 1800
- Hoxton
- BOUNDARY
- 1600
- 1440
- Run
- Visitor Center Start/Finish
- Locust Ridge Trail
- 1600
- 2000
- 1600
- FOREST
- 1600
- Wetland Loop
- 1600
- Covered Bridge
- 1440
- Lawrence Cem
- Ash
- Waterfall
- Martin's Mine
- 1600
- NATIONAL
- 1600
- Creek
- 1560
- 1400
- 1520

30. Martin's Mine Meander
at Smithgall Woods

N

• • • Side Trail

0 .... 1/2 mile

0 .... 1/2 kilometer

© The Countryman Press

foot-only paths. The road climbs a hill, then dips past a beekeeping area and fields, the first of many that are sown with crops favorable to wildlife. Dukes Creek is off to your right. Pass Tower Road on the left at 1.1 miles. Just ahead, near a field, is the Wetland Loop Trail. The main road then spans Dukes Creek on a scenic covered bridge.

The road becomes gravel beyond the bridge and travels closely alongside Dukes Creek, a special-regulations trout stream.

You may end up wishing you'd brought your rod. Whether you fish or not, take time to view this creek, one of the prettiest in the North Georgia Mountains. Pass the Hemlock Picnic Shelter just before reaching the Martin's Mine Loop Trail at 2 miles.

Cross the footbridge over Dukes Creek and turn right onto the loop trail, heading downstream. Just ahead, the trail passes a boardwalk overlooking a wetland. Turn up Black Branch, a tributary of Dukes Creek.

Covered bridge over Dukes Creek

Look around; the woods seem perfectly normal but something is out of kilter. It is the terrain. Trees grow atop odd-shaped hillocks. Linear mini-ridges of soil run against the contour of the natural drainage. These are mine tailings, displaced soil left over from the gold-extraction process.

Gold was first discovered on a tributary of Dukes Creek in 1828 here in White County. Over time, a gold rush began over the 60-square-mile area that yielded the valuable mineral. The Englund Mine was the first to operate in these parts. However, it was Lumpkin County and Dahlonega that got all the publicity. They had the town and, perhaps most importantly, the newspaper to get the word out. The great Georgia gold rush was on.

Most mining was done by placer–basically panning for gold on a bigger scale– and hydraulic mining–using gravity-driven water cannons to blast soil loose for later gold extraction. Martin's Mine, named after

Scottish transplant John Martin, used a third method, known as hard rock mining. He dug shafts and tunnels to get out the ore, and then used a process involving mercury and heat to extract the pure gold from the ore. The tailings were left over from the process, and they are even more visible during the winter months.

The Martin's Mine Trail continues winding among the tailings. The real surprise is how well the forest has recovered. Cross Black Branch on a footbridge, then come to the Martin's Mine upper loop. To your left, a bridge passes over the tributary and leads to the site of a mining stamp mill. Save this for later and keep right, looping uphill away from the stream and crossing small branches on wooden bridges.

Return to Black Branch at a pretty waterfall shaded by dense forest. The lower falls is but a 6-foot cascade. Above it is a five-tiered dramatic drop, made more impressive by winter rains and melting snows.

The largest gold nugget east of the Mississippi was found in the vicinity of these falls, spurring more interest in mining.

The upper loop follows the branch downstream, back to the bridge and stamp mill site. Cross the bridge and head west, passing through a man-made "gorge" of dug earth atop the Reynolds Vein, as this area of gold was known. You are running parallel to the Martin hard rock mine. On the climb, you pass one of the remaining shafts Martin dug into the ground. The other two have collapsed. From a perch, you can peer down into the shaft.

The trail descends away from the shaft, works through woodland, and then returns to Dukes Creek. Imagine this land a century or more ago: completely denuded of vegetation, open tailings lying everywhere, soil clogging Dukes Creek. It was this amazing recuperation of nature that led a radio magnate named Charles Smithgall to purchase the area and the lands surrounding it starting in 1981. It took 81 land transactions to save the tract from development. The land was eventually sold to the state of Georgia in 1994 for half its appraised value, and thus this historic park came to be.

Return to the road at 3 miles, and begin backtracking toward the visitor center. The Wetlands Loop awaits if you want to add 1 mile to your overall walk. Otherwise, return to the visitor center at 5 miles, then walk the 1.4-mile Laurel Ridge Interpretive Trail. The path passes a small picnic area, then works its way up toward the crest of Laurel Ridge. Interpretive stations, along with a helpful brochure from the visitor center, explain the changing nature of the forest as you climb to Laurel Ridge via small streams. From the top of the ridge, the path meanders back down to Dukes Creek and returns to the visitor center.

After your hike here you will surely want to return to Smithgall Woods again, whether to hike, bike, hunt, fish, or otherwise enjoy the natural beauty of this state conservation area.

31

Locust Log Ridge Lookout

Total distance: 7.4 miles there and back

Hiking time: 4 hours

Vertical rise: 750 feet

Rating: Moderate to difficult

Maps: USGS 7.5' Jacks Gap, Hiawassee, Chattahoochee National Forest, Brasstown Bald handout

This hike travels west along a rib ridge of Brasstown Bald to a viewpoint. Your venue is the Arkaquah Trail, one of the best, yet least-used, paths in the North Georgia Mountains. Along the way it travels through the Brasstown Wilderness in high-country forest and passes Blue Bluff, among other interesting outcrops on this path. More ridge-running along Locust Log Ridge, with some ups and downs, leads to an unnamed knob. The view from here extends north, but much of the enjoyment of this hike is in the journey itself.

HOW TO GET THERE

From Helen, drive north on GA 17/75 for 12 miles to GA 180. Turn left on GA 180 west and follow it for 5.3 miles to GA 180 Spur. Turn left again and go 2.4 miles to the Brasstown Bald parking area. This is a fee parking area.

THE HIKE

The Arkaquah Trail begins near the parking area entrance booth, by the rest rooms. A water fountain is located nearby in case you want to fill your water bottle before the hike. Walk the paved path to the rest rooms just a short distance, then veer left onto the Arkaquah Trail. Immediately descend through thick rhododendron along a spring branch that provided water for the Chero-kee who once camped where the parking area now stands.

The singletrack path enters the Brass-town Wilderness, curving right along the south slope of Brasstown Bald and heading

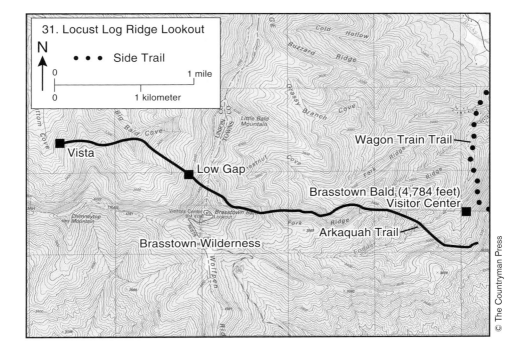

west toward Chimneytop Mountain. The trail is well above 4,000 feet and stays there for nearly 2 miles as it meanders among gray mossback boulders, underneath rhododendron, along open grassy stretches, and below some major bluffs forming the rampart that is Brasstown Bald.

At 0.6 mile, the Arkaquah Trail levels off in a gap on the west side of Brasstown Bald and continues its westerly ways. Cherry, mountain ash, and birch trees grow above the underbrush that crowds the undulating path, broken by gray outcrops with obscured vistas of the surrounding lands. In winter, the views are nearly continuous. This high-elevation environment is different than most ridge-running paths in Georgia, which are normally dominated by oak and hickory woodlands.

At times, the path travels over bare rock. By 1.2 miles, on the east end of Chimneytop

Mountain, the outcrops have become large enough to open vistas back to the east, where you can plainly see the observation tower atop Brasstown Bald. This view alone is worth the price of admission, in my opinion. These open rock areas also make for good stops to just sit back and enjoy the scenery.

Continue along Chimneytop Mountain, descending on switchbacks. Reach a spot where the trail twists between boulders on a "fatman's squeeze," at 1.4 miles. Just beyond the tight spot, a large overhanging bluff provides shelter from storms and is an interesting rock feature itself.

Wind down amid more boulders on the western shoulder of Chimneytop, dropping below the 4,000-foot mark. The ridge becomes knife-edged and quite craggy, with stunted trees hanging on where enough soil has gathered to hold their roots in place.

Chestnut oaks frame the view from Locust Log Ridge.

More exposed rock lies ahead. At 2.1 miles, the path slips over to the right of the ridgeline, the north side, and dips below a tall bluff extending 100 or more feet above the trail. This sheer gray rock wall faces north and is part of the greater Blue Bluff.

The Arkaquah Trail begins a serious descent on the north side of the ridge in cool thickets of rhododendron, passing a small overhang. It continues the downgrade by switchbacks, and eventually regains the nose of the ridgeline. The path has now joined Locust Log Ridge, and drops to reach Low Gap, elevation 3,505 feet, at 2.6 miles. The vegetational change is stunning here. In this relatively protected part of the forest the trees grow straight and tall, rising high overhead. This soaring linear forest contrasts with the stunted, windblown, sculpted trees and bushes of the narrow ridgelines and knobs emanating from Brasstown Bald.

The trail rises from Low Gap. Pines and oaks become more prevalent, and the more northerly species have dropped out. Work your way over a knob and then descend along a narrow ridge to reach Cove Gap at 3.3 miles. From here, the Arkaquah Trail makes a final climb to a second knob, the most westerly one on Locust Log Ridge. The trees on this rocky protrusion have no defense against the elements and so remain short in order to hold tight when winter winds pound the ridge.

Many rock outcrops and slabs begin to reappear on this final climb. Reach a high point at 3.7 miles. Just to the right of the trail, chestnut oaks frame a view to the north and into the Brasstown Creek valley from a stone perch. Is this view as good as the one atop Brasstown Bald? Absolutely not. However, the walk along the trail, the solitude, and the trailside scenery amid the Brasstown Wilderness make this destination one of the finest in the region.

On the return journey you will have to ascend a net of 800 feet. Of course, there are a few descents on the way back that add to the total amount of climbing. If you were to go west on the Arkaquah Trail you would drop 1,000 feet with no climbing back to Brasstown Bald to reach Track Rock Gap, but this route requires a shuttle.

Track Rock Gap is an interesting spot. It is the site of ancient aboriginal petroglyphs. Unfortunately, the rock drawings are now protected from theft or vandalism by a metal cage, tainting the atmosphere around them. It is these drawings that give the gap its name.

The Arkaquah Trail starts back at the Brasstown Bald parking area, which has a visitor center. From here, you can take a 0.6-mile paved hiking trail to the summit of 4,784-foot Brasstown Bald, Georgia's highest point. If you are too tired to hike to the top of Brasstown after going on the Locust Log Ridge Lookout hike, you can pay to take a shuttle to the top. And if you do, you will be shocked at all the able-bodied people that choose to ride rather than make the short walk to the lookout, with its 360-degree views. Furthermore, you will appreciate the solitude and natural contrast that the Arkaquah Trail offers.

32

Wagon Train Vista/
Brasstown Bald

Total distance: 3.6 miles

Hiking time: 2 hours

Vertical rise: 500 feet

Rating: Moderate

Maps: USGS 7.5' Jacks Gap, Hiawassee, Chattahoochee National Forest, Brasstown Bald handout

This book wouldn't be complete without a trek to Georgia's highest point, Brasstown Bald. However, the trail up to the summit is short, only 0.6 mile one way, so an added walk on the nearby Wagon Train Trail—into the Brasstown Wilderness and to a view—enhances this high-upon-high experience.

HOW TO GET THERE

From Helen, drive north on GA 17/75 for 12 miles to GA 180. Turn left on GA 180 west and follow it 5.3 miles to GA 180 Spur. Turn left here and go 2.4 miles to the Brasstown Bald parking area. This is a fee parking area.

THE HIKE

This hike traverses a variety of environments, both natural and man-made. The Brasstown Bald parking area, developed by the Forest Service, has a visitor center, book shop, and—believe it or not—a shuttle bus which, for a small fee, will take those who don't want to (or can't) make it 0.6 mile to the top of Brasstown Bald, where there is an interpretive center and an observation deck that offers a 360-degree view from Georgia's highest point at 4,784 feet. On a clear day, visitors can see all the way to Tennessee.

Aside from the developed area, the mountain also holds the 12,565-acre Brasstown Wilderness, which envelops nearly the entire mountain, top excepted. On these high ridges you'll find forests heavy with yellow birch and other species that replicate forests farther north. Parts of the Wagon Train Trail look, feel, and smell like ridge-running trails in the Smoky Mountains

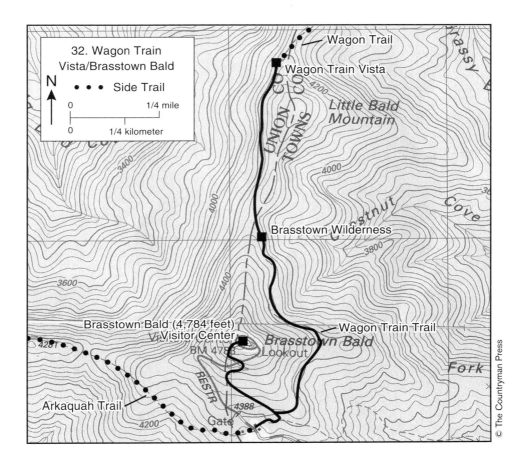

32. Wagon Train
Vista/Brasstown Bald

N

• • • Side Trail

0   1/4 mile

0   1/4 kilometer

Wagon Trail

Wagon Train Vista

Little Bald
Mountain

Brasstown Wilderness

Brasstown Bald (4,784 feet)
Visitor Center
BM 4768

Wagon Train Trail

Brasstown Bald
Lookout

Arkaquah Trail

4388
Gate

National Park. So get a taste of the Brasstown Wilderness on the trail and then appreciate the developed view atop Brasstown Bald, and you can say you have been to one of Georgia's most outstanding spots.

The hike starts on the Summit Trail, heading up Brasstown Bald. The trail is to the left of the visitor center as you face it. Take the paved path past some rest rooms and the shuttle bus that goes to the top of Brasstown and wind up a short piece to intersect the Wagon Train Trail. This trail crosses the Summit Trail at an angle, and is a wide, mown path. An interpretive sign explains how the trail got its name.

Early in the 19th century the powers that be in the town of Young Harris wanted a road built to the top of the Brasstown Bald, old Georgia Route 66. Using convict labor, they blasted and worked their way toward the top of the peak over many years. The road was never officially opened to vehicles, although wagon trains out of Young Harris used it to gather and camp on the peak. Over time, the failed road became known as the Wagon Train Trail. Today, the erstwhile road has reverted to a wilderness path that possibly has more man-hours of work on it than any other trail in the North Georgia Mountains.

The tower on Brasstown Bald

Turn right on the Wagon Train Trail, following the wide path that soon splits. Stay left. The sky is open overhead. Oddly enough, you pass a gravestone memorializing someone's pet on trail left before reaching a Forest Service gate and entering the Brasstown Wilderness at 0.6 mile. The canopy closes in and the trailbed narrows, becoming more of a footpath as it heads north on Wolfpen Ridge, which forms the Towns County–Union County line. More important is the ambiance of the trail. Cool breezes sift through the rhododendron, even on the hottest day.

This is the highest of the high country in the state. Grassy Branch Cove lies far below to the east. The lower elevation of the surrounding terrain enhances the perspective as you ramble downward on Wolfpen Ridge. The singletrack path winds beneath wind-sculpted yellow birch and sweet birch trees.

This trail is a good place to discern the difference between the two trees. Yellow birches, found infrequently overall though plentiful here, are easy to spot. They have yellowish-gold bark with horizontal stripes. This ragged bark peels off the tree. The larger yellow birches do not have peeling bark on their lower trunks, although it still appears on the upper branches. Sweet birch, also known as black birch, is common and has horizontal stripes on its bark, which is more brownish-gray. The bark does not peel, and it resembles that of a cherry tree. Scratch a twig of black birch and it smells like wintergreen. In Georgia, black birches grow in moist areas along mountain streams and also in higher elevations, especially on north-facing slopes. Yellow birches only grow at the highest elevations in the mountains here, generally at or above 4,000 feet and along cool streams.

The path becomes quite rocky as it descends along a wash, flowing from the crest of Brasstown Bald above. It continues north and gains the top of Wolfpen Ridge. The ridge then opens to the west side, into the Brasstown Creek drainage. Bluffs rise to your right, as does the bulk of Little Bald Mountain. The names here reflect the previously open nature of the area. The bluffs, shimmering with water and spotted with lichens, were partly blasted along the trail to widen the old roadbed. At 1.2 miles you reach a clearing and outcrop that opens due west. This is the Wagon Train Trail vista. The Brasstown Creek valley is below you, and the bulk of Brasstown Bald rises to your left. This is good place to turn around and proceed toward the mountain.

Reach the Summit Trail at 2.3 miles after backtracking on the Wagon Train Trail. Turn right and climb the paved path, which rises steeply to cross the paved access road leading to the top. It is not much farther as you climb amid stunted, wind-sculpted trees to reach the interpretive center, observation deck, and tower atop Brasstown Bald. The interpretive center is staffed and worth checking out, but only after you step up to the deck and enjoy the grand vistas. Plaques along the edges of the observation deck inform you of what lies in the distance. Unfortunately, the tower isn't open to the public, but the observation deck will more than suffice. The best views are on clear days in the fall, when colorful hues cloak the mountains.

33

Raven Cliff Falls

Total distance: 4.9 miles there and back

Hiking time: 2½ hours

Vertical rise: 700 feet

Rating: Moderate

*Maps: USGS 7.5' Cowrock,
Chattahoochee National Forest*

Raven Cliff Falls is one of North Georgia's most interesting cascades. It slices through a sheer rock bluff known as Raven Cliff, dividing it in two over the ages and continuing to cut deeper. Along the way to the falls you will be passing through the Raven Cliff Wilderness, where more waterfalls await. This can be a busy hike, so solitude seekers should make this trek during the week or in colder months. Also, take note that the short trail to Dukes Creek Falls is very near the Raven Cliff Trail, making it easy to bag two major falls in one trip.

HOW TO GET THERE

From Cleveland, take US 129 north/GA 75 Alternate for 3 miles. Turn right on GA 75 Alternate and follow it 5.1 miles to GA 348. Turn left and go 2.7 miles to the trailhead on your left. The trail starts near the bridge over Dodd Creek.

THE HIKE

The parking area has rest rooms and an information kiosk. Leave the parking area and begin the Raven Cliff Trail by heading upstream on the left bank of Dodd Creek. Enter the Raven Cliff Wilderness, established in 1986. The wilderness has numerous waterways and waterfalls, several of which you will see on this hike. Elevations range from 1,800 feet near Boggs Creek to 3,846 feet atop Levelland Mountain. Forty-one miles of trout water flow through the 9,115-acre wilderness.

Lush woods shade the track. To your right, a large hemlock camping flat lies

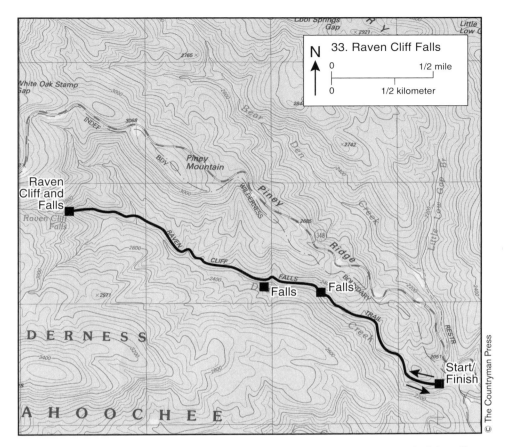

© The Countryman Press

beside the stream, and there is a deep pool in the bend. This big pool makes a refreshing post-hike swimming hole. The wide track continues beneath rhododendron and drops to cross Dodd Creek on a wooden footbridge. Continue upstream among scattered maple, birch, tulip trees, and hemlock, and the ever-present rhododendron. White pines form a superstory overhead. Even the brightest days will be a little dark in the deep mountain valley. This darkness enhances the white froth created by the falling creek. The upgrade is quite gentle, but the creek is crashing downstream, making quite a splash.

The rocky, rooty track curves around a bend to the right, tracing the stream in its meanderings through the mostly tight valley. Piney Mountain borders Dodd Creek to the east, while Adams Bald holds sway overhead to the west. Campsites are scattered where streamside flats open. Spindly, straight-trunked hemlocks shoot upward from these flats. At times the trail runs creekside; other times it is well above, such as when you arrive at the first major falls at 1.1 miles. To your left, the creek drops about 15 to 20 feet over a rock striation stretching across the waterway. Whitewater tumbles down, then takes a bouncing ride over a long, irregular rock slide to end in a pool. A user-created trail leads to the base of this falls.

Raven Cliff Falls

You are still well above the creek by the time you reach the second falls at 1.3 miles. The trail hangs nearly over the falls, which makes a 30-foot downward dash, hitting a rock before it journeys on. A very rough trail leads to the base of this falls, and another leads to the top, where you can lean over and nearly see the bottom of the falls. This is an excellent place for a daredevil to show off and get hurt. I know because I once broke my foot jumping way off a bluff into a mountain creek. Let the falls put on the show, and live to see Raven Cliff Falls down the trail.

Notice where rock was blasted to create the logging track over which the trail travels. This valley was logged in the early 1900s, and some evidence of this activity remains. Today the Dodd Creek area receives quite a bit of recreational use. What constitutes "wilderness," anyway? After 18,600 pages of testimony and the consolidation of 65 bills, the Wilderness Act of 1964 was passed to clarify the term. The legal definition of wilderness, spelled out in the bill, is as follows: "A wilderness, in contrast with those areas where man and his . . . works dominate the landscape, is hereby recognized as an area where the earth and its community of life are untrammeled by man, where man . . . is a visitor and does not remain."

Like all bills, it was a compromise. Far from land being forever preserved, the bill has loopholes allowing mining and grazing in wilderness areas. But such flaws are tolerated in passing laws to protect the land. Another fear, unfounded, was that wildernesses would be cut off from the citizens who backed their very creation. Ranging from 6 to 9.08 million acres in size, wilderness areas have multiple uses, such as hiking, hunting, canoeing, climbing, fishing, and camping—and going to see waterfalls.

Logging, road building, and damming are strictly prohibited.

The Raven Cliff Trail continues on, bridging a feeder branch. A plethora of dashing waters, rock slides, cascades, and straight drops continue along the creek. More spur branches come into Dodd Creek. At 2 miles, the trail bridges a major branch and then begins to climb steeply. You can see Raven Cliff ahead. The path braids because people have made their own way to the cliffs. This area needs some restorative work. Keep forward, moving uphill. All roads lead to Rome.

Reach Raven Cliff Falls at 2.5 miles. From afar it looks like a continuous bluff, but as you come nearer you see that a waterfall has cut the cliff in half, splashing downward in a ribbon of white between vertical rock walls. Imagine the time it took for the water to slice Raven Cliff in two.

A rocky, eroded path leads toward the top of the cliffs. It is dangerous when wet. The path leads up, then to the left, where hikers have climbed a braid of roots to ascend to the top. From here you can look not only back down the valley, but also at another waterfall above Raven Cliff Falls. Any hiking beyond this point should be considered off-trail. By the way, climbing the braid of roots is discouraged by the Forest Service and is part of the reason they outlawed rappelling in the Raven Cliff Wilderness. But another reason is getting back down the root braid; that's the tricky part.

At any rate, from the top of Raven Cliff you can see back down the valley and to the southeast. After your hike, stop by Dukes Creek Falls. The trailhead is just 1.3 miles south on GA 348 from the Raven Cliff Trailhead. The trail leads a little over a mile to an observation deck looking out on the 250-foot cascade.

34

Chattahoochee Headwaters Hike

Total distance: 9.4 miles there and back

Hiking time: 5½ hours

Vertical rise: 1,000 feet

Rating: Moderate to difficult

Maps: USGS 7.5' Jacks Gap, Tray Mountain, Chattahoochee National Forest

The Chattahoochee River is Georgia's most significant waterway and the state's contribution to great rivers of the world. This hike travels along the Appalachian Trail to the river's headwaters, Chattahoochee Spring, located high in the North Georgia Mountains. The spring is deep within the Mark Trail Wilderness, beneath the slopes of Jacks Knob. The ridge-running track has many ups and downs, but none are long or arduous. However, the hike out and back is nearly 10 miles, so be prepared. A trail shelter and campsites make overnighting on this trip a potential added adventure.

HOW TO GET THERE

From the bridge over the Chattahoochee River in Helen, take GA 75 north for 9.2 miles to Unicoi Gap. The parking area is on the east side of the gap. The Appalachian Trail crosses GA 17/75 at Unicoi Gap. This hike follows the AT across GA 17/75, southbound and toward Hogpen Gap.

THE HIKE

This hike can be done any time of year, and each season provides its own reward. Of course, the destination of this trip, Chattahoochee Spring, is the certain reward. Here, you can see the first flows of the "Hooch."

Cross over to the west side of GA 17/75 on the Appalachian Trail, southbound. Climb wooden steps away from the road and turn south to parallel it below you. The AT soon makes a big uphill turn to the right and enters the Mark Trail Wilderness, nearly

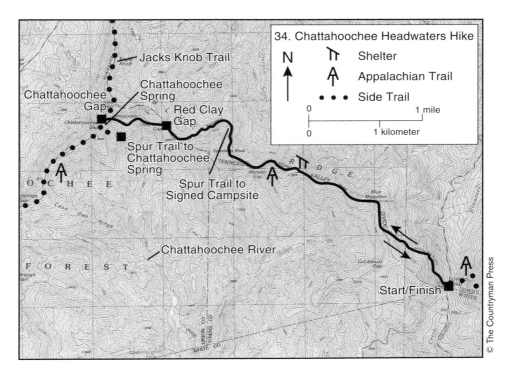

17,000 acres in size and established in 1991. The singletrack path crosses a boulder field, climbing through hickory-oak woods on a steep slope, the eastern shoulder of Blue Mountain. At times, the path is more rock than soil as you clamber upward. Enter a dry piney area and make a series of switchbacks. Between the fragrant evergreens you can see Rocky Mountain rising up across Unicoi Gap.

The path turns away from the gap and enters fern-floored woodland. Make the crest of the ridge at 1.2 miles. The climb moderates on the sandy and still-rocky track. Top out on Blue Mountain, 3,970 feet. Congratulations—you just ascended 1,000 feet from Unicoi Gap. The Appalachian Trail turns westward on a gentle, undulating grade, where hiking in the mountains is pure fun. The ridgeline narrows in an attractive thick forest with a heavy understory. Soon

the mountain flattens out and you reach a trail junction at 2.2 miles. A blue-blazed spur trail leads right a short distance to the Blue Mountain Trail Shelter, an open-front, board affair that extends to a covered porch with built-in benches. You'll find bear-proof food-storage cables and a fire ring to complement the shelter.

Ahead, the Appalachian Trail descends a short distance to reach a cool, clear spring just to the right of the trail. This spring serves those who camp at the shelter. Ironically, it feeds Henson Creek, which feeds Soapstone Creek, which is a tributary of the Hiawassee River, and therefore, it isn't even part of the Chattahoochee River drainage.

The AT descends beyond the spring to reach Henson Gap at 2.6 miles. The tread is narrower than other, more popular stretches of the master path of the East. You circle around the north side of Red Knob, passing

The foggy Appalachian Trail at Chattahoochee Gap

another marked spring at 3 miles and a spur trail to a campsite at 3.2 miles. From this point the trailbed is extremely rocky and travel slows as you negotiate each footfall on, around, and between gray boulders pocked with lichens and moss. Despite the rough track, the hiking is not tough because elevation changes are minor.

Drift into Red Clay Gap at 3.9 miles, just after passing through a dense mountain laurel thicket. The Appalachian Trail shifts over to the south side of the ridge and into the Chattahoochee River drainage. The forest now features dry species. A short distance beyond the gap, take a moment to stop and cup your ear as you face downhill. Do you hear flowing water? Below you, the Chattahoochee River and its tributaries are gathering and heading south to make the march on Atlanta and points beyond. It is the bulk

of Jacks Knob, rising to your right, which gives life to the Chattahoochee. The springs emerge from its south slopes, fed by rain and snow.

Your steps lead past Jacks Knob and to a trail junction at Chattahoochee Gap at 4.5 miles. This gap lies at 3,500 feet. To your right, the Jacks Knob Trail leads north to Brasstown Bald. Ahead, the Appalachian Trail continues circling around the headwaters of the Chattahoochee River to Hogpen Gap. To your left lies the trail to the prize: Chattahoochee Spring. The blue-blazed trail and a plain sign, WATER, are all that mark this important headwater spring.

Twist and turn downhill, dropping toward the flowing noise. And soon you are there. I will admit that in many ways this spring resembles innumerable others in the Southern Appalachians: a low flow of cool, clear, alluring water. But this isn't just any spring. It marks the humble beginnings of Georgia's master river, the Chattahoochee. This is the river that flows south into the splendid trout waters of the Chattahoochee Wildlife Management Area of the Chattahoochee National Forest; down through the tourist town of Helen, where tubers float its cool riffles; and down to Lake Lanier, where boaters pull water-skiers and lake homes overlook the impounded waters.

Freed of its reins, it goes on to Atlanta to become the centerpiece of the Chattahoochee River National Recreation Area, where rafters and canoeists and kayakers enjoy a slice of nature amid Georgia's most urban locale. From Atlanta it turns southwest, flowing to the Alabama state line, where it is dammed again as West Point Lake. It delineates the Alabama–Georgia state line and heads south into a series of dams before it reaches the river town of Columbus, Georgia. It then flows through the Fort Benning military base.

Now in southwest Georgia, the Hooch is dammed again as massive Lake Walter F. George. After leaving this lake and passing Fort Gaines it runs south, and at one point flows past the spot where Alabama, Georgia, and Florida all meet, "way down yonder on the Chattahoochee." Its final penning occurs at Lake Seminole, where another great Georgia river, the Flint, meets it. Together they form the Apalachicola River, which flows through Florida to the Gulf. And it all starts right here, at Chattahoochee Spring.

Northeast Georgia Mountains

35

Bottoms Loop of Unicoi State Park

Total distance: 2.2 miles

Hiking time: 1½ hours

Vertical rise: 200 feet

Rating: Moderate

Maps: USGS 7.5' Helen, Unicoi State Park Trail

The Bottoms Loop Trail is a good sampler hike in Unicoi State Park, located near the mountain town of Helen. It travels the low hills and flats in the Smith Creek valley, around which the state park is centered. Along the way it passes an old homesite and then runs along Smith Creek, a fine trout stream. It is likely that this hike will be but one of the activities you engage in at Unicoi, for this state park not only has a fine trail network, but also a good campground for tent and RV campers.

HOW TO GET THERE

From the Chattahoochee River bridge in downtown Helen, head north on GA 75 for 1 mile to GA 356. Turn right and continue 2 miles to the park. Stay on the main road and look for the right turn heading toward the park lodge. Turn here and pass under an overhang to the back of the lodge. The trailhead is located at the rear of the parking area, away from the lodge building.

THE HIKE

The hike starts at what is known as the main park trailhead. Leave the lodge parking area and descend on wooden steps toward GA 356. You soon reach a junction. The Lakeshore Trail leaves left, the Big Frog Nature Trail keeps forward, and you turn right to stay with the Bottoms Loop, which is blazed yellow. Descend on a dirt and gravel track, passing the other end of the Big Frog Nature Trail and the park tennis courts. On your return trip, the nature trail makes for a good final walk. Follow a little creeklet

Lodge
Start/Finish

Lakeshore Trail

Frog Pond Trail

Tennis Courts

Union Ch

UNICOI

STATE PARK

Bottoms Loop Trail

Helen Trail

Creek

35. Bottoms Loop of Unicoi State Park

N

• • •   Side Trail

0   1/4 mile

0   1/4 kilometer

© The Countryman Press

A meadow along Smith Creek

spanned by a footbridge to reach the paved Unicoi Bottoms Road.

Leave the road and enter white pine woods with an understory of mountain laurel. Work up a little hollow on a rooty path and leave the bustle of the park lodge well behind you. Reach a trail junction at 0.6 mile. Veer left, staying with the Bottoms Loop, and cross a clear branch bordered by doghobble and laurel. Soon you pass the site of an old mountain homestead. Look for the leveled spot and the pile of mossy rocks where a chimney once stood. Imagine the number of hours the homesteaders spent cooking their homegrown food over that fireplace.

Back then, in the "Land of Do Without," there was precious little money to buy manufactured goods from stores, and if it couldn't be made on the farm using nature's bounty, then it wasn't used. Often, families had just one skillet, one pot, and a few other things

that we would barely recognize, such as a spinning wheel, because we now make very little, if anything, that we use in our own daily lives. I wonder what they would think if they could see that their farm is now part of a state park where hikers travel by and ruminate on a forgotten past and a discarded way of life.

The path dips away from the homesite, winding in and out of small stream branches, each one creating its own hollow as it flows west into Smith Creek. Bridges span many of the creeks, which are separated by little rib ridges. Finally, the path follows one particular nameless branch due west. This full-fledged creek cuts a deep valley before opening into the bottomland of Smith Creek.

Come alongside this clear mountain stream, which is managed for trout by the state park. At 1.4 miles, you intersect the Helen Trail, which leads southwest along Smith Creek and beyond to the tourist town of Helen. A large footbridge constructed in 2005 crosses the creek and is followed by a second, longer one on the way to Helen. The Bottoms Loop turns up the flats of Smith Creek. Small spur trails lead to fishing spots along the watercourse. You may notice some of the fish enhancements, such as logs placed across the stream to create pools and bank stabilizers to prevent erosion.

Farther ahead, the trail opens to a wildlife clearing. You may see deer here in mornings or evenings. Notice how trees have been left to grow along Smith Creek to further stabilize stream banks and provide shade. A cooler trout stream is a healthier stream, not only for the trout but for all the other life that thrives in cool, clear, clean water. The open field allows for ridgeline views in the distance.

The Bottoms Loop turns away from the riparian area and climbs a feeder branch of Smith to reach a junction at 1.7 miles. Here, you begin backtracking toward the lodge. On your return, take the Big Frog Nature Trail. It passes a frog pond and another open area managed for wildlife. Interpretive signs help you learn more about the park. Complete this loop and ascend the wooden steps toward the lodge to end the hike.

While here, consider indulging in other activities and making use of the facilities at Unicoi State Park. You can also try the variety of eats in nearby Helen. And you can burn those calories by walking the 3 miles to town and back, although if you get too full you might have to call in a ride.

Other trail options are varied. The Unicoi Mountain Trail is designed for and used by mountain bikers. It makes a 7.5-mile loop, winding all over the park. A bike permit is required and can be purchased at the park lodge. The Lake Trail is probably the most popular trail here. It circles Smith Lake, making a 2.5-mile loop and passing many of the park facilities, from the swim beach to the trading post. The Chattahoochee National Forest hiking trail to Anna Ruby Falls is also nearby. In just 0.4 mile you can reach what many consider Georgia's most picturesque falls.

The state park campground offers many different options, from the walk-in tent sites to the unique wooden platforms of the Squirrel's Nest. Other campsites have water and electricity and are designed for RV and popup use. The campground fills on weekends during summer, but it makes a great base camp for exploring the area. The park also has two swim beaches. Or you can rent a canoe or paddleboat and go fishing for catfish, bass, and bream. Smith Creek is open to trout fishing, too. Tubing is a time-honored pastime in Helen, and there are plenty of outfitters for those who want to take a summer float right through town on the Chattahoochee. Considering all the above, you might want to bring more than your hiking boots for a trip to Unicoi State Park.

36

Rocky Mountain Loop

Total distance: 5.4 miles

Hiking time: 3¼ hours

Vertical rise: 1,000 feet

Rating: Moderate to difficult

Maps: USGS 7.5' Tray Mountain, Chattahoochee National Forest

This loop hike incorporates a section of the Appalachian Trail, which climbs from Unicoi Gap and tops out on Rocky Mountain for a good vista. It then descends to Indian Grave Gap, where you can pick up the Rocky Mountain Trail back toward Unicoi Gap on the rich north slope of Rocky Mountain, keeping the terrain new and fresh almost the entire walk. Be prepared not only for good views, but also for some ups and downs.

HOW TO GET THERE

From the bridge over the Chattahoochee River in Helen, take GA 75 north for 9.2 miles to Unicoi Gap. The parking area is on the east side of the gap. The Appalachian Trail crosses GA 17/75 here. This hike follows the AT away from GA 17/75, northbound and toward Addis Gap.

THE HIKE

This loop hike gets the main climb over with right off the bat. Head northward on the Appalachian Trail, away from Unicoi Gap, on the side of the road with the stone inscription for the AT. Enter rocky woods and keep putting one foot in front of the other, each one higher than the last. It is called climbing. It makes your heart pound and sweat pour from your brow. It also leads to rewards, like a good view and being in better shape. Of course, you may be focusing on cussing out an outdoor writer for convincing you to make such an ascent.

In the distance you will hear a stream over your pounding heart. You come near it, only to switchback away, ever upward. The path soon takes you back toward the stream,

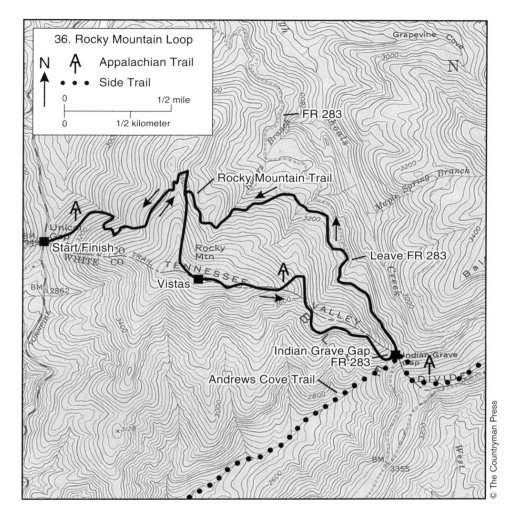

paralleling it and then turning left to cross it. This is a stream you might want to straddle, one foot on either side, because it will likely be your last opportunity to stand on both sides of the Hiawassee River at once. Yep. That's right. The USGS quadrangle maps indicate that this is the uppermost headwaters of the Hiawassee River. And to think, you can barely find a puddle deep enough to dip a cup into!

Sometimes rivers like this one have the designation "river" from their headwaters all the way to their terminus. The Hiawassee's terminus is at the Tennessee River on the west side of the Appalachians. Other North Georgia rivers—such as the Tugaloo, which forms part of the border with South Carolina—are only designated a river after the confluence of two other rivers; in this case, the Chattooga and the Tallulah. Apparently a river becomes a river when government mapmakers decide it is one. Actually, historical naming likely plays a larger role.

The bulk of the mountainside rises to your right. The AT continues uphill beyond the gurgling brook of a river and reaches a

The southern vista from Rocky Mountain

trail junction on the shoulder of Rocky Mountain at 1 mile. The blue-blazed Rocky Mountain Trail, your return route, leaves left. The white-blazed Appalachian Trail curves right (south), up the nose of the ridgeline, aiming for the crest of Rocky Mountain—and seemingly aiming for whatever ground it can find that is higher than the ground you are walking on.

The track levels out atop Rocky Mountain, falling just short of the 4,000-foot mark. A shaded campsite with a grassy floor makes for an inviting rest spot. Just ahead, the AT turns back east and begins to open onto a rock face like those scattered throughout the North Georgia Mountains. These faces are responsible for the many peaks named Rocky Mountain throughout these highlands. And this one deserves its name, not only for its bare rock faces, but also for the rocky soil in which the oak-dominated forest grows.

The outcrops fall south from the peak and open views into the Smith Creek drainage, across to Smith Mountain and to one of my personal favorites in Georgia mountain nomenclature, Crumbly Knob. No "crumbles" are visible from this vantage point, however. The AT passes several rock faces and actually travels directly over some, revealing more vistas. Oak woods cover the south slope of the hill as you begin working east and down off Rocky Mountain. It is an easy cruise from here, and you earned it.

At 2.1 miles the trail reaches a gap, but instead of climbing over the knob ahead, it swings around the right side, still dropping, to reach Indian Grave Gap and Forest Road 283 at 2.7 miles. The Andrews Cove Trail comes in from your right, having climbed 2 miles from Andrews Cove Campground. The Appalachian Trail crosses FR 283 and heads for North Carolina and points beyond, but this loop hike turns left on FR 283, following the blue blazes of the Rocky Mountain Trail painted on roadside trees.

The downgrade continues on the gravel forest road, which is shaded more often than not. Cruise along, watching for rivulets flowing under the road off Rocky Mountain above and to your left. You are circling the peak. At 3.3 miles, as the road curves to the left, look for a double blue blaze as the Rocky Mountain Trail leaves the forest road and enters the woods on that side.

The path now joins an old logging grade, passing beneath young woods. More small rivulets cross the path. Tulip and maple trees predominate on this north slope. Drop right off the old roadbed at 3.5 miles and join a singletrack hiking trail. The woodland is bisected by a stream—more rock than water—that trickles into High Shoals Creek. It is mostly uphill from this rocky branch, appropriately located on the slopes of Rocky Mountain. The climb amounts to 500 feet, less than half the elevation gain made from Unicoi Gap to the top of Rocky Mountain. And before you know it, at 4.4 miles, with a little more sweat on your brow and a faster heartbeat, you intersect the AT.

Backtrack toward Unicoi Gap, straddling the Hiawassee River one more time for cheap hiker thrills. Look around and enjoy the scenery on your downhill return, as there is no head-hanging huffing and puffing like there was on the climb up. Maybe you won't even curse this outdoor writer on the downgrade. Reach Unicoi Gap and complete your hike at 5.4 miles.

37

High Shoals Waterfall Walk

Total distance: 2.4 miles there and back

Hiking time: 1¾ hours

Vertical rise: 480 feet

Rating: Moderate

Maps: USGS 7.5' Tray Mountain,
Chattahoochee National Forest

High Shoals Scenic Area deserves its national forest designation. Flowing off the slopes of Rocky Mountain and Tray Mountain, High Shoals Creek gathers water and momentum for a crashing show over two major falls, plus a few others, on its way down and out of the Chattahoochee National Forest. It is not only the water but the surrounding woodlands that draw many visitors to this short, pretty walk. The forest is attractive and varied, from piney hillsides to lush streamside trees. Be aware that the access road has an auto ford that may prove troublesome for low-clearance vehicles.

HOW TO GET THERE
From the bridge over the Chattahoochee River in Helen, take GA 75 north for 11.2 miles to Forest Road 283, Indian Grave Gap Road. FR 283 is 2 miles past Unicoi Gap. You must make this hard right turn while going downhill, so keep your eyes peeled. The turn is signed for High Shoals Scenic Area. Turn right on FR 283 and soon cross over the vehicle ford on the uppermost headwaters of the Hiawassee River. Stay with FR 283 for a total of 1.3 miles to the trailhead on your left at a turn. Parking is limited, so if you are here on a busy weekend, please park close to allow room for other cars.

THE HIKE
Leave the parking area and enter part of the Swallow Creek Wildlife Management Area on a dirt and gravel track, blazed in blue. Descend into pine-oak-mountain laurel

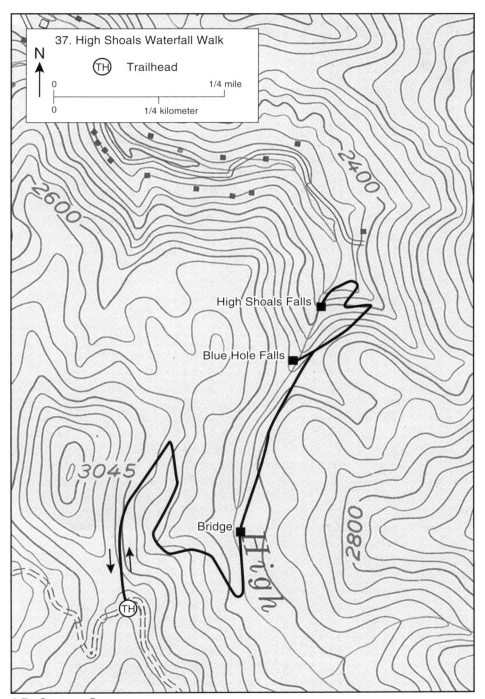

N

37. High Shoals Waterfall Walk

TH Trailhead

0   1/4 mile

0   1/4 kilometer

2400

2600

High Shoals Falls

Blue Hole Falls

3045

2800

Bridge

High

TH

© The Countryman Press

woodland. No water is in sight, but it can be heard making a low roar in the valley below. At 0.2 mile, make a hard turn to the right. The track becomes quite rooty before dipping into a lush cove with a tiny streamlet flowing toward High Shoals Creek, same as you. Curve deeper into the valley, where the moisture-loving species of Georgia's mountain woodlands are holding their appointed places. Hemlock and sweet birch trees tower over rhododendron thickets. Above it all stands a superstory of white pine.

The path turns back north after reaching a flat beside High Shoals Creek. This area makes for a good relaxation or picnicking spot. Just beyond this attractive area, at 0.5 mile, is a wooden footbridge spanning the creek. Peer down into the stream below. The clear, cool water is pure mountain elixir, flowing over time-smoothed stones. This water helped carve the mountains into their present shape; once-craggy stone peaks resembling today's Rocky Mountains are now aged, softened, rounded, and topped with a supple mantle of green. The water continues its endless quest to seek its own level and to cut these mountains down and wash them to the ocean, granule by granule.

High Shoals Creek feeds the Hiawassee River, which flows north into North Carolina, then west into Tennessee, slicing through the crest of the Southern Appalachian Range, where it joins the Tennessee River, which in turn feeds the Ohio. The Ohio then feeds the Mississippi, and thus silt that was once Georgia's high country ends up expanding the alluvial plain of the Mississippi River, down Louisiana way in the Gulf of Mexico.

The flat continues beyond the bridge as you follow High Shoals Creek downstream. A campsite here is shaded by white pine and hemlock. The valley deepens. Bridge a pair of trickling creeks coming in from your right, flowing off Hanson Mountain. Galax lines the path. Below you, the stream is cutting a deep "V" into the terrain. The falling water is increasing its noise and the drops between pools become steeper and more frequent. Through the rhododendron you can see white foaming water as it drops faster and faster. Cross another tributary on a sturdy wooden bridge.

At 0.7 mile, a spur trail leads acutely left and upstream to Blue Hole Falls. An observation deck makes viewing safe and easy. In front of you, the creek is making a single drop over a horizontal ledge into the Blue Hole. Rhododendron frames the cascade, and it is easy to see why the plunge pool got its name. The Blue Hole is extraordinarily deep for such a stream. It is open to the sun overhead and makes a nice swimming hole, especially on a sultry summer afternoon in Georgia. And if the water doesn't cool you off, the chill air emanating from the 20-foot waterfall will.

Return to the main trail and continue downstream. The trail can be wet here from oozing springs. The descent sharpens and the path switchbacks down a steep slope. Stone steps make the walking smoother. Down, down, down into lush woods to reach the creek again, and a viewing deck of the High Shoals Falls, elevation 2,350 feet, at 1.2 miles. The falls are so high that they aren't visible in their entirety. However, you can see most of the upper white drop.

It is the second part of the falls that will catch your eye, because it widens as the water drops. An irregular rock face, with some parts exposed and some buried beneath the flow, continues to defy the relentless fast-moving water wearing it smooth. The white foam pounds and crashes and roars against the seemingly immutable rock,

Blue Hole Falls

but ultimately the flow will wear it down long after this book has disintegrated and returned to the earth. For now, High Shoals Falls is the centerpiece of a wonderful scenic area where you can walk and see the power and beauty of nature at work.

There is but little pool below these falls, in contrast to the Blue Hole above. After High Shoals Falls, the creek quickly moves on, leaving the national forest to join the Hiawassee River, which has work of its own to do.

38

Tray Mountain

Total distance: 2.4 miles there and back

Hiking time: 2 hours

Vertical rise: 600 feet

Rating: Moderate

Maps: USGS 7.5' Tray Mountain, Chattahoochee National Forest

This hike starts high and gets higher. From Tray Gap, over 3,800 feet, it leads up the slopes of Tray Mountain through the Tray Mountain Wilderness to the apex and some great vistas. From the mountaintop, you travel east down the shoulder of the mountain to a trail shelter and yet another view, this time from a wide outcrop that is great for just hanging out and taking in the scenery. The Appalachian Trail takes you through this high-country haven.

HOW TO GET THERE

From the Chattahoochee River bridge in downtown Helen, head north on GA 17/75 for 2 miles to Forest Road 79, Tray Mountain Road. The right turn onto FR 79 is easy to miss; it occurs as GA 17/75 is curving left. Be careful here. Follow the gravel road mostly uphill for 8.1 miles to Tray Gap, where FR 698 leaves left. The northbound Appalachian Trail begins on the north side of Tray Gap.

THE HIKE

Tray Mountain is one of the most notable mountains in Georgia, in my opinion. Maybe it's because of the many enjoyable experiences I've had up here. Like the brutal winter night I spent near the shelter below the summit many years ago. You should've seen the stars, countless points of light shining down through the barren trees being battered by a bitter north wind. Or the time I sat looking out on the hazy green landscape on a warm summer evening from the outcrop near the shelter. The rock slab held heat

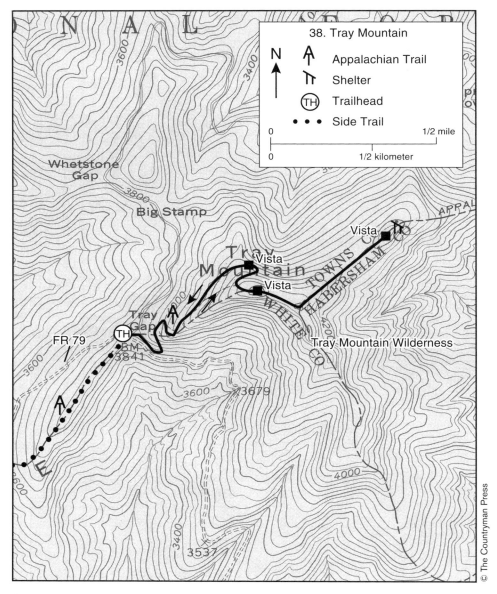

from the afternoon sun well into the evening, warming my back better than any spa treatment. Or the foggy morning when all I could see was the faint outline of a dirt path leading up to a stony crest, bordered by fallen rhododendron petals.

I clearly recall drinking the cold, clear water emanating from the spring downhill of the shelter. And the friends with whom I shared the above experiences. When I received the assignment to write this book, I immediately knew Tray Mountain would be

Tray Mountain offers views into North Carolina.

included among the fine destinations of these Southern Highlands.

Leave Tray Gap, elevation 3,850 feet, and walk north on the white-blazed Appalachian Trail. Pass an information signboard indicating your entry into the Tray Mountain Wilderness. The path angles gently uphill in oak-hickory-locust woods typical of the high country here. Shortly, switchback to the left and continue climbing. It isn't long before high-elevation flora begins to appear. Note the pale gold trunks of the yellow birch, which is more common to the north and found infrequently in Georgia. The path keeps ascending and is lined with rhododendron.

At 0.6 mile, on a switchback to the right, an outcrop extends to the left of the trail. You can step onto a boulder and look north to the Hiawassee River basin and beyond into the high country of the Nantahala National Forest of North Carolina. This view is a preview of things to come. The path turns south and gently ascends past more yellow birch and rhododendron.

Notice how stunted the vegetation is here. The winter winds are simply too much for trees to withstand, and they must bow to the blow. Soon you reach the crest of Tray Mountain where the rocky top is rimmed in a crown of greenery. In most directions you can see the mountains and valleys beyond. On my last trip, the dense, brushy vegetation had grown up somewhat, obscuring this vista, but one section had been cut back. Not to worry, though, as there are plenty of views to go around at this high point of 4,430 feet— less than 500 feet shy of Georgia's highest peak, Brasstown Bald. Tray Mountain is the second-highest point on the AT in Georgia, 31 feet lower than Blood Mountain. Two USGS markers are embedded in the stone. Small spur trails lead to other outcrops and sheltered areas on top of Tray.

The Appalachian Trail drops off the crown and winds steeply among jagged rock. Get to the next knob, which is more wooded than the official peak, before descending more forcefully off the east shoulder of Tray Mountain. Reach a trail junction at 1.1 miles. The AT splits right and downward, while a blue-blazed spur trail leads left toward the Montray Shelter. Follow the blue-blazed path, still traveling the ridgeline through low, broken woods. You are still above 4,000 feet.

Ahead, on your right, is a grassy clearing and campsite located next to an expansive rock outcrop. The outcrop has plenty of areas level enough to grab a seat and enjoy the easterly vista into the Goshen Branch drainage and to the mountains beyond. Break out a snack or maybe your dinner if you're spending the night at the shelter or in the vicinity. The trail shelter lies just beyond the outcrop. It is a three-sided Adirondack-style bunkhouse, open on the front. A trail leads down to the spring behind the shelter. The water emanates from a concrete box and drips into a small pool before heading north to enter the Hiawassee River.

Near the spring you may notice the stone foundation of an older, smaller shelter from the early days of the Appalachian Trail. The shelter is a good turnaround point and a great place to overnight, turning your day hike into a backpacking trip.

On your return trip, the climb from the shelter is less than 300 feet. And you can look for more things to appreciate in the Tray Mountain Wilderness, one of 10 federally designated wilderness areas wholly or partially within the North Georgia Mountains. (There are 14 wilderness areas in the state, totaling 486,055 acres; however, 75 percent of the acreage is held in the Okefenokee Wilderness of the famed Okefenokee Swamp in southeast Georgia.)

The Tray Mountain Wilderness, 9,702 acres, was established in 1986. It encompasses over 16 miles of Appalachian Trail, which is by far its biggest draw. The wilderness also holds the upper drainages of Left Fork Goshen Branch and Wildcat Creek, which, including all tributaries, adds up to around 41 miles of trout streams. And Tray Mountain is the shining diamond that stands over the streams and ridges of this protected swath of North Georgia. It is truly a notable mountain.

39

Wolfstake Knob from Dicks Creek Gap

Total distance: 5.4 miles there and back

Hiking time: 3 hours

Vertical rise: 1,150 feet

Rating: Moderate to difficult

Maps: USGS 7.5' Macedonia, Hightower Bald, Chattahoochee National Forest

This hike travels the Appalachian Trail, following a knob-and-gap pattern to a fine vista overlooking the greater Lake Burton area of northeast Georgia. This is a lesser-visited section of the AT in the state, far from the action atop Springer Mountain or the wilderness areas through which the master path of the East travels in the Chattahoochee National Forest. For some reason, many of those who do walk this part of the AT pass right by the spur trail to the lookout. But their loss is your gain, so grab your boots and try this hike.

HOW TO GET THERE

From Helen, take GA 17/75 north for 21 miles to US 76. Turn right on US 76 east and follow it 7.7 miles to Dicks Creek Gap, where the Appalachian Trail crosses. The parking area is on the left side of the gap as you approach.

THE HIKE

Now for a little truth in advertising: The destination overlook for this hike isn't really on Wolfstake Knob. It is actually on an unnamed knob just east of Wolfstake. But somehow the title "Unnamed Knob Just East of Wolfstake Knob from Dicks Creek Gap" just didn't sound right. Besides, Wolfstake Knob is such a catchy name. You can only imagine the story behind it. Was a wolf tied to a stake here? Or did a wolf stake out the knob? Or did someone get into a hand-to-paw battle with a wolf and do it in with a stake?

Red wolves were once present throughout the Southern Appalachians but have

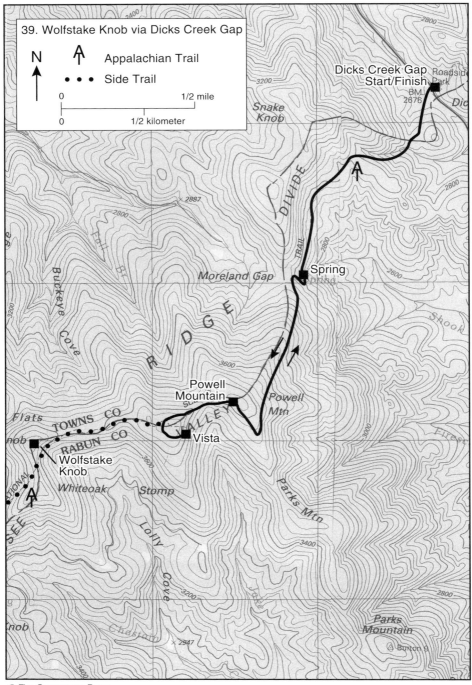

39. Wolfstake Knob via Dicks Creek Gap

N

Appalachian Trail

Side Trail

0   1/2 mile

0   1/2 kilometer

Dicks Creek Gap
Start/Finish

Roadside Park
BM.
2676

Snake
Knob

DIVIDE

TRAIL

Moreland Gap

Spring

RIDGE

Powell
Mountain

Powell
Mtn

Vista

Flats

TOWNS CO

RABUN CO

VALLEY

Wolfstake
Knob

Whiteoak

Stomp

Parks Mtn

Forest

Lolly Cove

Chestnut

2947

Parks
Mountain

Burton

© The Countryman Press

The Tallulah River valley from a rock face near Wolfstake Knob

been extirpated from the region for at least a century. There was a reintroduction attempt in the Great Smoky Mountains National Park in the 1990s, but the wolves could not sustain a population. The closest red wolves reside in the coastal swamps of North Carolina. Ironically, the common coyote has expanded its range throughout the Southeast, filling in the slot of the red wolf, which once kept coyotes from entering its domain. Sadly, all we have left in these parts is a place name with "wolf" in it. Name aside, though, the overlook is a worthy day hike.

Dicks Creek Gap (2,675 feet), your starting point, has a shaded picnic area beside a little stream adjacent to the hiker parking area. There is also a stone Appalachian Trail marker here at the saddle. Begin by crossing US 76 from the parking area, southbound on the Appalachian Trail. Briefly trace an old road, slipping between some vehicle barriers. Ascend a singletrack path bordered by white oaks and other hardwoods. The trail enters a thicket of mountain laurel,

where you see only twisted and gnarled brown trunks because the greenery is growing above your head. Beyond the thicket, the track enters a hollow and begins climbing along a little stream, the uppermost reaches of Dicks Creek flowing off Snake Knob above you.

The AT's grade sharpens along Dicks Creek before the path turns away from the water and enters dry woods. It tops out on a rib ridge emanating from Snake Knob and briefly descends, but you know this won't last for long. Step over a second intermittent stream. The trailbed is sometimes sand, sometimes clay, mixed with an array of ever-present, boot-catching roots and rocks. Volunteer trail crews keep it in good shape, though, leveling the trailbed, installing waterbars, and more. The path soon settles down, moving southwesterly on a level track in tall timber below Snake Knob.

At 1.1 miles, just below Moreland Gap, a spur trail leads left a few feet to a spring, the headwaters of Shook Branch. Marked springs such as this are located all along the Appalachian Trail. The AT is blazed in white, but spur trails to shelters, springs, overlooks, and trailheads are marked in light blue. Sometimes, when AT thru-hikers decide to take shortcuts or skip sections of the trail, they are said to be "blue-blazing." So even though blue blazes often take you to where you need or want to go, the term has a derogatory connotation. Some thru-hikers are purists, walking every foot of the white-blazed AT.

You continue climbing, breaking the 3,000-foot barrier in Moreland Gap above the spring. A campsite is located here. Keep ascending toward Powell Mountain. The trail first goes up the nose of the ridge, then makes use of switchbacks before taking a hard right turn on the edge of the mountain at 2.1 miles.

The path turns north here and tunnels below more mountain laurel. The trees on the ridgeline are a bit shorter here, stunted by wind. Notice the crazy shapes and contortions of the trunks and branches of this ever-green, which can be alternately described as a bushy tree or a tree-like bush. Reach a high point of 3,800 feet on Powell Mountain, then dip to a saddle that is quite weedy in summertime. Make one last climb; just as the trail levels out at 2.6 miles you will see a blue-blazed path leading left. The AT continues forward.

Follow the blue-blazed path uphill, where it levels out in grassy woods with another campsite. Continue left to an outcrop and clear view. The rock face spills down, preventing tree growth and opening the view before you. Jake Branch and North Fork Moccasin Creek form the valley just below. Parks Mountain is the rampart rising above Jake Branch. The Tallulah River valley lies in the distance, framed by the mountains of northeast Georgia.

Now, if you want to go to the actual Wolfstake Knob, return to the AT and leave southbound off the unnamed knob. The next knob you climb, about 0.25 mile away, is Wolfstake. This way, you can tell everyone truthfully about that hike with the cool name you took on the Appalachian Trail from Dicks Creek Gap.

40

Hemlock Falls

Total distance: 1.8 miles there and back

Hiking time: 1½ hours

Vertical rise: 300 feet

Rating: Easy

Maps: USGS 7.5' Lake Burton, Chattahoochee National Forest

Hemlock Falls is a powerful show of force in the North Georgia Mountains. After gathering waters from the north and south forks of Moccasin Creek, a rush of froth plunges into one of the biggest pools in the state. The walk to this falls is very scenic as well. Along the way you will see more cascades in a tight, deeply wooded gorge full of moving water that is a world unto itself.

HOW TO GET THERE

From Clarkesville, take GA 197 north for 23 miles to Moccasin Creek State Park. There is a bridge over Moccasin Creek. Turn left just before the bridge (just beyond the bridge and to the right is the Moccasin Creek State Park Campground). Immediately after the turn you will see a trailhead surrounded by a wooden fence next to a spillway dam on Moccasin Creek. This is the trailhead for the state park's Wildlife Trail. To reach the Moccasin Falls Trailhead, continue on the gravel road, passing a hunter check-in station and going 0.5 mile to a dead end. There is a vehicle turnaround and a large inscribed boulder that reads HEMLOCK FALLS TRAIL.

THE HIKE

Hemlock Falls is but one attraction in a scenic area adjacent to Moccasin Creek State Park and Lake Burton. There are many other lures nearby within the Chattahoochee National Forest, which nearly surrounds Lake Burton, such as Wildcat Campground, Rabun Beach, and the natural waterslide on

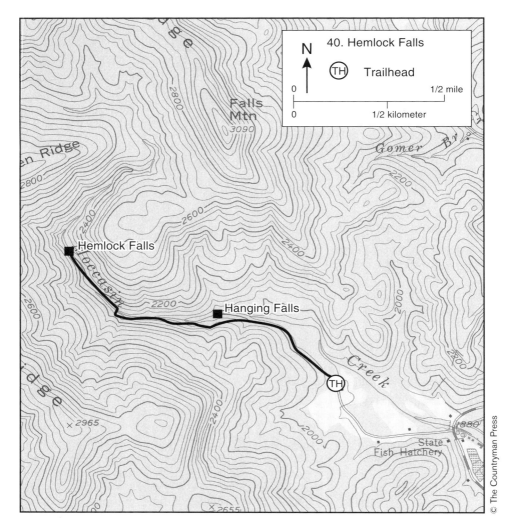

Wildcat Creek. But Hemlock Falls holds its own among all these places.

The first thing you will notice on your hike to Hemlock Falls is the inscribed boulder at the trailhead. Similar boulders can be found at many trailheads throughout the Tallulah District of the Chattahoochee National Forest in the northeastern corner of the state. These inscribed boulders are not only appealing but durable—I have never seen one vandalized, weathered by the elements, or chewed on by a bear like many of the wooden signs or newer Carsonite posts so popular today.

Beyond the boulder, the Hemlock Falls Trail enters the lower Moccasin Creek valley, which is bordered by Bramlet Ridge to the south, Falls Mountain to the north, and Hellhole Mountain to the west. To the east, Moccasin Creek flows into Lake Burton. The trail travels a berm above an old roadbed made wet by seeps flowing off

An inscribed stone marks the Hemlock Falls Trail.

Bramlet Ridge. Moccasin Creek is crashing loudly through the woods to your right. As an appropriate precursor to the falls, hemlocks thickly populate the woodland and shade the path.

The trail grade is moderate in the now-wide valley, where pines also grow. Ahead, however, the path gets pinched in by the ever-narrowing gorge. The moist trail is crowded with rhododendron, and climbs above Moccasin Creek. At 0.4 mile, look across the creek to view a stream descending off the aptly named Falls Mountain. It flows steeply to a rock ledge, then makes a translucent drop into a sea of rhododendron on the way to Moccasin Creek. The falls was actually created by Moccasin Creek, which cut its valley faster than the smaller side stream, leaving a hanging valley from which the water had to drop.

At the exact point where you stand on the trail to observe the hanging falls there is a large multitrunked basswood tree. Notice the heart-shaped leaves with their finely toothed edges. Not only do basswoods commonly have multiple trunks, but they also often have young shoots growing from the base. Cherokees used basswood for carvings and chair bottoms, and also for mats woven from the tough inner bark. Mountain pioneers made casks and vats from the hollowed wood.

Basswoods are uncommon in Georgia, and like many other trees from colder climates, they are at the southern end of their range here. They grow north to Maine and west to Minnesota and Oklahoma. When they flower in early summer they are often covered with bees, earning them the nickname "bee tree." Many claim that basswood honey is second in flavor only to sourwood honey.

The main stream roars and froths, dashing against sharp-sided boulders that give Moccasin Creek a rugged appearance. The trail is extremely pinched in. The track was

Hemlock Falls

blasted and watery seeps spill over onto it. Finally, the tight gorge forces you to the creek's edge, where a bridge awaits. Someone inscribed the date of construction, 1993, in the concrete base. Good thing this bridge was built, too, as this crossing is just above a rough cascade that drops into a swirling pool bordered by a logjam. It would be quite unpleasant to fall into the pool.

Cross to the right bank. To your left through green thickets, Moccasin Creek is racing down long rocky shoots in a white-water frenzy that drives kayakers to their boats. Of course, the volume and level of froth depend upon recent precipitation, and if you catch this creek after a big rain you'll be well rewarded. All these watery features give rise to the question: How good must Hemlock Falls be, to be *the* destination falls on this creek?

The answer lies not far ahead as you continue upstream. The valley widens again and you are well above the creek. At 0.9 mile, a spur trail leads left to the base of the pool below Hemlock Falls. The pool here is so large that it prohibits your getting too close to the drop. Hemlock Falls is more wide than tall. It descends about 15 feet over a rock ledge and bounces over a few rocks into the pool. Some folks consider this pool among the best swimming holes in the North Georgia Mountains. It has varying depths, is open to the sun, and has a pleasant flat bordered with large poolside sitting rocks. This flat is also used as a campsite.

The area around the falls seems to have no more hemlock trees than the rest of the Moccasin Creek valley, but maybe the preponderance of hemlocks on the way to the falls inspired its name. The official trail ends at the pool below the falls. However, a discernable, yet unmaintained path continues a little over 0.5 mile, with one ford, to reach Moccasin Creek Falls.

After assessing the power of the creek as you head up, consider whether or not you can make it across the ford to the falls. If the water is low and slow, it will likely be easy. The round-trip to Moccasin Creek Falls adds a little over a mile to your 1.8-mile round-trip hike to Hemlock Falls. You might also want to consider walking the 1-mile loop of the Wildlife Trail, located back at the turn to the Hemlock Falls Trailhead.

41

Southern Nantahala Wilderness Walk

Total distance: 6.2 miles there and back

Hiking time: 3½ hours

Vertical rise: 800 feet

Rating: Moderate

Maps: USGS 7.5' Hightower Bald, Southern Nantahala Wilderness, Chattahoochee National Forest

This hike joins the Appalachian Trail through the Southern Nantahala Wilderness. Begin the trek at remote Blue Ridge Gap in the far north of Georgia. Enter the wilderness and travel north over knobs to make the North Carolina state line. The elevation changes are gradual and gentle for the most part. Just over the state line, near Bly Gap, there is a rewarding view, as well as a camping area and spring that also can be used as a lunch stop for day hikers.

HOW TO GET THERE

From Helen, take GA 17/75 north for 21 miles to US 76. Turn right on US 76 east and go 5.2 miles to Upper Hightower Creek Road. (There is a sign for Mount Pleasant Church of God here; if you drive over Upper Hightower Creek on US 76, you have gone too far.) Turn left on Upper Hightower Creek Road and follow it 3.6 miles as it turns into rough, gravel Forest Road 72. Keep climbing on FR 72 for 1 mile, and a total of 4.6 miles from US 76, to reach Blue Ridge Gap, the high point on FR 72. There is room for two or three cars at this remote trailhead.

THE HIKE

Blue Ridge Gap, your starting point, lies just above 3,000 feet. The Appalachian Trail is blazed in both directions across the small staging area. This hike heads north on the AT, to your left as you approach the gap from US 76. Follow the white blazes up a few wooden steps and pass a sign indicating the Southern Nantahala Wilderness.

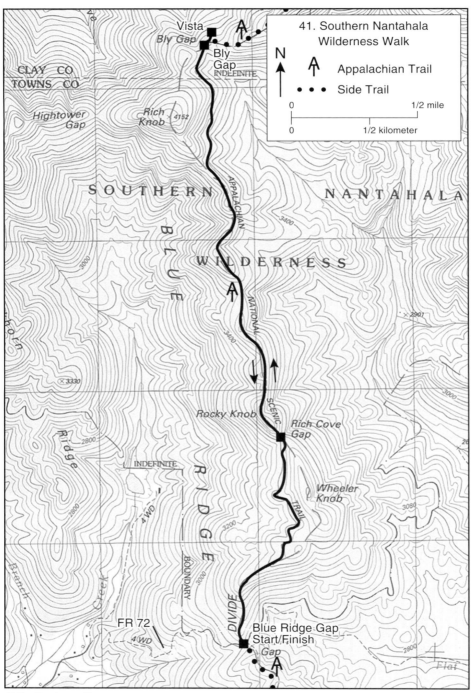

41. Southern Nantahala Wilderness Walk

N

Ⱥ Appalachian Trail

•••• Side Trail

0   1/2 mile

0   1/2 kilometer

Vista
Bly Gap

Bly
Gap
INDEFINITE

CLAY CO
TOWNS CO

Hightower
Gap

Rich
Knob   4152

S O U T H E R N   N A N T A H A L A

B   APPALACHIAN

L   W I L D E R N E S S

U   3400

E   NATIONAL

3400

3400

× 2901

× 3330

SCENIC

Rocky Knob   Rich Cove
Gap

Ridge   2800

INDEFINITE

R   Wheeler
Knob

I   3080

4WD

D   TRAIL

G   3200

3000

E   BOUNDARY

Branch

FR 72

4WD

D
I
V
I
D
E

Blue Ridge Gap
Start/Finish

Gap

2800

Flat

© The Countryman Press

The southern Nantahala Mountains from Bly Gap

The 23,339-acre wildland was established in 1984, and over 12,000 acres are in Georgia. The rest are in our destination, the Tar Heel State. The Georgia portion of the wilderness is as much as 12 miles wide east to west and 3 miles wide north to south. This section of the AT is the only developed trail on the Georgia side. However, if you like to follow old roadbeds or are an off-trail hiker, this place is for you. The North Carolina side of the wilderness has 32 miles of the Appalachian Trail coursing through it, and 14 miles of other trails. Thirty miles of pathway connect to the wilderness from the greater Standing Indian Basin. Standing Indian Mountain, at 5,499 feet, is the high point in the wilderness.

I find the forest here among the most attractive along the entire AT in the state. It has just the right mix of moist and dry species. The meandering trail passes through many transitional areas where different species have the opportunity to thrive. Interestingly,

American holly is a prevalent species. Growing primarily in the Southeast, this thorny evergreen extends west to Texas and northeast to Massachusetts. In the Southern Appalachians it is a common mountain tree. Best known for its red berries and green leaves in Christmas decorations, the normally small tree is often used as an ornamental shrub and is clipped to various shapes. Its finely textured wood is used to make handles and rulers, and in cabinetry. The red berries, though inedible to humans, are an important food for songbirds.

The trail ascends gently away from Blue Ridge Gap amid white pines, tracing a long abandoned roadbed toward Wheeler Knob. At 1 mile, a spring and campsite are located on the left flank of the knob, to the left of the AT. The spring is but a slow trickle.

Continue a moderate uptick and reach Rich Cove Gap at 1.2 miles. At this slender saddle the AT turns left and continues uphill toward Rocky Knob. But it ends up slipping over to the east side of the knob, where you gain obscured views east to the Tallulah River, born on the southern slopes of Standing Indian Mountain. Regain the crest of the ridge, which drops off sharply on both sides. The ridge marks the Tennessee Valley Divide. Waters to your left flow to the Gulf of Mexico, and waters to your right flow to the Atlantic Ocean.

The trail is shaded by patches of laurel and rhododendron. Reach a shallow gap at 1.8 miles. The abandoned roadbed you have been tracing leads right and downhill toward Charlies Creek, while the singletrack Appalachian Trail ascends the nose of an unnamed knob. This south-facing segment is warmer and drier, and is rife with oaks.

Top out and keep north, rising to the next knob. On the climb, at 2.3 miles, a spur trail leads left to a rock outcrop with partial views to the southwest. A little limb trimming could make this a great view, although barren winter trees do improve the vista. The AT levels off, then tunnels through brush, aiming for Rich Knob. The knob rises high to your left, while the trail's climb is much gentler, avoiding the steeper pitches. Look for rock bluffs along the slopes.

Cross the Georgia–North Carolina state line at 2.9 miles. It is marked with a sign nailed to a tree. Just uphill, an overhanging rock makes for a great rain shelter or photo backdrop. Appalachian Trail thru-hikers have completed their first state at this point, so many stop here to record the event. There is plenty of reason to celebrate this milestone, though they have over 2,000 miles left in their journey.

Keep forward to soon reach a level area and a spring. This spot, encircled by yellow birch trees, doubles as a campsite and lunch spot. The AT turns left here and climbs a bit to reach Bly Gap at 3,840 feet. Here it makes a hard right and travels past a particularly gnarled oak tree before opening to a clearing where you can look northeast toward the higher peaks of the Southern Nantahala Mountains. Your return trip from here is a mere 3.1 miles, whereas an AT thru-hiker is just getting started.

42

Three Falls of the Tallulah River Valley

Total distance: 2.4 miles there and back, both hikes

Hiking time: 2 hours

Vertical rise: 450 feet

Rating: Easy to moderate

Maps: USGS 7.5' Tallulah Falls, Tiger, Chattahoochee National Forest

The Tallulah River cuts quite a swath through the mountains of North Georgia. It starts high in the Southern Nantahala Wilderness in North Carolina, and then heads south into Rabun County on a beautiful run to meet another legendary Georgia watercourse, the Chattooga River. Along the way it is dammed by Georgia Power. Near similarly-dammed Lake Rabun, the valley cuts deeply enough for the Tallulah's tributaries to form waterfalls of their own.

This trek takes you to three waterfalls along two creeks separated only by Lake Rabun. The first, Joe Creek, features Panther Falls and Angel Falls. The second creek, Falls Branch, is but a short drive away and displays Minnehaha Falls. The aggregate hiking distance of the two trips isn't much. Furthermore, the Joe Creek Trailhead is located at Rabun Beach, a fine camping destination where you can add to your fun by camping out and enjoying the still waters of the lake.

HOW TO GET THERE

From just north of Tallulah Falls, keep north on US 441 to Old US 441. Turn left on Old US 441 at the signed turn for Rabun Beach Recreation Area and follow it 2.5 miles to Lake Rabun Road. Turn left and go 5 miles to Rabun Beach Camp Area No. 2, on your right. Enter the campground and turn right on Camping Loop B, heading past Spur B to reach the Angel Falls Trailhead, near campsite No. 74. The parking area has four spots and is near a small picnic area. The campground is open from late April through October. During the rest of the year, you will

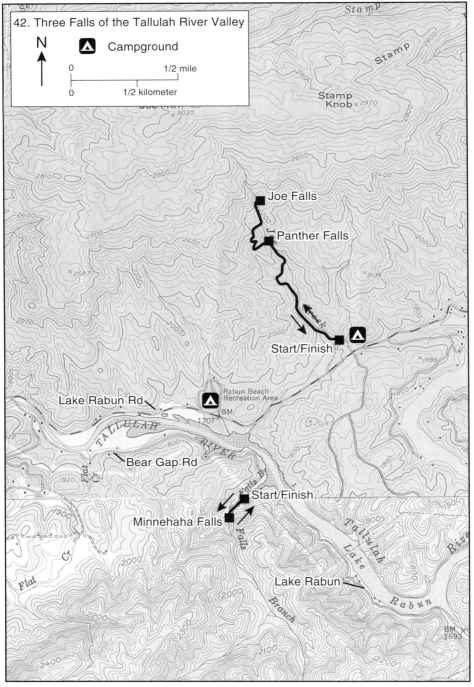

42. Three Falls of the Tallulah River Valley

N

🔺 Campground

0 ——————————— 1/2 mile

0 ——————————— 1/2 kilometer

Stamp

Stamp

Stamp Knob ×2970

Joe Falls

Panther Falls

track

Start/Finish

Rabun Beach Recreation Area

BM 1707

Lake Rabun Rd

TALLULAH RIVER

Bear Gap Rd

Start/Finish

Minnehaha Falls

Lake Rabun

© The Countryman Press

have to carefully park along Lake Rabun Road, then walk through the campground to reach the trailhead.

To reach Minnehaha Falls, continue west on Lake Rabun Road, passing Rabun Beach Camp Area No. 1 and traveling a total of 1.6 miles to Low Gap Road. Turn left and continue over the bridge spanning the Tallulah River to shortly reach Bear Gap Road. Turn left and continue 1.6 miles to the Minnehaha Falls Trailhead, on your right as Bear Gap Road turns left. A small parking area is across from the trail.

THE HIKE

The parking area for this trailhead was once the site of Civilian Conservation Corps F-9, one of four such Great Depression–era camps located in Rabun County. This 1930s work program developed Rabun Beach Campground and other roads and recreation areas, including the trail you are about to walk. The CCC boys were here from June 23, 1933, until May 11, 1942, when all available hands were recruited for World War II.

Leave the Angel Falls parking area on the Rabun Beach Trail and begin walking up the right bank of Joe Creek, which is fairly small. It flows off the slopes of Joe Mountain and Stamp Knob to the north. Soon you cross a bridge over the creek and come to a series of multitiered, evenly spaced ledges over which the water drops, making a pretty sight.

Continue up a narrow rhododendron-choked hollow. Notice the remains of an old dam across Joe Creek. Walk up steps and rise well above the creek. The hollow opens a bit as the wide path runs beneath hemlocks aplenty. Take note of a wooden bench built into a stone foundation on the hillside. There is a cut where a spring once flowed near the bench, but you can see the spring has sprung itself a new passage beside the

stone inlay. This stone masonry is the handiwork of the CCC. Parts of the trail are wet.

Ahead, a small bridge spans a tributary that widens the valley, and drier species of trees like sourwood appear. The valley closes again and the trail bridges Joe Creek twice in quick succession. Just ahead, at 0.6 mile, you reach Panther Falls. Stone slabs extend to the base of the falls, which is a two-tiered drop over horizontal ledges cutting a 40-foot swath through the greenery.

The path turns away from Joe Creek and climbs steeply, working its way above the high falls. Cables aid in keeping hikers on the steep-sided trail. You can look down onto Panther Falls from here and see that it is steeper than it appeared from the bottom. Open out of a precipitous gorge, still climbing, to cross Joe Creek on a footbridge.

Just ahead, the trail splits. Stay right to reach a viewing platform and Angel Falls. This wooden platform is located in the middle of the extremely tall waterfall, which is obscured by rhododendron above. It too has multiple horizontal ledges over which the water stair-steps down, from far above the viewing platform to well below it. Angel Falls makes the most of the water it has to work with.

Finish the upper loop trail, then backtrack to the trailhead.

Now it is time for Minnehaha Falls. Follow the driving directions to the trailhead, then climb away from Bear Gap Road on wooden steps with a railing. You are just across the lake from Joe Creek. The path works its way around private land in mountain laurel, Fraser magnolia, and pines. Falls Branch is audible in the hollow to your right.

Drift into Falls Branch, covered in rhododendron. Resume a climb to reach Minnehaha Falls at 0.3 mile. The waterfall starts narrow and widens as it descends, kicking up quite a mist on its impressive 100-foot

Panther Falls

drop. There is no pool below the falls; the water just keeps moving on its descent to the Tallulah River, which is dammed to form Lake Rabun and bordered by many vacation homes. The Forest Service has some lake frontage on Lake Rabun in the Rabun Beach Recreation Area.

Rabun Beach Campground has two major areas, with electric hookups available at some campsites. Camp Area No. 2, near the Rabun Beach Trail, has electric sites and hot showers. The recreation area swim beach is popular in summer. A changing house overlooks the swim area, which is bordered by buoys. There is a floating dock within swimming distance of the shoreline. A boat launch is available for those with watercraft who want to ply the narrow lake. Or you can fish for bass, bream, catfish, and trout from the Forest Service pier. All of the above makes the Three Falls of the Tallulah River Valley a more alluring place.

43

James Edmonds Backcountry Loop

Total distance: 7 miles

Hiking time: 4¼ hours

Vertical rise: 960 feet

Rating: Moderate to difficult

Maps: USGS 7.5' Dillard, Black Rock Mountain State Park

This is a solid day hike or an overnight backpacking loop. The trail starts in the high country of Black Rock Mountain State Park and travels nearly the length of the park, dipping to a mountain stream before climbing to a vista at the appropriately named Lookoff Mountain. It then loops back toward its beginning, passing near Black Rock Lake and by a pretty falls on Greasy Creek to return to the high country and its terminus. Four backcountry campsites are situated along the route, making overnight trips of different lengths a breeze.

HOW TO GET THERE

From Cornelia, take US 441 north for 32 miles to Clayton. Continue north just a few miles to Mountain City. Turn left onto Black Rock Mountain Road from US 441 and follow it 3 miles to dead-end at the state park. Once inside the park, veer right toward the visitor center. After this turn, the parking area for the James Edmonds and Tennessee Rock Trails is on your right. The path begins beyond a small picnic area.

THE HIKE

The trailhead starts out quite high, less than 400 feet from the park's highest point. Leave the parking area and walk up some steps to a trail junction. Here the Tennessee Rock Trail and the James Edmonds Trail (JET) part ways. Stay right with the JET. The single-track path begins descending through rich fern-floored woodland. The forest is quite thick from top to bottom. Maples, tulip trees, and the ever-present oaks and hickories

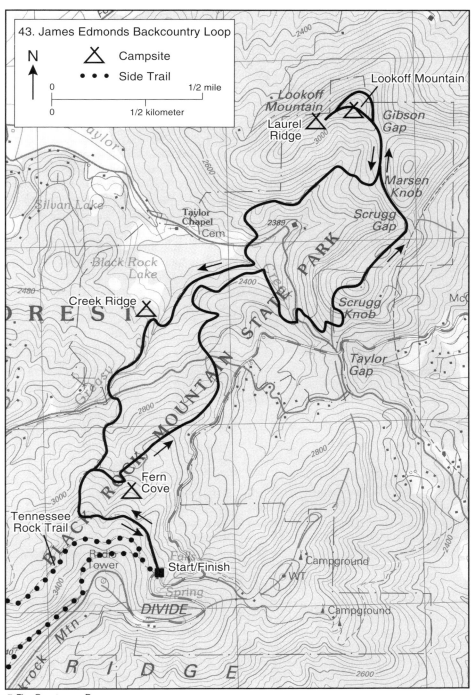

43. James Edmonds Backcountry Loop

N

△ Campsite

••• Side Trail

0 ——— 1/2 mile
0 ——— 1/2 kilometer

Lookoff Mountain

Lookoff Mountain

Gibson Gap

Laurel Ridge

Marsen Knob

Scrugg Gap

PARK

Taylor Chapel Cem

2389

Black Rock Lake

2400

Creek Ridge

Scrugg Knob

Taylor Gap

O R E S T

BLACK ROCK MOUNTAIN STATE PARK

2800

2800

Fern Cove

Tennessee Rock Trail

Radio Tower

Falls

Campground

Start/Finish

WT

Spring

DIVIDE

Campground

R I D G E

2600

© The Countryman Press

shade the path. Underbrush crowds in too, especially in mid- to late summer.

Curve into a streambed and continue descending. Switchbacks take you to a narrowing ridgeline dominated by white pines. Reach a trail junction at 0.7 mile, where the James Edmonds Trail splits. Stay right with the East Fork JET and shortly cross an unnamed feeder branch of Greasy Creek to reach the spur trail to the Fern Cove backcountry site. It is located in pine woods near the stream.

Leave Fern Cove, ascending on a small branch to pick up an old roadbed, which makes for easy, level hiking, and continue north. The easy hiking ceases as the path dips to meet Germany Mountain Road at 1.3 miles. Cross the road and resume the downgrade on a rooty track. Join a branch heading downstream. You begin to wonder when and where you are going to make the inevitable climb. Despite the lush woods, a good eye can see the shimmer of Black Rock Lake between the trees to the left.

Roaring Taylor Creek greets you at 1.9 miles. This rhododendron-cloaked branch is racing down the mountain to feed Black Rock Lake. You, however, head up the branch, tunneling beneath green shrubbery. Tree cover is thick overhead. Taylor Creek is open enough to show off some rocky cascades. Bridge the creek after a sharp left and meet Taylor Chapel Road at 2.3 miles. Cross the road and begin the climb to Lookoff Mountain. The climb leads into drier piney woods, at times tunneling through mountain laurel. Level out in a gap and join the Eastern Continental Divide. Waters to the right drop to the Atlantic Ocean via the Tugaloo and Savannah Rivers. Waters to the left drop into the Gulf of Mexico via the Tennessee, Ohio, and Mississippi Rivers.

Beyond the gap, Marsen Knob rises to your right. Join a roadbed and reach the end of the East Fork James Edmonds Trail. The West Fork JET leads left. This is your return route, but first, it's time to climb to Lookoff Mountain. Keep forward at this junction and begin the short but sweet ascent, which has its own mini-loop and two backcountry sites, Lookoff Mountain and Laurel Ridge. Stay right as the mini-loop begins curving around the north side of the mountain. Boulders stand amid the thick woods. Curve around to reach a rock slab and the spur trail to the "lookoff" of Lookoff Mountain. The spur trail drops to a wide rock face where you can look north and west into the uppermost portion of the Little Tennessee River valley.

Return from Lookoff Mountain and continue your mini-loop, walking directly through the Lookoff Mountain campsite, which stands at the mountain's wooded peak. This campsite has the standard wooden benches and fire ring you find at each backcountry campsite in the park. The path completes the mini-loop. Continue backtracking to the James Edmonds West Loop. The trail begins descending, passing a small spring to the left of the trail where backcountry campers can obtain water. This spring may dry up in late summer or early autumn.

The path drops steeply on a bed of clay, then levels off to step over the spring branch. From here, the West Fork JET heads down a well-watered valley. The main creek slides over rock slabs. Unexpectedly, the trail splits right and climbs over a laurel ridge to wander seemingly without purpose on a rocky slope before meeting Taylor Chapel Road at 5 miles. Black Rock Lake is visible to the right, and you can easily walk down to it from here. A short nature trail loops around the lake.

The JET crosses the road and drops to Taylor Creek. This is the low point of the loop, so it is almost all uphill from here.

The Little Tennessee Valley from Lookout Mountain

Circle around the side of a mountain after crossing the creek. White pines dominate the forest here. Black Rock Lake is visible through the trees. Curve to Greasy Creek, which flows beneath the rhododendron. Cross on a footbridge, then turn upstream to reach a pretty waterfall at 5.6 miles. This wide cascade slides over a mossy slope into a small pool. Just ahead, a spur trail leads right to the Creek Ridge backcountry campsite. This site is located on a level roadbed and open to the sun overhead.

Continue up the Greasy Creek valley, which is audible but not visible through the evergreens. A high bridge spans Greasy Creek just before you reach Germany Mountain Road at 5.9 miles. The JET resumes its steady uptick, winding back and forth amid oak-hickory-pine woods and dipping to a feeder branch of Greasy Creek eventually intersecting the East Fork James Edmonds Trail at 6.3 miles. You have now completed the loop portion of the hike. From here it's a steady 0.7-mile climb back to the trailhead.

44

Tennessee Rock Loop

Total distance: 2.2 miles

Hiking time: 1¾ hours

Vertical rise: 960 feet

Rating: Moderate

Maps: USGS 7.5' Dillard, Black Rock Mountain State Park

The Tennessee Rock Loop explores the highest reaches of Black Rock Mountain State Park. Not only do you visit Tennessee Rock and the highest point of Black Rock Mountain, but you also learn a thing or two on this walk. The state park has a brochure coordinated with numbered stops that turn this afternoon stroll into an outdoor classroom and interpretive hike. So be prepared to stretch your brain in addition to stretching your legs. Black Rock Mountain State Park also offers a quality campground with sites for big rigs or walk-in tent campers.

HOW TO GET THERE

From Cornelia, take US 441 north for 32 miles to Clayton. Continue north just a few miles to Mountain City. Turn left from US 441 onto Black Rock Mountain Road and follow it 3 miles. The road dead-ends at the park. Once inside, veer right toward the visitor center. After this turn, the parking area for the James Edmonds and Tennessee Rock Trails is on your right. The path begins beyond a small picnic area.

THE HIKE

A nice little picnic area is available at the trailhead, which the Tennessee Rock Trail shares with the James Edmonds Backcountry Trail (see Hike 43). The path heads up some steps away from the picnic area to a trail junction. The Tennessee Rock Trail turns left. It is wider than the James Edmonds Trail and receives more use. Ahead the path splits again at the loop portion of the hike. Stay right here, following the

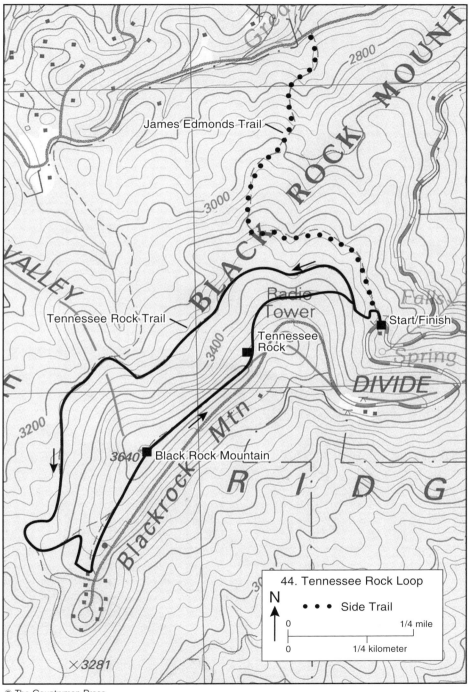

James Edmonds Trail

Tennessee Rock Trail

Radio Tower

Tennessee Rock

Start/Finish

Black Rock Mountain

3640

3281

VALLEY

BLACK ROCK MOUNT

DIVIDE

RIDG

Blackrock Mtn

Falls

Spring

2800

3000

3200

3400

44. Tennessee Rock Loop

N

● ● ● Side Trail

0   1/4 mile

0   1/4 kilometer

© The Countryman Press

numbered posts in ascending order. It is well worth picking up the accompanying booklet for this hike back at the trading post in the park campground. This way you can be the smart one, and the group's naturalist on the hike.

Cruise around the north slope of Black Rock Mountain, which rises to your left. Pass a spring that creates its own microhabitat. Chestnut oaks and saplings of the American chestnut grow in the area. The American chestnut tree was once the dominant giant of the Southern Appalachians. It ranged from Maine to Mississippi, and in the mountains it grew to massive proportions. Some of the largest trees in this area required a tape measure of more than 30 feet to determine their circumference.

The fruit of this tree was very important. Chestnut acorns were the staple food for everything from bears to birds. Of course, humans ate them, too. But the tree also provided some of the best wood for everyday use by pioneers, like those who settled in Rabun County. It was also coveted by the timber companies that harvested the hills.

Sadly, just as the pioneer days in the Appalachian backwoods are gone, so are the mighty chestnuts. In the early 1900s, Asian chestnut trees were imported to the United States, bringing a fungus with them. The Asian trees had developed immunity to the fungus, but the American chestnut was helpless. Before long, chestnuts were dying in the Northeast, and the blight worked its way down to the Southeast in the 1920s. Two decades later, the chestnut trees had been decimated.

To this day, chestnut trees sprout from the roots of the ancients, growing up but always succumbing to the blight. Hopefully, these chestnuts are building a resistance and will one day tower over the Southern Appalachians again, long after we're gone. Scientists are expediting this process, and experiments are under way to graft American chestnut trees with the Asian chestnuts in an effort to develop a blight-resistant American chestnut.

Ahead, a spur trail leads left to stop No. 7. This stop is at the base of a botanically rich, high-elevation boulder field. These Southern Appalachian boulder fields normally occur only above 3,000 feet on the north sides of mountains. Wildflowers, mosses, and herbs thrive here. These boulders were created during the last ice age by the repeated freezing and thawing of the rock bluff up the ridge. This action broke rocks free from the top of the mountain and they came to a rest here.

Reach a gap at post No. 10. White pines become more prevalent here. Pass a trail junction leading to the park cabins, then begin the climb to the crest of Black Rock Mountain. A few switchbacks lead to the peak, elevation 3,640 feet, and a marker is posted at the high point. Five mountains combine to make this the highest state park in Georgia. Black Rock gets its name from the sheer cliffs and outcrops of dark granite, called biotite gneiss. For us, this means open views of the Carolinas and Tennessee, as well as Georgia. Due to its high elevation, the mountaintop enjoys the same average summertime temperatures as Burlington, Vermont.

From here, it is an easy walk along the crest of the mountain and along the Eastern Continental Divide. Ahead, steps lead to Tennessee Rock, where you can look north and west. There is a view across the trail to the east, as well. On a clear day you can see the high points of Georgia and Tennessee: Brasstown Bald (4,784 feet) and Clingmans Dome (6,642 feet), respectively.

Ferns line the Tennessee Rock Trail.

The valley of the Little Tennessee River is below. The park handout includes a detailed map showing each point in the distance.

Pass more outcrops that make good relaxation spots before dropping through rhododendron to come along Black Mountain Parkway. The Eastern Continental Divide runs east, but you continue downhill to the north, making a steady descent to intersect the other end of the Tennessee Rock Trail. Backtrack just a short distance to the trailhead.

Black Rock Mountain Campground offers a little something for everybody, in addition to hiking. It has 48 sites with water, electricity, and cable TV hookups for RVs, and on a dead-end road on a mountaintop rib ridge there is an 11-site, walk-in, tents-only area. There is a lake up here, too. You can fish 17-acre Black Rock Lake from the bank for bass, bream, catfish, and trout. Boating and swimming are not allowed.

But the most popular activity at Black Rock is hiking. In addition to the Tennessee Rock Trail and the James Edmonds Loop, there is the short Ada-Hi Falls Trail. This trail dips into a cool cove about 0.2 mile on the way to the falls. Since the trail and creek are so high on the mountain, there is not a whole lot of water going over the falls.

45

Panther Creek Falls of Habersham County

Total distance: 6.8 miles there and back

Hiking time: 3¾ hours

Vertical rise: 450 feet

Rating: Moderate

Maps: USGS 7.5' Tallulah Falls, Chattahoochee National Forest

There are two Panther Creek Falls in the mountains of North Georgia, and both are detailed in this guidebook. The Panther Creek Falls of the Cohutta Wilderness is in Fannin County (see Hike 42). Both of these waterfalls are fine destinations that should be on your "must-do" hike list.

This Panther Creek Falls is a high-volume, powerful affair that dumps over a large and ragged rock face into one of the largest pools in the Georgia mountains. Along the way you descend into an ever-deepening gorge, where rock faces and overhangs have been worn smooth over time. The trail travels through places so narrow that handrails have been installed for safety. Such beauty and excitement draws the crowds, however. This is a very busy trail, so try to come on a weekday or during the winter. Cold temperatures are not an issue on this hike, as the elevations are low and bridges keep your feet dry.

HOW TO GET THERE

From Cornelia, take US 441 north for 14 miles to the sign for Panther Creek Trailhead. Turn left here on Glenn Hardeman Road and follow it a short distance before turning right onto Historic Old US 441. Go 1 mile, then turn left into the signed parking area on Forest Road 174. The trail starts on the east side of Old US 441.

To reach the trailhead from Clayton, at US 76 west and US 441, drive south on US 441 for 13 miles to a signed right turn for Panther Creek Trailhead. Turn right on Historic Old US 441 and follow it 1.3 miles to the trailhead, on your right.

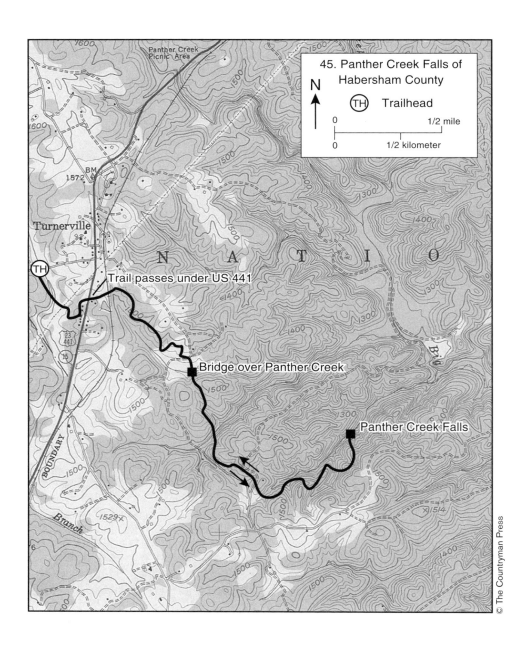

Panther Creek Falls

THE HIKE

Leave the parking area and cross over to the east side of Historic Old US 441. The Panther Creek Trail immediately enters the woods, and Panther Creek is crashing to your right, wasting no time in its downward quest for the Tugaloo River. The creek drops noisily over rocky rapids, almost drowning out the traffic on US 441's twin bridges, which the trail soon passes under. The wide sand-and-dirt trail passes a prominent USGS metal survey marker before entering a gorgeous flat of white pines with an understory of hemlock and maple. Partridgeberry covers the forest floor, along with pine needles. The creek is out of sight on the far side of the flat.

You soon come alongside the stream again as it begins to cut a gorge. Step over a pair of feeder branches and pass under a power-line clearing at 0.5 mile. The clearing gives you a good view of the stream, which is now far below. The gorge tightens and the creek is continually falling, barely taking time to gather into pools. Mountain laurel grows thick along the path, which is shaded by maple, oak, hickory, and pine trees. By the way, campsites are plentiful along the creek.

The trail reaches a pair of rock overhangs where a backpacker might have trouble squeezing through. Just past the overhangs, the creek drops over a couple of ledges and then it narrows into a long, steep chute that curves to the right. It is quite a sight, especially in high water. The path curves to the right as well, coming to a rock ledge. It used to go forward here, but was washed out. Now the trail takes an unexpected hard left turn up a steep rock face, where hikers have to use hands and feet to scramble up a root-covered ledge. The path works its way downhill, rejoining Panther Creek in a streamside flat at 1.4 miles. Just ahead, the trail has a bridge to the right bank. Little Panther Creek comes in below, on the left.

The valley widens and the gorge opens. The stream quiets down accordingly, flowing over small riffles and actually pooling up from time to time. The woods are quite brushy, rising in the wake of many dead pines, the result of a major southern pine beetle infestation years back. This cycle is natural; the pines will tower over the valley again one day, but for now, rotting trunks will continue to fall over the path, allowing sunlight to reach the forest floor.

The path is quite sandy in spots, a result of creek overflow during times of flood. Cross two branches by bridge at 1.9 and 2.1 miles. The path reenters heavy woods and then comes alongside a rocky valley wall. The creek resumes its falling ways, showing off a long, impressive cascade. Another creek comes in just below the falls, and the path keeps curving along a rock bluff above the creek. It briefly opens again, only to reach another bluff where wire railings strung together by posts help hikers stay on the trail and out of the water below. It is steep here, and the walking is exciting. Rock overhangs above the trail add to the ruggedness. Shoals increase on Panther Creek where the gorge narrows.

The gorge becomes increasingly scenic, and the trail hangs right along the creek, except for where it circles around a tributary. Pass more railings stretched out along the narrow track. Just after the tributary, at 3.2 miles, a spur trail comes in from the right. This is a shortcut path to the falls from an area known as Hollywood—named for the holly tree, not the glamorous lifestyles of the famed city's inhabitants.

The path switchbacks down and emerges onto a rock slab facing upstream. This is your viewing platform for some wide cascades above. Below these, Panther Creek briefly pauses in a deep pool before the trip over its namesake falls. Leave the rock platform (a great picnicking spot), and descend through rough terrain, aided by more railings. Panther Creek Falls is rip-roaring just out of sight.

Soon the trail arrives at a flat, and the base of the falls at 3.4 miles. What a sight! The waterfall is tall, wide, and powerful. It rivals Jacks River Falls for volume, High Shoals for its drop, and Hemlock Falls for breadth. Catch Panther Creek Falls after a heavy rain and you will see the power of nature at work. Your viewing area is a sand/gravel bar overlooking the huge mist-covered pool, perhaps the largest in all of North Georgia. The sky is open over the pool, which makes it a first-rate swimming hole. Shaded woods back the gravel bar. As alluring as the spot is, please don't camp here. First, you won't get any solitude; and second, the area could use a break from the heavy visitor traffic.

46

Tallulah Gorge Loop

Total distance: 1.9 miles

Hiking time: 2 hours

Vertical rise: 300 feet

Rating: Moderate

Maps: USGS 7.5' Tallulah Falls, Tallulah Gorge State Park

The Tallulah River Gorge, cut by water and time, is one of the most spectacular features in the region. Near the historic town of Tallulah Falls, the river drops deeply into a steep and scenic canyon, where waterfalls continue to cut the gorge ever deeper. Legendary aerialist Karl Wallenda once balanced on a wire over this deep chasm. Today you can make a loop along the rim of the gorge and into its depths, where an impressive hiker's suspension bridge crosses the river. Be advised that although this is one of the most scenic hikes in the book, it is also one of the most developed. And it is very near US 441 and the town of Tallulah Falls.

HOW TO GET THERE

From Cornelia, take US 441 north for 22 miles to the Tallulah River. Tallulah Falls Lake is on your left as you cross the bridge. Shortly past the river and lake, turn right to enter the state park and follow Jane Hurt Yarn Road to the Jane Hurt Yarn Interpretive Center. The hike begins on the left side of the lower parking area (as you face the interpretive center).

THE HIKE

Bring your camera on this hike, as clear days offer huge rewards for photographers. Even hazy summer days have allure in this gorge. Descend from the parking area on a wide path to meet the North Rim Trail. Turn left here and walk east on a wood-chip track to a footbridge over a little creek. Pines

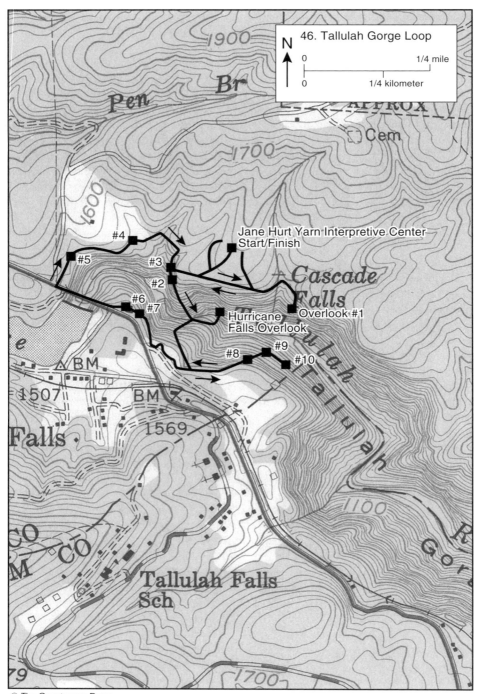

46. Tallulah Gorge Loop

N

0 .... 1/4 mile

0 .... 1/4 kilometer

1900

Pen *Br*

Cem

1700

1600

Jane Hurt Yarn Interpretive Center
Start/Finish

#4

#5

#3

Cascade Falls

#2

Overlook #1

#6

#7

Hurricane
Falls Overlook

BM

#8

#9

#10

1507

BM

Falls

1569

1100

Tallulah Falls Sch

1700

79

© The Countryman Press

dominate at the top of the gorge. Soon you reach Overlook No. 1. The overlooks are numbered to help you track your progress on this very developed trail. The fallen tower beside Overlook No. 1 is the north tower Karl Wallenda used to string wire across the gorge when he walked across in 1970. The view is a long look into the deeper south end of the gorge.

Backtrack on the North Rim Trail, passing around the back of the Jane Hurt Yarn Interpretive Center to join a springy path made of recycled tires. Descend to Overlook No. 3 and begin the loop portion of your hike on the Hurricane Falls Trail. Overlook No. 3 reveals Ladore Falls, also known as L'Eau d'Or Falls, which is French for "water of gold." Begin descending the 750 steps to the suspension bridge over the Tallulah River, stopping at Overlook No. 2, which also has views of Ladore Falls. These steps may represent the most complexly constructed footpath in the state, perhaps the entire Southeast.

You can see the bridge below, but also admire the natural features that make the gorge so spectacular—steep-sided rock walls, sheer cliffs, crashing water below. The forest becomes increasingly moist as you near the river, with hemlocks a regular feature of the landscape. Reach the suspension bridge, and linger if you dare. Below you, Hurricane Falls makes its way over striated rock. There is a platform under the bridge, too.

Another set of steps await across the river—450 steps down to the bottom of the gorge. A viewing platform allows a bottom-up look at Hurricane Falls. To continue down the gorge you need a permit, which you can get at the interpretive center. Only a finite number of permits are issued, though. If you have one, you can cross the river here if flows allow.

You will break your first big sweat ascending those 450 steps back up to the suspension bridge. More climbing is ahead as you make your way up to the top of the south rim. This rim faces north, so more lush vegetation shades the path than on the north rim. Look for old cables around which trees have grown. The cables aided the climb out of the gorge in days gone by, for Tallulah Gorge has been a tourist attraction for quite some time—well before the state park was established in 1992 in a cooperative effort between Georgia Power and the state.

Reach the crest of the gorge and the South Rim Trail at 0.8 mile. The gorge rim up here is more sparsely vegetated and the trail is open to the sun. Turn left and make your way toward Overlooks 8, 9, and 10. Notice the obviously newer stone steps and benches among the older ones. A side trail leads right and uphill to the Sliding Rock Trail, which also requires a permit from the state park. The Sliding Rock Trail leads down to Bridal Veil Falls.

Overlook No. 8 allows you to see where you've been. Check out the suspension bridge below, and Hurricane Falls. Also, look downstream for the interpretive center and across to Caledonia Cascade, a side-stream waterfall plunging into the gorge. From Overlook No. 9, gaze downstream at Oceana Falls. Beyond here, the path passes a neat undercut bluff with a stone bench. Overlook No. 10 opens to Caledonia Cascade and a 1,000-foot bluff across the gorge. Rails and fences are situated along all the overlooks, allowing worry-free viewing.

Backtrack to the Hurricane Falls Trail and keep on the South Rim Trail, now heading upriver. The trail passes older rock steps and benches. Overlook No. 7 provides a view of Tempesta Falls, while Overlook No. 6 opens

Overlook at Tallulah Gorge

down the gorge. The trail now comes very near US 441, and soon reaches it. Walk along the road, northward, crossing the bridge on a pedestrian walkway. The old US 441 goes under the new bridge and over the dam at Tallulah Falls Lake. Veer right across the dam, joining the North Rim Trail. A spur trail leads left to the picnic area and beach on the lake. The North Rim Trail passes a spur leading left to the state park campground, then comes to Overlook No. 5, which opens to the upper gorge.

Overlook No. 4 offers a view of the Tallulah Falls Dam, which was finished in 1913. The lake is visible behind the dam. The man-made cascade makes quite a fall from the lip of the dam. From here, the trail crosses a small creek and soon comes to Overlook No. 3, ending the loop portion of the hike. Backtrack to the trailhead.

Make sure to visit the interpretive center, which has many historic and natural displays about the area. A helpful staff is available to answer your questions.

47

Becky Branch Falls and Martin Creek Falls

Total distance: 4 miles there and back

Hiking time: 3½ hours

Vertical rise: 180 feet

Rating: Moderate

Maps: USGS 7.5' Rabun Bald, Chattahoochee National Forest

This hike follows one of Georgia's longest trails, the Bartram Trail, north from Warwoman Dell Picnic Area to two pretty waterfalls that seem to be bypassed for other more popular falls closer to the population centers of North Georgia. The Bartram Trail is located in the northeastern tip of the state. A hike on this trail can be extended into backpacking trips with solitude aplenty.

HOW TO GET THERE

From just north of the junction of US 76 west and US 441 in Clayton, Georgia, head east on Rickman Road and follow it a short distance to Warwoman Road. Turn right and go 3 miles to Warwoman Dell Picnic Area. Turn right into the picnic area and continue 0.1 mile to a covered shelter on your left. The northern portion of the Bartram Trail begins a little up the road and leaves right, near an information kiosk.

THE HIKE

Warwoman Dell Picnic Area is a good place to have a meal and enjoy the falls and a short interpretive trail that starts at the top of the dead end of the gravel road. The southern portion of the Bartram Trail (BT) leads uphill and to the left from this dead end. But for this northbound hike on the BT you need to leave right from the gravel road, well before the dead-end, and just before an information kiosk, which describes the old fish hatchery constructed from 1933–37. Walk just a few feet beyond the turn and inspect the old rearing tanks, once full of feisty trout. This was built by some of the

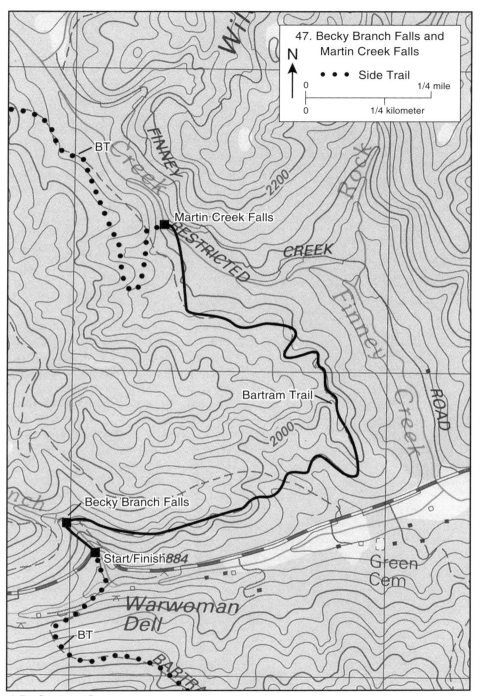

Martin Creek Falls

"CCC boys" from the Civilian Conservation Corps camp located near here.

Return to the Bartram Trail and ascend along Becky Branch, reaching Warwoman Road at 0.1 mile. Pass a roadside metal plaque commemorating William Bartram just before crossing the road. Enter the woods and the Warwoman Wildlife Management Area, climbing sharply along Becky Branch. Pass a small building related to the water supply at Warwoman Dell.

Soon you reach Becky Branch Falls and a bridge. This cascade makes an impressive drop, fed by waters flowing off Raven Knob and Pinnacle Knob. It is a long, narrow falls set amid lush greenery. The trail splits beyond the cascade: The right fork returns to Warwoman Road, and the BT stays left to enter a burned area. The trail itself acted as a firebreak. Ahead, you can see where the flames jumped the trail. The broken woods offer views toward an unnamed knob near Warwoman Dell. At 0.5 mile, bisect a bull-

dozed firebreak heading straight up the ridgeline. The forest was spared beyond the firebreak. This firebreak is growing over now, but it's still visible to a keen eye.

The BT parallels Warwoman Road below in north-facing woods rich in ferns and Fraser magnolia. Many stately white pines and hemlocks shade the trail. Cross a footbridge over a streamlet at 1 mile before turning north into the Finney Creek valley in maple-pine-laurel woods. At 1.7 miles, the singletrack path merges left onto an old woods road. Martin Creek, a feeder branch of Finney Creek, crashes below, shooting through a mini-gorge where cascades slide over rock walls.

The valley opens and the trail reaches a camping flat across Martin Creek at 1.9 miles. Ahead are more campsites in hemlocks and white pines. At 2 miles, the Bartram Trail heads right over a wooden bridge spanning Martin Creek, and passes a rock house before crossing the creek a second time on another footbridge. An elaborate wooden deck is attached to the bridge. To the right, the deck leads to an observation area below Martin Creek Falls. To the left, you can continue on the BT.

Martin Creek Falls is a two-tiered cascade framed in rhododendron. The upper tier has a rocky fall and a slide cascade, while the lower tier includes a delicate veil drop on the right and a curtain-type drop on the left. The BT soon leaves the flat, turns left up a small side branch, and then picks up a woods road. It climbs to near the top of the falls, where you gain a new perspective.

This hike is just a sampler of the Bartram Trail, which offers the consummate Southern Appalachian experience as it makes a 110-mile trek from northeast Georgia's Chattahoochee National Forest to western North Carolina's Nantahala National Forest. Though the BT passes through no designated wilderness areas, it certainly exudes a wilderness aura. The path begins along the wild and scenic Chattooga River, then turns north onto the Blue Ridge, culminating in a 360-degree view from a stone tower atop Rabun Bald. (The Rabun Bald Trail to the tower is detailed in Hike 48, and the Bartram Trail route from Wilson Gap in Hike 49.)

The BT then moves into North Carolina amid incredible stone-faced mountains, where the views are all natural. After crossing the Little Tennessee River valley it heads back into the high country, offering another 360-degree view from the old stone tower at Wayah Bald. From here, it goes downhill to Nantahala Lake before entering the gorge country of the Nantahala River, and topping out with a climb along numerous waterfalls to the trail terminus at Cheoah Bald, which functions as a grandstand for the Smoky Mountains.

The Bartram Trail is well marked, well maintained, and mostly easy to follow. Quality camping opportunities are many and well spaced from one another, making an end-to-end traverse very doable. Natural features extend from beginning to end, keeping the hike interesting.

The trail is named for 18th-century naturalist William Bartram. Inspired by his naturalist father, John, son William set out in 1773 to explore the southeastern United States. For four years he cataloged and described the flora, fauna, and Indians of the region. He is credited with identifying over 200 native plants. His adventure was later published as *Travels of William Bartram.* The Bartram Trail roughly follows his journey through the mountains of North Georgia and western North Carolina. It attempts to offer a wilderness opportunity reminiscent of Bartram's experience, while promoting knowledge of the Southern Appalachian region.

Bartram's accomplishments continue to be celebrated to this day. Bartram Societies have sprung up throughout the Southeast; his home place and botanical garden is a Philadelphia landmark; and his travels are noted and commemorated in Alabama, South Carolina, and Florida, in addition to Georgia and North Carolina.

48

Rabun Bald

Total distance: 5.8 miles there and back

Hiking time: 3½ hours

Vertical rise: 2,100 feet

Rating: Moderate to difficult

Maps: USGS 7.5' Rabun Bald,
Chattahoochee National Forest

Rabun Bald is the second-highest point in Georgia and the highest foot-access-only mountain. Located in the northeastern corner of the state and reached via a relatively obscure trailhead, Rabun Bald is often overlooked. Rabun is no longer an open field, but it still features a grand vista from a wooden deck perched above a rustic stone lookout tower at 4,696 feet. The rating "moderate to difficult" may be misleading. Though the climb is 2,100 feet, the hike is less than 3 miles one way, making it doable by most anyone with patience. So make time to climb this Georgia landmark.

HOW TO GET THERE

From just north of the junction of US 76 west and US 441 in Clayton, Georgia, head east on Warwoman Road 10 miles to Forest Road 7, Hale Ridge Cemetery Road. Turn left and go 5.6 miles to a gap. The trail starts on the hill to the left of the gap. There is roadside parking on the right, just past the trail. Watch carefully; this trailhead is not well marked.

THE HIKE

The trail takes you west and uphill in a wooded gap dominated by white pines. Leave the gap and ascend into thick woods. Gray plastic diamonds nailed to trailside trees mark the singletrack path. Galax is the dominant ground species. You would expect the trail to climb hard and fast at any moment, but instead it undulates along the ridgeline. You can hear Addie Branch off to your right. This creek flows off the eastern

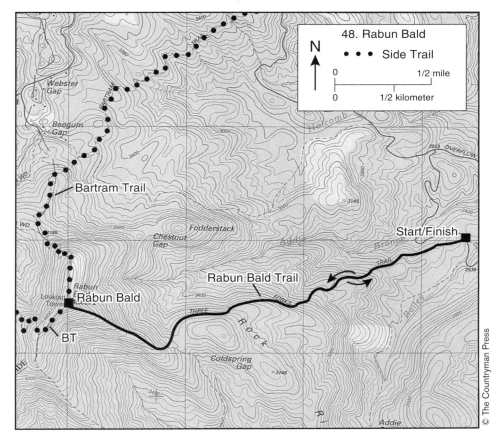

slopes of Rabun Bald, between Chestnut Ridge and Rock Ridge.

The first pitch comes about 0.75 mile up the trail. It is steep but not long. Continue up in beautiful, lush woods reflective of the rainfall here. Rabun Bald is the wettest spot in the wettest county in the state of Georgia. Actually, Rabun County is not only the wettest place in Georgia but in the eastern United States. The immediate region, which also includes a slice of South Carolina and North Carolina, averages between 60 and 80 inches of rain per year. In very wet times, Rabun Bald will get over 100 inches of rain per year. This helps make northeastern Georgia such a botanically rich area. Fall is

usually drier, and the clearer skies reveal fantastic views atop the mountain.

Both red and sugar maples thrive in the understory on this ridgeline, and there are many ferns. You begin to hear water, and then come alongside a tumbling high-country creek at 1.4 miles. There is a little campsite to the left of the trail beside this tributary of Addie Branch.

The trail leaves the creek behind, swinging around its headwater spring to pass through Coldspring Gap at 1.7 miles. An unnamed knob rises to your right. The name Coldspring is common throughout the Southern Appalachians—Coldspring Branch, Coldspring Knob, several Coldspring Gaps—

A grassy gap along the Rabun Bald Trail

as there are many tasty, clear, cold springs flowing off the mountains. The trail becomes rockier, and the south-facing slope to your right reveals the usual suspects in this environment: azaleas, chestnut oak, mountain laurel, and hickory.

The three dominant species of hickory in this area are mockernut, pignut, and bitternut. All three grow upwards of 80 feet. Their leaves are much longer than wide and have fine teeth along the edges, with either five or seven leaflets at the end of each branch. The end leaf sticks out and the others extend directly across from one another. Animals love hickory nuts, and they are a staple for turkeys and squirrels. Hickory wood is highly prized and quite strong. President Andrew Jackson was known as "Old Hickory" for his strength and resilience.

The knob falls away to your right as you continue forward on a mostly level track. Cruise into pretty Grassy Gap at 2.1 miles, where there is another campsite. True to its name, grass grows in the flat among the young trees. This area was an open field at one time, much like Rabun Bald, which has since become fully forested.

Grassy Gap makes a good resting spot because it is all uphill from here, with 900 or so feet of elevation gain ahead. Begin working up the eastern shoulder of Rabun Bald; the path takes the straight-up-the-ridgeline approach. Notice how the trees become more stunted as the ridge narrows and rises. The sparse tree cover allows underbrush to grow tall in summer.

The trail steepens as it winds its way amid boulders, rhododendron, and stunted trees. Views begin to open just before you reach the peak at 2.9 miles. A stone tower bordered by grass stands at the center of the apex, and an inscribed rock is to the left. Climb the tower to a wooden platform and look out in all directions. To the west are the towns in the Little Tennessee River valley, including Clayton; to the north stand the stone-faced mountains of North Carolina; to the east are the Cherokee Foothills of South Carolina and the Piedmont beyond; and to the south are the North Georgia Mountains and the distant lowlands.

The inscribed rock near the tower refers to the Rabun Bald Trail as the "Three Forks Trail," its former name.

This area will always be quieter than Brasstown Bald, Georgia's highest point by less than 100 feet, which has a vehicle-accessible visitor center and only a short trail. Rabun Bald is for hardier peak lovers who like to earn their vistas. Below you the Bartram Trail crosses the bald. From here, the path leads 13.5 miles south to Warwoman Dell Picnic Area or 4.2 miles to the North Carolina border.

49

Rabun Bald and Flat Top Mountain via Bartram Trail

Total distance: 9 miles there and back

Hiking time: 6½ hours

Vertical rise: 1,300 feet

Rating: Difficult

Maps: USGS 7.5' Rabun Bald, Chattahoochee National Forest

This is a secluded and forgotten part of the Bartram Trail (BT) that travels to two of my favorite vistas in the Southern Appalachians. A long gravel drive leads to Wilson Gap and the hike's starting point. From here, the BT runs north to a view of the rock face of Flat Top Mountain, where you soon will be standing and looking south. From this point, the hike has some ups and down, eventually leading to the final up at Rabun Bald, where a stone tower awaits with incomparable 360-degree views. Campsites with water along the way make this a great one-night backpack. Be aware that the drive to the trailhead includes a ford of Sarahs Creek that is best suited for high-clearance vehicles.

HOW TO GET THERE

From just north of the junction of US 76 west and US 441 in Clayton, head east on Warwoman Road for 9 miles to Sarahs Creek Road—easily missed on a downhill curve to the right. Turn left onto Sarahs Creek Road (FR 156) and follow it 2 miles to Sarahs Creek Campground, where there is an auto ford. Just beyond the ford, turn left onto Forest Road 155, and go 7 miles to the Bartram Trail. Look for the yellow blaze markers on trees to the right at the gap. The trail is on your right, marked with an inscribed boulder. If you go too far, you will see another inscribed stone to the left of the road at Wilson Gap, 0.5 mile beyond the correct trailhead for this hike.

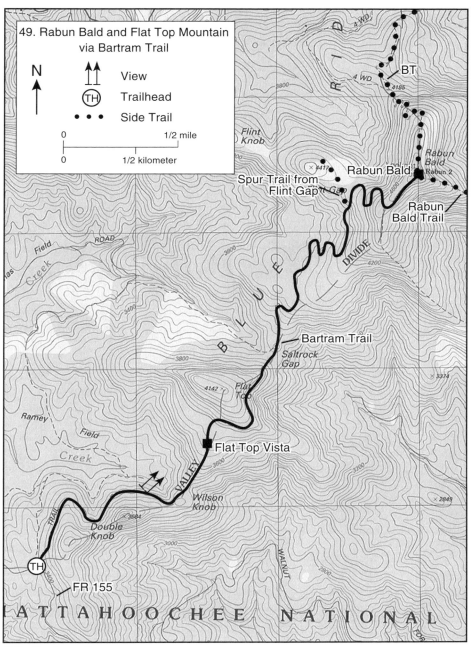

49. Rabun Bald and Flat Top Mountain
via Bartram Trail

N

View
Trailhead
Side Trail

0   1/2 mile
0   1/2 kilometer

BT

Flint
Knob

Rabun
Bald

Spur Trail from
Flint Gap

Rabun Bald

Rabun 2

Rabun
Bald Trail

DIVIDE

BLUE

Bartram Trail

Saltrock
Gap

Flat
Top

Flat Top Vista

VALLEY

Wilson
Knob

Ramey

Field

Creek

Double
Knob

TRAIL

TH

FR 155

ATTAHOOCHEE   NATIONAL

© The Countryman Press

Doubletop from Flat Top Mountain

THE HIKE

If you want to day-hike this trek, consider car camping down at Sarahs Creek Campground, which you passed on the drive in. It has some attractive sites with lots of privacy and is located along the pretty, crystalline trout water of Sarahs Creek.

The hike goes north from Forest Road 155 on a singletrack path through gorgeous woods with just the right mix of trees and brush. It starts out with a moderate climb around the west side of Doubletop, with far-reaching views north and west. Ramey Field is below you. Previously logged areas are discernable by the different heights of the trees.

Ramey Creek has cut a deep valley, allowing you to see the rock face of Flat Top Mountain, where the Bartram Trail soon leads. That is what makes this hike so special: You get an early look at the place where you'll shortly have an even better view. And the view from Flat Top is a good one.

The trail continues to circle around the headwaters of Ramey Creek, keeping north below Wilson Knob. The BT passes over some small rock slabs that are a preview of things to come. At mile 1.2, you reach a gap between Wilson Knob and Flat Top. This dry gap has a horizontal rock slab that is a decent spot to take a break. The trail switchbacks up from the gap. At the eighth switchback, stop for a moment to catch your breath and enjoy a view to the south of mountains fading into the Piedmont. On a clear day you can see into South Carolina.

Beyond the switchbacks, at 1.6 miles, look left for a side trail to a fantastic view from a rock face. This is one of my favorite views anywhere. I used a picture from this point for the cover of my book, *Long Trails of the Southeast*. Craggy pines hang on to the margins of the rock slab, providing a green frame for the vista. The two knobs of Doubletop are visible and you can see where you hiked from. Below, the valley of

Ramey Creek opens the mountains to the south and west.

Flat Top is a great place to view fall colors and is one of those special out-of-the-way places that will remain less visited no matter how much publicity it receives.

Beyond the vista, the BT comes alongside a trickling branch. This spring creek runs beneath laurel and rhododendron with an overstory of squat oaks. A small, but mostly level campsite lies on the far side of the creek. The path begins ascending the south slope of Flat Top Mountain, passing through a prescribed burn area. The young trees are regenerating—chestnut oak and pine. They grow close to the trail, crowding the foot bed along with briars and brush. Some views open in uncanopied spots as the trail switchbacks up. Better views are available where the trail levels off along the east slope of Flat Top. A spur trail leads right to a spring here.

Flat Top Mountain soon runs out of mountain, so the BT descends to Saltrock Gap. This gap got its name from the salt licks left for cattle that once grazed high in the mountains during the summer. Often, a farmer would dump the salt in a hollowed-out log or in a natural rock depression. These cattle are part of what kept Rabun Bald an open grassy peak. The forest quickly began regenerating after the cattle were removed.

Continue through the wide gap to a split in the trail at 2.8 miles. You go sharply right, while an obvious roadbed keeps forward through a rhododendron thicket and on to a small brook. The BT switchbacks uphill, and

a tiny spring crosses the trail at 3.3 miles. Keep ascending to Flint Gap and a trail junction at 3.7 miles. An inscribed boulder marks the spot. To the left, a blue-blazed trail leads toward Flint Gap, but the BT keeps forward, then turns right and begins switchback after switchback.

The trail is working up the west side of Rabun Bald through low-slung mountain laurel, oak, and birch. Just when you think the mountain has no top, you make the knife-edge crest and an inscribed rock at 4.5 miles. Uphill to the right is the stone viewing tower—elevation 4,696 feet, making it Georgia's second-highest peak. Steps lead to the top of the tower and a wooden platform. I believe the 360-degree view here is the best in Georgia. Part of this rating is based on the effort necessary to get here, as opposed to the 0.6-mile trek up Brasstown Bald, the state's highest point, which also has a shuttle to the top.

To the north stone-faced mountains form a rampart in North Carolina, while the Little Tennessee River valley is dotted with small communities to your west. To the east are the Cherokee Foothills of South Carolina and the Piedmont beyond. And to the south, the North Georgia Mountains and the Piedmont fade into the sky. The Three Forks Trail mentioned on the inscribed rock is now called the Rabun Bald Trail (see Hike 48). It leaves right 2.9 steep miles to Hale Ridge Cemetery Road. From this point, the Bartram Trail soon enters North Carolina and makes its way to meet the Appalachian Trail at Cheoah Bald.

50

Chattooga Wild and Scenic River Ramble

Total distance: 19.2 miles end to end

Hiking time: 10 hours

Vertical rise: 350 feet

Rating: Difficult

Maps: USGS 7.5' Rainy Mountain, Whetstone, Satolah, Chattooga National Wild and Scenic River, Chattahoochee National Forest

The Chattooga River deserves its wild and scenic designation—and then some. Running through Georgia's Chattahoochee National Forest, the Nantahala National Forest of North Carolina, and the Sumter National Forest of South Carolina, this 50-mile-long river corridor protects one of the most significant free-flowing streams in the Southeast. The river rises in North Carolina and heads southwest to serve as the Georgia–South Carolina border before meeting the Tallulah River to form the Tugaloo River.

The Chattooga is perhaps best known for being the backdrop of the Burt Reynolds movie, *Deliverance.* It was around this time, in 1974, that the Chattooga was designated a wild and scenic river, a place where rafters, canoists, kayakers, and anglers could enjoy this valley of massive boulders, clear trout and bass waters, and deep forests. Hikers have 36 miles of river trails to enjoy, and many more in adjacent national forest lands, which include the Ellicott Rock Wilderness. This hike covers the lowermost 20 miles of river corridor, all on the Georgia side of the Chattooga, from the US 76 bridge to the GA 28 bridge.

HOW TO GET THERE

From the junction of US 76 west and US 441 in Clayton, Georgia, head east on Rickman Road a short distance to Warwoman Road. Turn right and go 14 miles to GA 28. Turn right and continue 2.1 miles to the Bartram Trail parking area on your left, just before GA 28 crosses the Chattooga River into South Carolina. This is the end point for

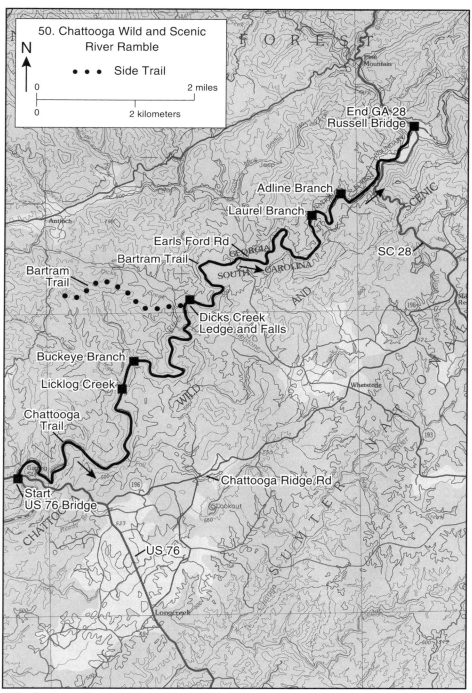

50. Chattooga Wild and Scenic
River Ramble

N

• • •   Side Trail

0 _____ 2 miles

0 _____ 2 kilometers

End GA 28
Russell Bridge

Adline Branch

Laurel Branch

SC 28

Earls Ford Rd

Bartram Trail

Bartram
Trail

Dicks Creek
Ledge and Falls

Buckeye Branch

Licklog Creek

Whetstone

Chattooga
Trail

Chattooga Ridge Rd

Start
US 76 Bridge

US 76

the one-way hike, so leave a shuttle vehicle here.

To reach the start point, continue east on 28 into South Carolina for 5.6 miles to Chattooga Ridge Road. There will be a sign here marked TO 76. Turn right and go 9.2 miles to US 76. Turn right again on US 76 and continue 2 miles to the bridge over the Chattooga River. The parking area and trailhead are on the west side of the bridge.

THE HIKE

Leave the US 76 bridge heading north, passing around some vehicle-barrier boulders. The gray-diamond-blazed Chattooga Trail begins winding in and out of hollows. Spur trails lead down to the river near the trailhead. Cross Pole Creek on a footbridge at 0.6 mile and follow it downstream. A rich forest of white pine, hemlock, and tulip trees shades the galax-lined path. Fraser magnolia, beard cane, partridgeberry, and ferns add to the mix. The trail passes on and off old roadbeds continually, so watch carefully for the gray blazes.

The Chattooga is frothing in the distance. The path winds up and down, and many wooden steps have been installed. The dry ridges between watersheds harbor pines, sourwood, and red maples. By now you have noticed the blue bands painted around some of the trees. These mark the wild and scenic river corridor, which averages 0.25 mile wide across the river. Auto traffic is blocked from the corridor, except in a few spots.

Wind in and out of more hollows before descending along a loud stream with many small falls to come near the Chattooga at 3.6 miles. A hemlock-laden flat with campsites is located 50 yards off to the right. Continue descending to cross some sluggish streambeds in a flat, then come directly along the river to a campsite at 3.7 miles.

If you want to camp by the river near here, the area you just passed is your best chance, for the Chattooga Trail turns away from the water, climbing directly up a dry ridgeline. The trail tops out at 4.8 miles and works down along a streamlet to reach the Chattooga again at 5.6 miles. This begins an extended stretch of river rambling beneath a superstory of white pine, with beech, holly, hemlock, and doghobble beside the path. In places, the trail is sandy from flood overwash and it jumps up a little bluff from time to time. You may see colorful whitewater boats bobbing along on the river.

Cross Licklog Creek, easily the largest stream you've traversed, at 6.1 miles. Watch for an ATV track leaving the river. Stay right here, soon spanning Buckeye Branch in thick rhododendron. Leave the river on a sharp left turn at 7.2 miles, and switchback uphill onto a roadbed. (If you're looking for riverside campsites you can just keep forward beyond the hard left.) Join a north-running ridgeline. You can hear the river roaring below before you drop through dry woods to step over Rock Creek and reach Sandy Ford Road at 9.1 miles.

Cross the road and climb into ragged piney woods, meeting the Bartram Trail (BT) at 9.9 miles. This is the end of the Chattooga Trail, and an inscribed stone marks the spot. The BT headed toward North Carolina curves sharply left to climb Rainy Mountain. You, however, keep forward on the yellow-blazed portion of the BT, going north up the Chattooga River corridor toward GA 28. Travel amid white pines to span Dicks Creek at 10.2 miles. A spur trail leads right over a second bridge to the top of 60-foot Dicks Creek Falls, then onward to the Chattooga River and Dicks Creek Ledge, a Class IV rapid. Don't pass on the bottom-up view of the waterfall. Campsites are available in the vicinity.

Dicks Creek Ledge on the Chattooga River

The BT jumps a gap beside a knob and returns to the river at 10.9 miles. It traces the watercourse for 0.6 mile as it sweeps to the right, availing more camping opportunities. Next you leave the Chattooga, ascend to another gap through laurel-oak woods, and then drop to meet Warwoman Creek–a large and scenic stream in its own right–at 12.1 miles. Cruise along this trout stream to Earls Ford Road and degraded campsites at 12.6 miles. The going gets pretty again, especially after you cross Warwoman Creek on an iron bridge at 12.9 miles. Continue upstream with the diamond blazes, traveling under dense hemlocks.

Turn right, away from Warwoman, heading for the hills once again. Bisect the road-like Willis Knob Horse Trail at 13.4 miles and keep ascending to the highest point on the entire hike–just under 1,900 feet and just under Willis Knob. Keep an easterly tack on the slopes of Willis Knob, passing a few streamlets. Traverse an old burn; look for burn marks on standing trees amid brushy undergrowth. Next, you enter the dark rhododendron hollow of noisy Laurel Branch, crossing on a footbridge at 15.1 miles. The Chattooga is on a major bend away from the trail.

You work toward more gently rolling terrain to span Bynum Branch at 15.9 miles. There is a campsite below the bridge. Cross Adline Branch at 16.6 miles amid many holly trees. The trail joins a roadbed here and the walking remains level and easy. Briefly share the path with a horse trail before turning uphill and left, then descend to a large flat.

White pines, both living and dead, dominate the landscape. The southern pine beetle has killed many of these trees. This area was once a farm, and many old roadbeds converge here. Look left just before a board-walk that crosses over a shallow branch to see a standing stone chimney that once served as someone's hearth. The wide track soon passes an old hay baler. Continue in bottomland to rejoin the Chattooga. Look across the river for the SC 28 boat launch at 17.8 miles.

At 18.1 miles you cross Holden Branch on a footbridge. Ragged, brushy woods border the trail, and kudzu is trying to take over where it can. Open areas allow views of Russell Mountain across the Chattooga. The trail comes alongside the river again, and you can look down on an island. Climb a hill above a flat before turning into the West Fork Chattooga River drainage.

At 18.9 miles, the trail turns abruptly right to cross the sand-bottomed West Fork on an iron bridge. Turn back along the Chattooga, which at this point is technically the West Fork, and pass an old bridge abutment. Finally, leave the roadbed you have been following and shortly reach GA 28 near Russell Bridge, at 19.2 miles, to complete the hike.

Index

Let The Countryman Press Take You There

Follow our experienced authors to the finest trails, parks, and backroads in these areas:

50 Hikes Series
Northeast
50 Hikes in Connecticut
50 Hikes in the Maine Mountains
50 Hikes in Coastal and Southern Maine
50 Hikes in Massachusetts
50 Hikes in the White Mountains
50 More Hikes in New Hampshire
50 Hikes in the Adirondacks
50 Hikes in the Lower Hudson Valley
50 Hikes in Central New York
50 Hikes in Western New York
50 Hikes in Vermont
Mid-Atlantic
50 Hikes in Maryland
50 Hikes in New Jersey
50 Hikes in Central Pennsylvania
50 Hikes in Eastern Pennsylvania
50 Hikes in Western Pennsylvania
50 Hikes in Northern Virginia
50 Hikes in Southern Virginia
Southeast
50 Hikes in Central Florida
50 Hikes in North Florida
50 Hikes in South Florida
50 Hikes in Kentucky
50 Hikes in Louisiana
50 Hikes in the Mountains of North Carolina
50 Hikes in the Tennessee Mountains
50 Hikes in West Virginia
West & Midwest
50 Hikes in Arizona
50 Hikes in Colorado
50 Hikes in Michigan
50 Hikes in Ohio
50 More Hikes in Ohio
50 Hikes in Oregon
50 Hikes in Washington
50 Hikes in Wisconsin

Hiking, Climbing, Fishing & Travel
Alaska on Foot
American Rock
Arizona Trout Streams and Their Hatches
Backwoods Ethics
The California Coast
Crossing Arizona
Fishbugs
Fly-Fishing the South Atlantic Coast

Bicycling
Northeast
Backroad Bicycling in Connecticut
25 Bicycle Tours in Maine
Backroad Bicycling on Cape Cod, Martha's
  Vineyard, and Nantucket
25 Mountain Bike Tours in Massachusetts
Backroad Bicycling in Western Massachusetts
Bike Rides in the Berkshire Hills
Backroad Bicycling in New Hampshire
25 Bicycle Tours in the Adirondacks
25 Mountain Bike Tours in the Adirondacks
Backroad Bicycling in the Finger Lakes Region
Backroad Bicycling in the Hudson Valley and
  Catskills
Backroad Bicycling Near New York City
25 Bicycle Tours in Vermont
25 Bicycle Tours in the Lake Champlain Region
The Mountain Biker's Guide to Ski Resorts
Mid-Atlantic
25 Bicycle Tours on Delmarva
25 Bicycle Tours in Maryland
30 Bicycle Tours in New Jersey
25 Mountain Bike Tours in New Jersey
Backroad Bicycling in Eastern Pennsylvania
25 Bicycle Tours in and around Washington, D.C.
Southeast
Backroad Bicycling in the Blue Ridge and Smoky
  Mountains
Backroad Bicycling in Kentucky's Bluegrass
25 Bicycle Tours in the Savannah & the Carolina
  Low Country
West & Midwest
Bicycling America's National Parks: Arizona &
  New Mexico
Bicycling America's National Parks: California
Bicycling America's National Parks: Oregon and
  Washington
Bicycling America's National Parks: Utah and
  Colorado
25 Bicycle Tours in the Texas Hill Country and
  West Texas
25 Bicycle Tours in the Twin Cities &
  Southeastern Minnesota
Backroad Bicycling in Wisconsin
Latin America
Bicycling Cuba

. . . and more!